DALIT'S INHERITANCE IN HINDU RELIGION

DALIT'S INHERITANCE IN HINDU RELIGION

Mahendra Singh

Publications

KALPAZ PUBLICATIONS
Delhi-110052

Dalit's Inheritance in Hindu Religion

Rs. 720

ISBN: 81-7835-517-5

Published in 2006 in India by
Kalpaz Publications
C-30, Satyawati Nagar, Delhi-110052
E-mail : kalpaz@hotmail.com
Website : http://www.gyanbooks.com
Laser Typesetting at: Tact Computer Graphics, Delhi
Printed at : Salasar Imaging System, Delhi

The unreal has no existence
And the real never ceases to be;
The reality of both has been perceived
By the Seers of Truth

.... Bhagwad Geeta II : 16

Contents

Preface 11

Introduction 19

1. **Creation of Universe, beings and Social Division** 21

• A Song I Sing to Thee • Involution and Evolution • Struggle for Existence • Cosmic Creation and Dissolution • Scientific Discoveries on Creation • The Eternal Cycle • Division of Society • Illogic of Hereditary Caste Derived from Purusha Suktam.

2. **Hindu Sources of Religious Knowledge** 37

• System of Indian Philosophies or Darshans • Vedas and Vedanta • Epics • Sutras and Dharam Shastras (Smritis) • Manu Smriti • Puranas.

3. **Shudra's or Low Caste's Right to Supreme Knowledge** 47

• The Adikarvada (Right to Knowledge) • Knowledge Versus Rituals-Position of Vedas • Untouchable as Guru of Adi

Sankracharya • Composer of Rig Veda • Position of Bhagwad Geeta • Universality of Truth Revealed in Upanishads.

4. **Aryan Gods Versus Caste** **57**

• Lord Krishna • Universal Equality in Bhagwad Geeta • Lord Rama • Lord Rama's Love for Low Castes • Sambuka Episode • Lord Shiva • Realised Souls • Sages and Personalities of Mahabharta.

5. **Worship of God-Impersonal, Personal and Social** **81**

• What is God • Worship of God-Impersonal • Worship of God-Personal • Worship of God-Social • Worship by Shudras and Low Castes.

6. **Shudra's Concept of Indian History - Glorious Spots are Their's or the Periods of Social Homogeneity** **93**

• Vedic Period • Epics Age(Mahabharta Period) • Dharam Vyadha • Buddist Period • Maurya Empire • Era of Manusmriti • Medieval India-of Defeat and Disaster for Hindus • Maharana Pratap-The True Kshatriya • End of Aurangzeb's Theocracy / By Shudra's Rising • Chhatrapati Shivaji and Guru Govind Singh Challenge Mughal Empire.

7. Real Merits and Demarits **121**

• Merit • Higher Merit • The Meritorious state • Negative thoughts weakens Merit • Materialism Taints Merit • Positive Software Brings about Results.

8. Shudras to Ati-shudras **131**

• Shudras before Manusmriti (322-185 BC) • Shudras after Manusmriti • Categories of Castes in Manusmriti • Mixed Caste of Manu • Vrityas • Shudras Brought Down • Caste by Worth • Constituents of Caste • Period of Gupta's (320-413 AD) and Harshvardhan's (629-647 AD) • Al-Beruni's Period (1000-1030 AD) • Period of Sant Ravidas (1411-1527 AD) • Medieval Saints Against Caste • Chhatrapati Shivaji's Period (1627-1680 AD) • Era of Starvation, Foreigner's loot, Famine Deaths and Mass Untouchability (1707-1947 AD.

9. Working of Nature's Laws **157**

• External World • Internal Universe • Wider Circulation of Blood for Healthy Progeny • Casue and effect.

10. Modern India - Background Personalities of its Universal Constitution **165**

Socio- Religious Reformers :- Raja Rammohun Roy (1772-1833 AD), Swami Dayanand Saraswati (1824-1883), Swami

Vivekananda (1863-1902) Naryana Guru (1854-1928) *Spiritual Saints* :- Shri Sai Baba of Shirdi (1854-1918), Ramana Maharishi (1879-1950 AD), Swami Shivananda of Rishikesh (1887-1963 AD), Baba Sawan Singh founder Radha Soami Satsang Beas (1858-1948 AD), Shri Pramahansa Yogananda (1893-1952 AD), Swami Chinmaynanda founder of Chinmaya Mission *Social Reformers*:- Jyotiba Phule (1827-1892 AD), Justice Mahadeo Govind Ranade (1842-1901), Swami Sardhananda Saraswati (1856-1926 AD), Dr. B.R. Amedhkar (1891-1956), *Philosephers and Thinkers*:- Sh. Aurbindo Ghosh (1872-1950), Rabinder Nath Tagore (1861-1941), Smt. Annie Basent (1847-1933), Bakim Chandra Chatterji (1838-1894), Ishwar Chandra Vidya Sagar (1820-1891), *Revolutionaries*:- Lokmanya Bal Gangadhar Tilak (1856-1920), Lala Lajpat Rai (1865-1928), Saheed Bhagat Singh (1907-1931), Chander Shekar Azad (1906-1931), R.P. Bismal (-1927), Roshan Singh (-1927), R. Lahiri (-1927), A. Khan (-1927), Jatindra Nath Das (1904-1929), Khudi Ram Bose (1893-1908), Vir Savarkar (1833-1960), Netaji Subhash Chander Bose (1897-1945), Jai Prakash Narayan (1902-1979) *Other freedom fighters: Persons connected with Destiny of India* Mahatma M.K. Gandhi (1869-1948), Pt. Jawahar Lal Nehru (1889-1964), Sardar Vallabh Bhai Patel (1875-1950), Lal Bahadur Shastri (1904-1966) *Smritis are submerged into the Ocean of Human Liberty*

11. Glimpses of Universal Science of Life 183

• Qualifications • Yoga Vashistha • The Upanishads • Isavasya Upanishad, Katho Upanishad, Mundaka Upanishad, Mandukya Upanishad, Chandogya Upanishad, Keno Upanishad • Srimad Bhagwad Geeta • Patanjali Yoga Sutras • Raja Yoga • Viveka Chudamani of Adi Sankracharya • Western Philosophies on the mystery of life

12. Towards the Source of Light and Power 207

• The life-giving source • Incarnations of God-Avtaras • The Temple of Universal Religion • The Supreme Power

13. Lawlwss State-A Dalit Girl Protects Her Honour by Losing One Arm 215

• The integrity in Public Service • Demoniacal Traits • A Dalit Girl put up brave fight in a corrupt system • System of Vigilence in India • Is the Vigilence Serving Public Interest? •How India has Survived. • National Integration with Social Justice.

14. Basic Tenets of Hindu Philosophy 239

• Reincarnation of Soul or Laws of Karma
• Towards Evolution.

15. The Liberator of Indian Slavish Psyche - Swami Vivekananda **257**

• The Lifting up.• Swami Vivekananda – His Life Sketch.

Appendices

1. Caste of Guna and Karma in Bhagwad Geeta. 275
2. Important Dates of Indian History. 281
3. Rendering the Public Service. 311

Index 323

Preface

The Hindu Society is divided into innumerable castes under four basic *Varnas,* i.e., Brahmin, Kshatriya, Vaishya and Shudras. The first three *Varnas* form *Dwija* or the twice-born class having right to various religious sacraments in varying degrees. The last *Varna* ie Shudra forms the service class who have limited rights in religious and social matters, bulk of it forming the 'Untouchables' class as lower Shudras. Due to discrimination against them, the Shudra class have struggled and are struggling against the tyranny of higher castes, some going to the extent of denouncing the Hindu religion itself. Strange are the ways of Providence that despite the efforts of separation by some Shudras and suppression by *Dwijas,* the bond of lower Shudras with Hindu religion remains unbreakable. There is something deeper that refuses to separate this social monolithic despite pulls of the two opposite sides. An attempt has been made in this book to identify these forces of homogeneity which enables the Shudras class, upper and lower, to remain part of the Hindu religion, impossible to set apart even in the worst circumstances. My quiet observations for more than three decades reveal that the Laws of Mother Nature are working in its own ways, independent of the injunctions of Brahmincial social laws given by Manu etc. The working of nature has been revealed by the sage Kapila in *Samkhya Yoga* as constituting of three Gunas, i.e., Sattva, Rajas and Tamas in their infinite combinations.

Similarly says Bhagwad Geeta "Earth, Water, Fire, Air, Space, Mind, Reason and also the Ego-these constitute My nature eight-fold divided" (VII:4).

Srimad Bhagwad Geeta is believed to be a revealed scripture given by the God himself who appeared on the earth in human form. The caste in it is given by worth based on Gunas and Karma while it is by birth as propagated by Brahmanic authors of Smritis and Dharma Shastras. The independent working of Nature outside the dictates of Brahmanic Scriptures seems to be going in accordance with the revelations made the God, as would be seen in various chapters of this book like 'Aryan Gods Versus Caste', ' Shudras concept of Indian History-Glorious spots are theirs ....' One of the greatest and most important personalities in Hindu religion comes from Shudras, as Ved Vyasa, the author of Mahabharta containing Bhagwad Geeta, some Puranas and compiler of Vedas (before him these were transferred orally from one sage to another). Likewise, other great and powerful personalities, ancient medieval and modern who shaped destiny of India leading to glorious eras came from Shudra class. I have used in this book the Brahmanic labels of *Varanas* by birth for the greatmen, even though the Nature's one for them would be different depending upon their worth.

I have relied upon the substantial, large, authentic and non-controversial facts, as gathered from the religious and historical books, and not on the remote, invented and estray ones. This is because the Nature's message is vivid to any impartial mind, needing no built-up props.

Swami Vivekananda has been quoted in several religious and social contexts in the book, as I believe that only a person of deeper understanding, capable of penetrating through material layers of mind, reaching spiritual vision, can bring the truth on worldly plane through doses of reality from higher realms. The words are not the satisfactory medium to express the higher state of wisdom but Vivekananda through his sharp and rational intellect has conveyed to humanity as best as he could the subtler thoughts on various subjects. At times Vivekananda seems to be giving contradictory version on a subject at different occasions. This is to be understood in its true spirit and the particular context. Any motivated reading on apparent words will be the case of devil interpreting scriptures to suit its pre-conceived notions. The rise of India happens to coincide with rise of Swami Vivekananda. His world-shaking speeches on universal religion in the Parliament of Religion in America (Chicago 1893), dipped into modernity and science, could not but have inspired the Indian leaders engaged in freedom struggle, immediately after the above period of 1893-1902 AD.

Says Subhash Chandra Bose, "I came across the works of Swami Vivekananda. I had hardly turned over a few pages when I realized that here was something which I had been longing for... I was thrilled to the marrow of my bones". With this inspiration Netaji as a student would walk 3 miles on foot back form college and give the money thus saved to a begger woman, to render practical help to a sufferer. Pt. Jawahar Lal Nehru in his address at Rama Krishna Mission, Delhi on 20 March 1949 said, "There were great man and one of them, better known than the others, not only in India but in other parts of the world is Swami Vivekananda......But I can tell you that many of my generation were very powerfully influenced by him and I think that it would do a great deal of good to the present generation if they also went through Swami Vivekananda's writings and speeches and they would learn much from that". Mahatma Gandhi after visiting Belur Math in 1921 said "On going through the works of Swami Vivekananda the love that I had for my country became a thousand fold". The deeply influenced Rabindra Nath Tagore said "If you want to know India, study Vivekananda". Due to the teachings of Vivekananda even in social, religious and political matters having link to spirituality, the contents of this book also have some spiritual leaning. In fact one full chapter on "Universal Science of life" has been made part of the book, attempting to give glimpses of higher wisdom as propounded by Indian sages and some western philosophers, leaving the interested readers to fall back on the original sources.

I have hardly any knowledge of Sanskrit, but relied upon credible sources of translation of its verses into English, having clarity of meaning, without scope of controversy. The general reference to Shudras in the book includes the low castes called untouchables, though separate chapter is given to bring out the relationship between the two, which is, ' Shudras to Ati-Shudras'. As regards the Brahmins, my emphasis is more on Brahmanism than on present Brahmin caste. 'Brihm' is entirely a different concept of a state of Infinite and Eternal Being. Brahmanas are the ritualistic portion of Vedas and by Brahmanism is meant the social order given by laws of Manu and other Smritis, with high privileges for Brahmin caste by-birth unrelated to their acts and deeds. This Brahmanism is not limited to Brahmin caste, but goes down to others in hierarchical order. Such privilege-mindedness dries up the sense of general social belonging, ultimately making its influential people selfish, ready to ditch their society, religion and nation, even by condemning themselves to prove their loyalty elsewhere.

I have dealt on the religious, social and cultural aspects of Hindu religion and not on current political themes and their perverted applications where some Dalit leaders are not behind others in exploiting caste system for the sake of their personal power rather than rendering selfless service to ameliorate the condition of the poor and down-troddens. They convert their individual political convenience into the vacillating ideologies of love and hate with respect to other castes.

In this political scenario, it is strange to see that some section of Brahmins who through their self-centeredness brought darkness and gloom on the nation and society in the past, have conveniently shifted to the other extreme as followers of Karl Marx and its materialism in all its twisted form. They formed the nuclelus of Marxism in India in the formative years. The negative concept of a Brahmin (knowledge power), a Kshatriya (military power) and Vaishya (wealth power), all pooled together, will create the worst form of caste bourgeoisie, leaving the Shudra proletariat entirely to their mercy. But the problem with Indian Marxist is that they do not want to believe in Hindu caste system and wishfully desire to cover it up with artificially conceived classes of rich and poor, purely on economic criteria. This ideology has made no dent whatsoever (except in a small pocket) on the Indian Psyche. How could it, when it appeals only to the belly (though important it is) and not the other hungers of human personality, viz. the intellectual, moral and spiritual. In India the prince of a kingdom willingly abandons the riches and worldly power to rigorously practice, without proper food for years, the penances to seek enlightenment as Buddha.

Dalit bourgeois and Dalit proletariat are a matter of fact today, but instead of working on cross purposes, they should work complimentary to each other. Only the Dalit elites have to understand that they have to retain their root in the ancient culture of this land and not remain rootless. No superstructure can ever be built without strong foundation. Even the few hundred years old America, the present day superpower, proudly claims its link to England and English culture, despite having fought a war with the British in 1776-1781 AD under the leadership of George Washington. Healthy past linkage is that which enables one to adopt modern outlook on matters which are subject to change.

What is my qualification to write on such an important subject involving spiritual, religious and social aspects of Hindu religion? It is nothing academic or literary. There had been practically no occasion in my life time to come up on any social or spiritual platform and least of all on any political one. But as a common man, I do claim to have rendered public service of more than 35 years selflessly with clean conscience, paying price to uphold certain values, in terms of career, postings and even life itself as indicated in Appendix-3 of this book. This was done not in a negative sense of causing confrontation for its sake or for selfish motives or for publicity sake but for applying corrections to the derailed tracks. It was like working of a wheel which moves on rugged or plain ground keeping its core or axle at rest ie to have a progressive out(er) look without compromising on basic values of public ethics.

I believed in the following words of Swami Chinmayananda (of Chinmaya Mission):-

> "Wanted; men:
> Not Systems fit and wise,

Not faiths with rigid eyes,
Not wealth in mountain piles,
Not power with gracious smile,
Not even the potent pen:
Wanted; Men!"

Alongwith other authors mentioned in the book, I express my gratefulness to the publications on Swami Vivekananda by Advaita Ashram, Calcutta. I also express my gratitude to the coincidental forces which placed some rare material from books, like Satnami Revolt, before me through chance.

New Delhi

Mahendra Singh

Introduction

The purpose of this book is to bring out as to what a Dalit inherits in Hindu religion of the contribution made by his forefathers or of the teachings contained in the scriptures. This may show them that they inherit a great spiritual treasure, which is so necessary today to balance materialistic mind-set. It is true that due to sever distortions in Hindu religion in the past, he inherits presently his social ostracization too. All chapters of this book except the two on Hindu philosophy, bring out either directly or indirectly, the role played by sages, kings and people of the so-called low castes in enriching the Hindu Dharma-which term includes Hindus, Buddhists, Jains and Sikhs, as per Constitution of India. By Dalit is meant the people of Shudra class, many of which became 'untouchables', as outlined in the chapter 'Shudras to Ati-Shudras'. Some of the ancient personalities mentioned are; Kavasa Ailush a composer in Rig Veda; Satyakama Jabala and Raikva the seer/ Rishi in upanishads; Sabri and Nishad Raj Guha, one devotee and another friend in Ramayana; Ved Vyasa, Vidur and Dharma Vyadha respectively the author of Mahabharta, Prime Advisor of Kaurvas and teacher of the most learned Brahmin Kaushik; Chandra Gupta Maurya of Maurya Period the first great king of India in the recorded history; Sant Ravi Das the great spiritual saint, Chattrapati Shivaji the greatest fighter in Medieval Period and Rani Rasmani the builder of Dakshineswar Kali temple, Calcutta whose priest was

Rama Krishna Pramahansa, in early Modern Period. Recorded proofs from authentic sources in history/ religious books have been provided in support of those whosoever were in the area of doubt regarding their caste status. Approximation of Pandavas (Chapter VIII-Shudras to Ati-shudras) and lord Krishna (Chapter IV-Aryan Gods Versus Caste) to the Shudras, has been brought out in necessary details. The thoughts of Swami Vivekananda in the matter forms the background of the book. He has not been included in this category as such, though he himself has said that some orthodox elements of Hindus call him a Shudra to question his right to teach shastras to them. Perhaps he was called so as a reaction of his sharp attack on social rigidities of Hindus. But Swamiji has said "——but I am not at all hurt if they call me a Shudra. It will be a little reparation of the tyranny of my anscestors over the poor. If I am a Pariah, I will be all the more glad, for I am the disciple of a man who- the Brahmin of Brahmin – wanted to cleanse the house of a Pariah". (C.W. Vol. III p. 211).

The hard words of Swamiji in social matters were not in a negative sense of destroying the religion itself alongwith the evils. Even a modern psychologist like Norman.V. Peale says "A negative thinker engages ultimately in a self – destroying process. The negative thinker, projecting negative thoughts, tends thereby to draw back to himself negative results. This is a definite and immutable law of mind". So, Swami Vivekananda said that *forming* part in religion should be brought into play after the *reforming* one.

Mahendra Singh

1
Creation of Universe, Beings and Social Division

A Song I Sing to Thee

"I am present" At Pralaya time,
When this vast universe is swallowed up,
Knowledge, and knower, and the known
Merged into one.

The universe no more
Can be distinguished or can be conceived
By intellect. The sun and moon and stars are not.
Over the bosom of the darkness, darkness moves
Intense. Devoid of all the threefold bonds,
Remains the universe. Gunas are calmed
Of all distinctions. Everything deluged
In one homogeneous mass, subtle,
Pure, of atom-form, indivisible—
There I am present.

"Once again, I unfold myself—that 'I';
of my 'Shakti' the first great change is Om;
The Primal voice rings through the void;
Infinite space hears that great vibrant sound.
The group of Primal Causes shakes off sleep,
New life revives atoms interminable;

Cosmic existence heaves and whirls and sways,
Dances and gyrates, moves towards the core,

From distances immeasurably far.
The animate Wind arouses rings of waves
Over the Ocean of great Elements;
Stirring, failing, surging, that vast range of waves
Rushes with lightning fury. Fragments thrown
By force of royal resistance, through the path
Of space, rush, endless, in the form of spheres
Celestial, numberless. Planets and stars

Speed swift; and man's abode, the earth revolves.[1]

And thus our globe, the earth came into the existence

Before discussing the question of differentiation in human race, it is very important to know as to how the universe and human beings were created. It is a baffling question and the philosophers, saints and scientists have been trying to find some credible answer to it through ages. There are references on creation in scriptures like Vedas and Bible. Both attribute this creation to the will of God. In the beautiful poem "A song I sing to Thee" Swami Vivekanand – a gareat spiritualist, philosopher and social thinker — has brought out as to how the cosmic creation takes places (upto plant stage). The life evolves from plant upto the man under the law of evolution of species, as propounded by the great scientist Charles Darwin (1809-1882 AD). Concludes Darwin in his 'Origin of Species' as, "I have now given the facts and considerations which have thoroughly convinced me that species have been modified during a long course of descent. This has been effected chiefly through the natural selection of numerous successive, slight, favorable variations, aided in an important manner by the inherited effects of the use and disuse of parts; And as natural selection works solely by and for the good of each being, all corporeal and mental endowments will tend to progress towards perfection ——— There is a grandeur in this view of life, with its several powers, having been originally breathed by the creator into a few forms or into one ; and that, whilst this planet has gone cycling on according to the fixed law of gravity, from so simple a beginning endless forms most beautiful and most wonderful have been and are being evolved.[2]

The anthropologists believe that whole of human race is the creation of Black African Eve, who lived some 2 lakh years ago in Africa. The latest Chinese fossils shows that Homo Erectus and Homo Sapiens had appeared on earth even at much earlier period than 2 lakh years and modern humans evolved gradually in many parts of the world, i.e., Asia, Africa and Europe. Whatever be the period of human appearance on the earth, the scientist consider their evolution from other spices of living creatures, that is, they believe that human beings are evolved from a very long chain of different form of lives and just not descended in the present human from sky or appeared through magical chance creation. Even the Hindus believe that a person comes to human form after passing through 84 lakhs *yonies* (wombs).

Involution and Evolution

The life appeared on this planet in the form of protoplasm—the smallest unit of living organism. It developed through countless forms to a perfect human being endowed with Super Intelligence. Now, something can not come out of nothing. This Intelligence must have been involved even in the protoplasm, which evolved gradually till it came to its fullest manifestation in the perfect human being. Every creature in the world expresses some part of this Intelligence in a given form. This evolution stops ones the creature reaches the perfection in human form and realizes itself as this Cosmic Intelligence present in all living beings. The ancient people called this Intelligence as God. It is He who is present in all living forms. This was the theme of Swami Vivekanand's Lecture delivered at New York on 19th January 1896. "This evolved freedom of consciousness is perhaps the ultimate destiny of creation" says Rabinder Nath Tagore in his Book 'Our Universe'. The French Scientist Louis Pasteur has also established through experiment that "Life comes from pre-existing life only".

Struggle for Existence

The living beings before they evolved sufficiently to express social consciousness, must have passed through a great struggle for existence, within their own species, as well as with other species of the environment. They came to that level of existence following the law of Darwin's theory "Survival of the Fittest" . Undoubtedly, they must have defended themselves from all sorts of dangers under the jungle law. They would not have come to that existence unless they were the fittest to survive. Alas, in the period which resulted in social division (in India, out of all places in the world), this natural right of self-defense of a living being was transferred to a particular group called 'Kshatriyas'. There would have been some sense in it had this category been used only for the protection of the nation and masses. But what has been revealed in the later history of India is that a particular group called 'Shudra' was totally made defenseless and quite often the state power was used against them. This arrested their natural growth as evolving beings.

Cosmic Creation and Dissolution

Srimad Bhagwad Geeta Says:

"Those who know from realization Brahma's day as extending to a thousand Mahayugas and Brahma's night to another thousand Mahayugas they alone know the reality of time" VIII : 17

"Arjuna, this multitude of being born again and again, under compulsion from prakriti, is dissolved at the commencement of Brahma's night and rises again at the commencement of his day" VIII : 19

The Philosophers and Scientist if ponder over the above theme, should get enlightened in their search to solve the mystery of creation. The 'day' is the period of grosser manifestation while 'night' of equal duration is the period of finer inactivity—of dissolution. The nature (prakriti) is fully governed by the law of cause and effect. That which is beyond nature is the abode of Supreme Intelligence – the God. The nature is being governed by an invisible law of this alternate cycle of manifestation and dissolution. We can see this in any creation. Seed is a very fine form of big tree, yet it is only in the seed that the whole tree is involved. Tree is merely the grossification of the finer form of seed. The law of becoming grosser and finer is applicable to the whole creation of sentient and insentient forms. Grosser from is the effect and finer the cause. That which is 'created' is only the changing of forms. No creation comes out at random and abruptly. It follows the perfect law of cause and effect. One starts fresh exactly from where he took rest, in this eternal journey till he reaches 'My abode'. He the Supreme Intelligence alone is at the beginning of all beings as involved background, while these beings are in extremely finer form, ready to emerge again at the beginning of the 'day'.

Scientific Discoveries on Creation

As on the date almost all scientists believe the creation of universe to be based on theory of 'Big Bang' as discovered by them through scientific methods. According to this theory, there was a great explosion after which the universe came into existence. The universe is expending ever since. In his master piece "The Mind of God"[3] the renowned Professor of Mathematical Physics, U.K. Paul Davies has analysed all aspects of creation scientifically. He states (page 49) "In other words, the entire cosmos would have been squeezed into a single point. At the point the gravitational force and density of material, were infinite. A point of infinite compression is known to mathematical physicists as a 'singularity'." This is an extremely complex subject though simplified to a large extent by Paul Davies. He further states "Because all our laws of physics are formulated in terms of space and time, these laws can not apply beyond the point at which space and time cease to exist. Hence, the laws of physics must break down at the singularity". "The picture that we then obtain for the origin of universe is a remarkable one. At some finite instant in the past the universe of space, time and matter is bounded by space – time singularity. The coming into existence of universe is therefore represented not only by the abrupt appearance of matter, but of space and time as well". He further writes "The bang did not occur at a points in space at all. Space itself came into existence with the big bang. ———— There was no before. Time itself began at the big bang". He mentions about a famous Russian Scientist Alexander Friedmann who after studying Einstein's equations discovered that the universe either expands or contracts. "One set of solutions corresponds to a universe that starts out at a big bang, expands at an ever-diminishing rate, and them starts to contract again. The contracting phase mirrors the expending phase, so that the contraction gets faster and faster until the universe disappears as "big crunch" – a catastrophic implosion like the big bang in reverse. This cycle of expansion and contraction can then be continued into another cycle, then another cycle and so on ad inifinitum __." Interestingly, Paul Davis while describing various views on creation mentions about the life cycle of Brahma as 311 trillion years.

Our planet earth of course came to the state of bearing life after billions of years of the Big Bang and will cease to bear life billions of years before the final dissolution of the universe. Having lived life of 5000 millions years, the sun is said to still go equal 5500 million years before it becomes a red giant and start enveloping in it all planets upto Mars, to where its diameter will extend before it becomes a white dwarf to fade completely or explode into a supernova. The sun is constantly converting hydrogen into helium and thus emitting light in the process. Once this supply of hydrogen is exhausted, the star will increase its diameters manifold, to become a 'red giant', as said above.

The Eternal Cycle

To quote Swami Vivekanand from the chapter 'cosmos' of 'Jnana-Yoga' , Advaita Ashram, Calcutta, "So rising and falling, the cycle goes on. So with all lives, so with all existence that we can see, feel, hear, or imagine. Everything that is within the bounds of our knowledge is proceeding in the same way, like breathing in and breathing out in the human body. Everything in creation goes on in this form, one wave rising, another falling, rising again, falling again. Each wave has its hollow, each hollow has its wave. The same law must apply to the universe taken as a whole, because of its uniformity. This universe must be resolved into its cause; the sun, moon, stars and earth, the body and mind, and everything in this universe must return to their finer causes, disappear, be destroyed as it were. But they will live in the causes as fine forms. Out of these fine forms they will emerge again as new earths, suns, moons and stars. "(a lecture delivered in New York, 19th January 1896 AD).

Piecing together all the views that of philosophers, scientists and scriptures, following form emerges out as the likely state of creation and dissolution, going on eternally.

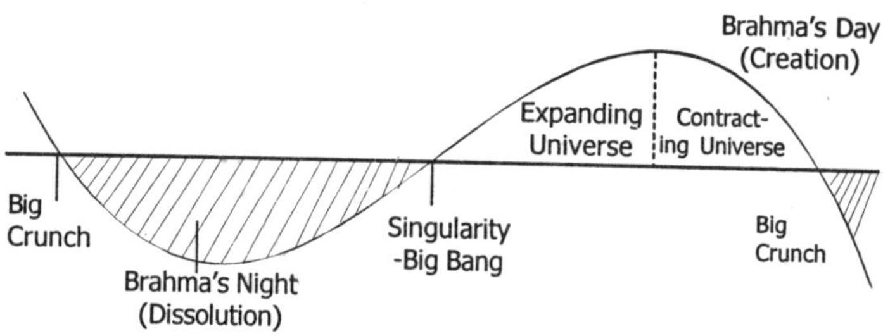

The Eternal Cycle

It seems the 'Creation' and 'dissolution' is the breathing out and breathing in of the Divine Being, as indicated above by Swami Viveknanda. And how poetically the Rig Veda says about the state of dissolution:

"There was neither death nor immortality. That one alone breathed in its own bliss and by its own powers inspite of absolute vacuum. That alone was, naught else".

There is no creation, animate or inanimate in the universe, therefore, outside the one existence. This existence seen at different plane is matter, mind and spirit, is governed by Cosmic laws. The static concepts like once shudra all time a shudra do not fit into this cycling universe of continuous evolution (of involved Super Intelligence) in all its laws.

Division of Society

How has this system of four-fold caste come into existence? Or, rather, how can such a system come into existence in a human society? We have two guides on this; One the scriptures and second the irrefutable logic. Let us first take up the logic.

Logic: Creation of caste system through a non-religious process, by natural development, does not appear to be a possibility but the same is being mentioned below for the sake of covering one view-point.

Here is society of Homo-sapiens that knows nothing of caste system. Small family group becomes bigger group under a tribal chief, either by consent or by force. This becomes still larger group until, imperceptibly, it develops into a state to be ruled by the like of a king. Now the king decides either on his own or on the advice of some saint-like person to classify the society into four castes; of Brahmins, Kshatriyas, Vaisyas and Shudras. How does he go about doing the job? If it is to be based on permanent merit, then an instant survey is to be conducted of all people in the state to determine as to who are all intellectuals by measuring their Intelligent Quotient through some device in hand. Even this is not sufficient as here the Intelligence is not merely worldly but divine. So some extra ordinary method had to be invented to classify some people as intellectuals whose progenies are going to be classified eternally in this category. Once so classified initially, subsequently the problem is easy – just make it hereditary.

If it is considered that there was no such super device developed to exactly measure the human intelligence at that primitive stage, the other alternative is to presume that various groups of human beings were created all of a sudden, instantly, intact with their identification mark for easy recognition and easy classification into the four categories.

Considering that such possible causes create absurdities, in all likelihood the four-fold classification should have been based on occupation of an individual, as it is easy and natural to classify people on this basis. This appears to be the universal basis of classification all over the world, by whatever name they may be calling such professionals. Even the Vedic period in India had this classification based on occupation, that is why a rishi of Rig Veda says "I am a composer of hymns, my father is a physician, my mother is a corn-grinder. Means are different but we all live together though engaged in different professions". — IX/112(3)

Subsequent hereditary concept of four-fold caste is peculiar to India, which came into existence after the Vedic age, to develop and promote the interests of particular group of society.

The Scriptures

As regards, the scriptures, it is only at one place in Rig Veda (Mandala X : Purusha Sukhtam 91 to 94) where the theory of creation is given. It is stated there that Brahmins came out of the mouth, the Kshatriya from the arms, Vaisyas from the thighs and shudras from the feet of the cosmic person. Another scripture is Srimad Bhagwad Geeta, where in sloka 13 of chapter IV, Lord Shri Krishna declares "The four-fold varnas have been created by Me according to the differentiation of Guna and Karma ; though I am author thereof know Me as non-doer and immutable". Since these are the fundamental and most revered scriptures of authority in Hindu religion coming in the category of 'Shrutis' , let us confine out attention only to these. The divine basis of caste is here only, elsewhere it being mostly man-made. Dharma-Sutras and Dharma-Shastras (Smritis) etc. are a later day creation of Brahmin writers. These are not the revealed texts but only the manuals of social, religious and family conduct, for a certain period of history. A detailed, dedicated and sincere study is called for the Shrutis, as the scriptural statements can not be brushed aside lightly. First let us take Rig Veda. Now, the shudras are said to have come out of the feet of Cosmic Person. Not taking it in the hierarchal and vertical order, from top to bottom, let us see it in following aspects. One, that the feet are of the Cosmic Person himself and not joined at his knee of other's after taking out the same from some Rakshasa (Devil). Two, the feet are considered the most sacred part of the God in Hindu religion, as even today we touch His feet only in any temple and never the hands or any other part. It is by touch of feet that Lord Rama released Ahilya from the life of a stone. Bharat ruled Ayodhya for 14 years during exile of Rama, by Placing sandles *'Charan-Khadaou'* of Rama on the throne. Krishna worshiped Sudama by washing his feet. Krishna himself was worshiped in the first honour ceremony by Yudishtra, by the washing of his feet (and no other part of body). Till date we show honour to our elders by touching his feet. In TATTVA BODHA, Adi Sankaracharya says under 3.2.2. 'KARMA INDRIYAS" that while presiding deity of hands is Indra, of the feet it is VISHNU :

पाद्योविष्णुः

In any case, there is no mention in the Suktam that the classification is hereditary i.e. by birth. Swami Vivekanand says "The doctrine of caste in the Purusha-Shuktam of the Veda does not make it hereditary" (complete works Vol. VI p. 208). It is only in the end mandala that such a sloka on creation occurs, the entire Rig Veda is free from caste references. Even for this mandala, composer of Sukta 30 to 34 (containing 58 Mantras) is Rishi Kavash Ailush, who was a Shudra according to the great German philosopher Prof. F. Max Meullor, (Ancient Sanskrit Literature). Shanti Parv of Mahabharta, Chapter 318 sloka 90 says on this creation "Brahmins were born from the mouth of Brahma, the Kshatriyas born from the arms of Brahma, the vaisya born from the navel of Brahma and the Shudras born from the feet of Brahma, therefore, people of all varnas are 'Braham Swaroop', i.e., identical with one Braham. No varna should be considered separate from the Braham".

Since it is unscientific and irrational to believe that instant creation of human beings took place from various parts of the body of the Cosmic Person at some point of time, the meaning of Suktam seems to be that a man is born in the world from respective part of the body of Cosmic Person, depending upon his nature which has different place value in its body. It does not refer to static conception of one time creation but to dynamic creation all the time again and again. Scientists tell us that there had been extinction of life on the planet earth many times due to cosmic phenomenon of great deluge, Ice age, drifting continents and movement of heavenly bodies. A recent collusion of comet Levy-9 with Jupiter in mid July 1994 drew the following comments from the scientists "If such a comet hits land, it would incinerate the whole world and kick up a cloud of dust that would blot out the Sun and bring a nuclear winter which in turn would destroy humankind". One such collision 65 millions years ago led to extinction of most living species including dinosaurs on earth.

Purusha Suktam itself says "Three-quarters of Purusha extends beyond the universe of change. The one-quarter of Him again and again come to play as universe———)" As per Matsya Avtar of Vishnu, a little fish comes to Manu for protection. Manu puts it in a pot, but it grows bigger. Manu then puts it in a tank next day but it grows as big and finally Manu puts it in the ocean considering its size now. The fish growing bigger, declares "Manu I am the creator of this universe. I have taken this form to warn you that I will deluge the world soon. You build a big boat and put a pair of every kind of animal and let your family enter it". The world was totally deluged but Manu saved his own family and two of every kind of animal and seed of various plants. Manu conducted an Yagnya, where a girl named Ida was born. She became the source of creation of the whole human race (See the modern concept of creation from African Eve as already detailed above). Similar story is contained in Old Testament of Bible where each pair of beings are saved from the great deluge by putting them on the great wooden ark.

There is therefore, no one time creation but it take place again and again.

Illogic of Hereditary Caste Derived from Suktam

Hereditary caste as assigned to Purusha Suktam through some motivation does not stand to reason as below:

1. This by-birth classification applies only to the land of Vedas. What about the creation of

human beings all over the world who do not follow this classification of Vedas. Does it mean that no creation of human beings took place elsewhere. So, unless the universal meaning of creation is assigned to Suktam, it shall be reduced to a sectarian scripture of Brahmins. The man of knowledge, strength and wealth have been born outside the vedic society and they are not very keen to relate themselves to the creation by birth of Pursha Suktam. An Albert Einstein will remain as great without the label of 'Brahamin' upon him, unless the word be in the universal sense of a learned man.

2. It is utterly foolish to establish relative importance of various parts of one's own body. The feet are considered as the lowest part of the body, but they alone provide the movement capability to a human being, as otherwise they will remain fixed at one place like trees, reverting back to the stage of low evolution. One never pities or whips up one's legs for bearing the load of upper three parts. Only a lunatic would do so. The four parts perform different functions and to an individual all are equally necessary for his healthy and active life.

As regards *Bhagwad Geeta*, it merits complete analysis of the term "according to differentiation of Guna and Karma". The meaning is clear that caste classification is based on merit of an individual (Guna and Karma) and it is so accepted universally as such by scholars. This is however, discussed in the Appendix-1 of this book in all its details. Other verses of Bhagwad Geeta on the caste/varna are to be read in this background. But before going into this question, it will be necessary to have an overall view of Indian Philosophical system as well as that of Hindu religious scriptures, to know their relative merits and importance.

References

1. From the poem 'A Song I Sing to Thee' by Swami Vivekanand, complete works Vol. VIII.

2. Origin of spaces by Charles Darwin, abridged and introduced by Richard E. Leakey, Faber and Faber, London.

3. 'The mind of God' by Paul Davis Penguin Books.

2
Hindu Sources of Religious Knowledge

There are basically two sources of knowledge with us, (1) Secular (2) Religious. In the category of secular fall the present day science, metaphysics and all other knowledge not dealing with any religion. It is not being dealt here. In the category of religious are various scriptures and Darshans (Philosophies). The religious knowledge in the Hindu context is that with which we are presently concerned. The chart 1 shows the system of Indian Philosophy (Darshan) and chart 2 the overall view of Hindu scriptures. The scriptures are basically divided into two parts; Shrutis and Smritis. Shrutis deal with eternal principal of religion and Smritis with the ephemerals. Whenever there is conflict between the two, the version of Shrutis prevails over that of Smritis, as the latter is not the revealed (divine) text.

Vedas and Vedanta

There are four Vedas, Rig Veda, Yajur Veda, Sama Veda and Atharv Veda. Vedas are divided into two main sections, the Karma-kand and Jnana (Knowledge)–Kand. Karma-Kand consists of two portions; Samhitas or the Mantra portion and 'Brahamanas' or Ritualistic portion. Mantra portion is the wonderful poetry particularly in Rig Veda invoking the deities of nature like sun, moon, fire, wind, water, Indra (ruler of heaven), earth, dawn etc. 'Brahamanas' are said to be the later day additions to the Vedas and contain the ritualistic details for various purposes and occasions. Every Veda has different number of 'Brahmanas' attached to it. Rig Veda is the most ancient scripture, perhaps even in the world, Containing 1028 Mantras.

Chart-1
System of Indian Philosophy

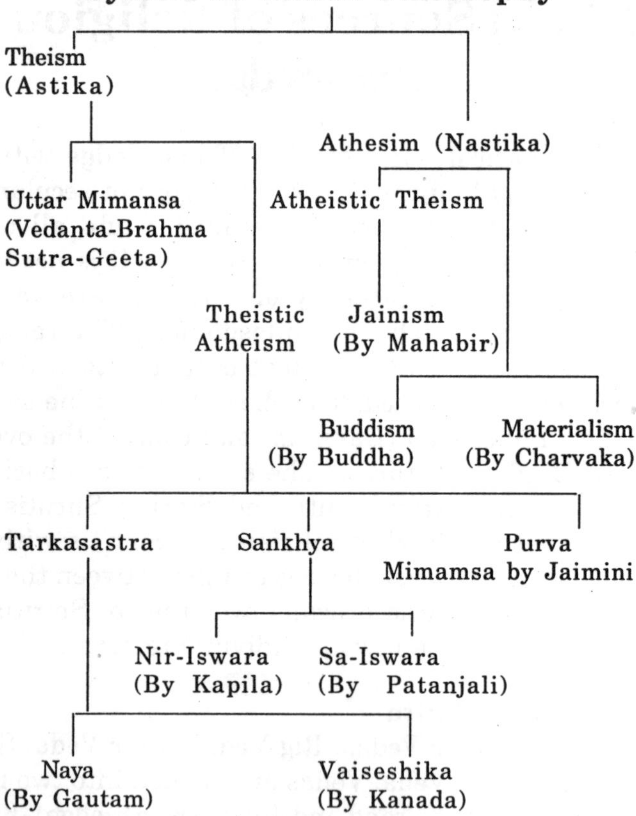

Explanation:
Theistic-Theism : belief in Vedas and God.
Theistic-Atheism:- belief in Vedas but not in god.
Atheistic –theism:- belief in Divine principle but not in Vedas.
Atheistic-Atheism:- belief neither in Vedas nor in God.
Source : Commentary of Swami Chinmayananda on Bhagwad Geeta, Chap. 2.

Chart-2
Hindu Scriptures

- Shrutis (Dealing with Eternal Principles)
  - Four Vedas (Rig, Yajur, Sama, Atharva)
    - Karma Kanda
      - Samhitas (Mantra Portion)
      - Brahmanas (Ritualistic Portion)
    - Jnana Kanda (Knowledge)
      - Upanishads (Aranyakas)

  Geeta is Essence of All Upanishads

  Aryankas are the stage in between Brahamanas and Upanishads

- Smritis (Dealing with Changing Times)
  - Itihas — Ramayana, Mahabharata
  - Puranas — 18 Puranas
  - Smritis- or Dharam Shastras — 18 Smritis Including Manu Smriti
  - Veda-Upanga — Various Darsans
  - Vedanga-(Six) — Like Grammers, Astrology, Kalpa Sutra, Ritual etc.
  - Upa Vedas- — Ayurveda (Mediciens), Dhanur Veda (War), Gandharv Veda (Music), Stapathya Veda (Yantra)

Chart - 3

The Brahminism

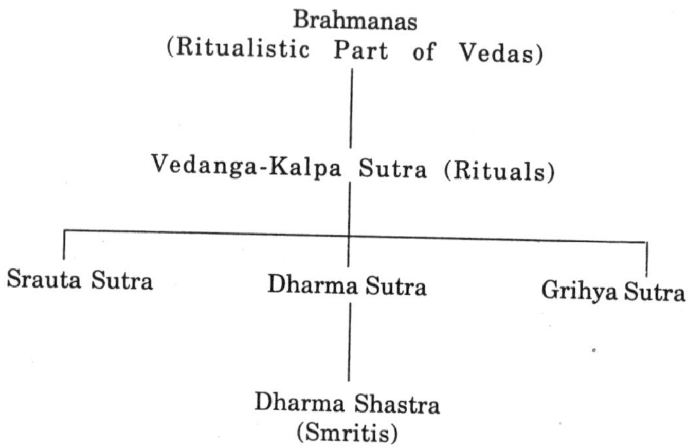

Note:- Vedangas are not the part of the Vedas, i.e., these are not Srutis, but are the supplementary applications of Vedas.

Rig Veda's 'Brahmana' is Aitereya. Sama Veda has 1810 Mantra, though many of these are common to Rig Veda. It has three Brahmana, popular being Jaiminey. Yajur Veda has two parts ; Shukla and Krishn. Shukla Yajur Veda is also known as Vajasney Samhita. Krishn Yajur Veda has four parts. Its Brahmana is sathpatha. Atharva Veda contains 6000 mantras. Its Brahmana is Gopatha.

Last or the concluding part of the vedas is Upanishad, which is its philosophical and spiritual portion. There are said to be 108 upanishads, important among them being: Brhadranyaka, Chandogya, Keno, Katho, Kaivalyo, Isavasya, Mandukaya, Mundaka, Prasana, Taittriya and Aitareya Upanishads. Srimad Bhagwad Geeta is the essence of Upanişhads. That is perhaps the reason why it is considered as the most sacred scripture of Hindus, even on present day, the law courts requiring to take oath on it by Hindus, before giving one's deposition as a witness. The importance of Bhagwad Geeta being self-evident, its slokas on division of society have to be gone through carefully in all its details to know the mind of God.

Epics

The two epics are Ramayana and Mahabharta. The former revolves around the personality of Lord Rama and the latter around the personality of Lord Krishna. Srimad Bhagwad Geeta is part (rather core) of Mahabharta. The epics contain the account of God in human form. Common points to be noted in both epics are:

1. The human form of God's manifestation is Kshatriya.
2. The teachings are universal in nature without any element of sectarian appeal.
3. There is combination of action, devotion and knowledge in these manifestations.
4. Their authors are connected to Shudrahood.
5. There is victory over the evil after the epic war, in each case.

The stories of the two epics are too popular to merit detailed narration here. Though historicity in both cases is not established in the sense of direct proofs, but this does not count much in view of the depth of appeal of the messages contained in the epics. If there is anything like reality in the world, the teachings and the quality of epics messages touch that reality; else these create their own reality for the salvation of human race.

The historians rate the age of epics anywhere beyond 1000 BC. Some proofs like the NASA report of a submerged bridge between Rameshwaram and Sri Lanka [Zee News 11 October 2002 and picture reproduced in an Article in *The Pioneer* dated 13 Oct. 2003] and the Govt. of India's project to discover the remnants of submerged Dwarka are emerging slowly. But, as said earlier, even without such proofs their perception is more than reality.

Sutras and Dharma Shastras (Smrits)

These are in continuation of Brahamana portion of Vedas, being ritualistic in nature. Root of present Hinduism based on Brahminical order of caste-by-birth, lies in these books. All this literature is the creation of Brahmin authors well-versed in Sanskrit literature but not necessarily in spiritual philosophy. The books contain the family, social and religious laws for Hindus. These are not revealed or sacred books like Srutis.

Sutras are: Grihya Sutras, Gautam Dharma Sutras, Srauta Sutras, Apastamba Sutras and Baudhyam Sutras. The authors are Baudhyana, Apastama, Gautam, Brahaspati, Vashista etc. Likewise there are smritis like Manu smriti (also called manav Dharam Shartra or Laws of Manu), Vishnu Smriti, Narad Smriti etc. written between 2nd and 7th century A.D.

Dharam Shastras are in continuing tradition of Sutras. Most of these are written in or around 1st Century A.D.

Manu Smriti or Laws of Manu

This was the most important law book of Hindus for centuries and contains the caste classification of Hindus, based on birth. Brahmanis are on the top, 'he is a deity even for the Gods' and shudras at the bottom, 'nothing belongs to a shudra'. The concept of outcastes appear predominantly, with strict prescription against them forcing to live outside Village. This book contains social laws in matters of marriages, occupation and other conducts with description of penalties against various offences and violation of laws by different castes.

Considering the names of races and other material in it, historians almost unanimously accept the period of creation of this Hindu law book called 'Manu smriti' as between 200 AD and 200 BC. The book 'Cultural History of India' Vol.V by Shri Sunit Kumar Chatterjee, with a forward by Sh. K.M. Munshi (a publication of Rama Krishna Mission, Institution of Culture, Calcutta) give the period of Manu smriti, as:

"The present text possibly took its shape during the Brahmanic revival in the first Century BC".

Similarly the 'Ancient History of India' by B.P. Saha and K.S. Behera gives about the period as "The famous book on Hindu law, 'Manu smriti' was completed in those days (sunga period)". Other historians also place the period in the vicinity of the above. Buddisht period of Ashoka came to end during 185 BC, when king Brihdratha, the grandson of Ashoka was killed on the prade ground by his Brahmin general Pusyamitra Sunga. Manu Smriti seems to be the product of sunga's period or other Brahmanic dynasty's period following the Sungas. The author of Manu Smriti is not the ancient progenitor of human race Manu, but a Brahmin who used his name for this work. Writing on Manav Dharam Shastra, Sh. S.V. Ketkar in his book. 'History of caste in India' published 1909, reprint by Low Price Publication, says "our author endeavors to pass his work off as that of somebody else, namely Manu, and this motive has had a great deal of influence on the treatment. He nearly succeeded in deceiving the readers till merciless historical criticism of modern times stepped in (Chapter. IV). S.V. Ketkar places the period of Manu Smriti as 227 AD. The ancient Manu is a different personality, who existed even before Ramayana period, as Iksvaku was the ancestor of Lord Rama, from which solar dynasty came. Lord Krishana says in Bhagwad Geeta "I taught this immortal yoga to Vivaswan (Sun-God); Vivaswan conveyed it to Manu (his son); and Manu imparted it to (his son) Iksvaku". Geeta (IV/1).

The German philosopher F. Max Mulleur, great admirer of and commentator on Hindu Scriptures, says about this Smriti, "The argument in support of the authenticity and authentativeness of Manu Smriti are extremely weak" (Sacred books of East-Laws of Manu Vol XXV {P. XVI}, Published 1886). Max Muller also says "Does caste as we find it in Manu and at present day, form part of the religious teachings of Vedas ?. We answer with a decided "No". Further, there is no authority whatsoever in the Vedas for the complicated system of Castes, no authority for the offensive privileges claimed by the Brahamins, no authority for the degraded position of Shudras ..... no law to prohibit the marriage of people belonging to different castes, no law to brand the off spring of such marriage with an indelible stigma" (India caste, Vol. I by John Wilson, K.K. Book Distributers).

Puranas

There are 18 Puranas, falling equally under three categories, namely, Vishnu Purana, Shiva Purana and Brahma Purana.

Vishnu Puranas are: Vishnu, Narad, Garud, Padama, Bhagvata and Vraha.

Shiva Puranas are: Matsya, Agni, Linga, Vayu, Kurma and Skanda.

Brahma Puranas are: Brahma, Markandeya, Bhavishya, Vamana, Brahmanda and Vaivarta.

These books are also not revealed texts but contain faithful account of the dynasties and glimpses of other historical events of kings, saints and religious personalities. The books try to illustrate the philosophical principles of Vedas and other scriptures, for the understanding of common people.

Darshans or System of Philosophies

These have been illustrated in chart 1 of this chapter. The two extreme philosophies are Uttar Mimansa who believe in Vedas as well as God and charvaka who believe that there is no life other then that of material enjoyment on this earth without any restraints of ethics and morality.

The *Jains* do not believe in Vedas, but believe in the Eternal Truth which is perfect and the ultimate aim of human salvation.

The *Buddist* deny any authority to Vedas but believe in the Moral Laws following which man obtain release from sufferings and attain the Nirvana.

Tarka philosophy is based on 17 gunas which is inherent in any substance. It is based on common sense which accepts the visible world as real and therefore analyses it in detail through the concept of anus (atoms).

Sankhya philosophy is scientific in its details and analytical in approach. It says nothing comes out of nothing. The world is the manifestation of Prakriti, which consists of its three basic gunas, i.e., Sattva, Rajas and Tamas. These in their different combinations produce infinite variety in life. The Purusha is in bondage of Prakriti and liberates itself through sattvic predominance. It does not consider God as necessary for philosophy, which the Patanjali philosophy requires.

Jaimini philosophy (Purva-Mimansa) believes in Karma- Kand portion of Vedas, according to which if man follow the rituals prescribed in Vedas, he obtains merit to enjoy heavenly pleasures.

3
Shudra's or Low Caste's Right to Supreme Knowledge

It it in the books written by priests that madness like that of caste are to be found and not in books revealed from God. Let the priest enjoy the fruits of their ancestor's achievement, while I follow the word of God, for my good lies there

Swami Vivekanand
Complete works Vol.VI, P. 395

An individual has full right to know himself. This is a divine right given to him which no one can take away. In fact this is the only purpose of a human life and all other creature's, as brought out in chapter-1. "Each soul is potentially divine. The goal is to manifest this divinity within by controlling nature, external and internal. Do this either by work or worship, or psychic control or philosophy- by one or more or all of these- and be free. This is the whole religion. Doctrines or rituals or books or temples or forms are but secondary details" said Swami Vivekananda. Vedanta is the perfect science of Self-knowledge. This is contained in Upanishads.

"And the Upanishads are the great mine of strength. Therein lies strength enough to invigorate the whole world, made strong, energized through them. They will call with trumpt voice upon the weak, the miserable and downtrodden of all the races, all creeds and all sects to stand on their feet and be free. Freedom, physical freedom, mental freedom and spiritual freedom are the watchword of Upanishad. Ay, this is the one scripture in the world of all others that does not talk of salvation but of freedom" – Swami Vivekananda, complete works, Vol. VIII P. 238.

About the authorship of Upanishads Swamiji Says: "You speak of meat eating kstriyas.... It is they who are the fathers of all that is noble and beautiful in Hinduism. Who wrote Upanishads? who was Rama? Who was Krishana? who was Buddha? Who were the Tirthankaras of the Jains? Whenever the Kstriyas have preached religion, they have given it to everybody, and whenever the Brahmins wrote anything, they would deny all rights to others". (Complete works Vol.-IV P. 358)

The Brahamins till now claimed the sole right to scriptural knowledge and its creation. How incorrect is their claim, particularly to the Brihm-Vidya-the Supreme Knowledge-will be evident from the contents of Chandogya Upanishad. First, it gives the description of Raikva-the cart puller-who imparts knowledge of Brihm to the king Jansruti, then it contains the teachings relating to satyakam Jabala- the son of a maid-servant-who attained this Supreme knowledge as a disciple of Rishi Haridrumata Gautam. According to Rishi Gautam, truthfulness is the only test to determine one's real lineage. The Upanishad then reveals how this knowledge was imparted to Brahmins for the first time by kstriyas.

Let us see the question of right to knowledge (which had been denied to Shudras for centuries) in a different light. The idea is not to say that no restriction be attached to the process of gaining such high knowledge.

It demands total commitment and dedication of an individual and the pearls of wisdom obtained are to be safe-guarded from those who have no interest in the subject. But it is said about Brihm-Vidya that it itself safeguards its secrets from the unqualified persons, just as the Einstein's Theory of Relativity safeguards its secret from those who have not developed the required sharpness of mind to comprehend subtler thoughts.

The Adhikarivada (Right to Knowledge)

What rights have the Shudras and other common people to the highest knowledge contained in Upanishads and other such texts. Listen to the voice of divine soul – Swami Vivekananda, "In most cases where Shankaracharya quotes Smirti in his commentaries on Vedanta-Sutra, he cites the authority of Mahabharta. But seeing that we find clear proofs about caste being based on qualifications both in Bhism Parva of the Mahabharta and in the stories of Ajagar and Uma and Maheshwara has he made any mention in his writings of this fact?

The doctrine of caste in the Purusha-Suktam of the Veda does not make it hereditary – so what are those instances in the Vedas where caste has been made a matter of hereditary transmission?

The Acharya could not adduce any proof from Vedas to the effect that Shudra should not study the Vedas. He only quotes". यदोऽनवकलस (Tai Samhita) to maintain that when he is not entitled to perform Yajnas he has neither any right to study the Upanishads and the like. But the same Acharya contends with reference to" अथातो ब्रह्मजिज्ञासा (Vedanta Sutra I i 1) that the word here does not mean "subsequent to the study of Vedas", because it is contrary to proof that the study of Upanishad is not permissible without previous study of Vedic mantras and Brahmnas and because there is no intrinsic sequence between the Vedic Karma Kand and Vedic Janana Kand. It is evident, therefore, that one may attain to the knowledge of Brahmn without having studied the ceremonial parts of the Vedas. So, if there is no sequence between the sacrificial practices and Janana, why does the Acharya contradict his own statement when it is a case of the Shudras, by inserting the clause "by force of the same logic". Why should the Shudras not study the Upanishads?" (complete works Vol. VI p. 208).

Knowledge Versus Rituals- Position of Vedas

There had been going an intense though unseen struggle between the Karam Kand portion and the Jnana Kand (the knowledge portion) of Vedas. This is indeed a conflict between the priestly hold on society and divine will to liberate human beings through direct path of knowledge. Evidence of this struggle are met in all times. Some of these are given as below:-

(a) In Upanishads

- There are two kinds of knowledge to be acquired- the higher and the lower.
- Of these the lower comprises the Rig Veda etc., the science of pronunciation, code of rituals, astrology etc. Then there is higher knowledge by which is attained that Imperishable.
- The deluded fools, believing the rites inculcated by the Vedas and Smirtis to be the highest, do not understand the other thing that leads to liberation. They having enjoyed the fruit of actions, enter this world or an inferior one.

Mundaka Upanishad

(b) Lord Shiva's Curse

- Enraged by Daksha, the attendant of lord Shiva Nandiswara cursed the Brahmin race that they shall find gratification only in wealth and physical comforts devoted to learning only for the sake of livelihood.

The sage Bhirgu uttered counter curse to Lord Shiva on behalf of Brahman race as " Because you denounce the Vedas which lay down the bounds of prosperity for man (following the conduct prescribed for different grades and stages in life) and thereby preserve the society as well as Brahmins, therefore you will take the path of heretics."

Lord Shiva, therefore, never liked the ritualistic portion of Vedas.

(c) Lord Krishna's Actions and Teachings

- Lord Krishna was not kind to the chief Vedic God, Indra. He stopped his worship by lifting Goverdhan mountain and again defeated him at Khandavprastha, renamed as Indraprastha. His teachings are :
- "Arjuna, those who are obsessed by desire and devoted to the letter of the Vedas, who look upon heaven as the supreme goal and argue that there is nothing beyond heaven are unwise. They utter flowery speech recommending many acts of various kinds for attainment of pleasure and prosperity with rebirth as their fruit. Those whose mind are carried away by such words, and who are deeply attached to pleasure and worldly prosperity, can not attain the determinate intellect concentrated on God". (Geeta Chapt. II/42-44).

'Untouchable' As Guru of Adi Sankracharya

For all his great learning and exceptional brilliance in philosophical matters, Adi Sankracharya happened to believe in prevailing caste system. The God did not like that such a wonderful mind should be tainted with this thinking. There is a famous incident which occurred in the life of the Acharya where God removed this colored patch from his mind. One day while at Kashi, Sankaracharya went to take a bath in Gangas. While returning to the temple of Vishvanath after bath he saw an untouchable standing in his way with four dogs. In his unguarded moment and going by the tradition, he asked this Chandala- the untouchable, to get aside quickly and give him the way. For a Brahmin, after all, this will be the most inauspicious thing to happen after a bath. The Chandala counter-questioned Acharya "which I should remove from your path, the body or Atman. The contents of your body and my body are the same (both made from five elements) and the contents of your Atman and my atman are the same (it is one universal spirit)". The Acharya felt a thunder bolt falling on his head and out of reverence for such a learning went into an ecstasy composing the famous *'Maneesha Panchakam'* – my five convictions, while giving following reply to this untouchable:

"This indeed is my deep conviction: he who has realized that he is not the seen, but that he is the one consciousness that illumines all experiences, the one consciousness that is the sole witness of the entire play of the universe, the one consciousness which is the very life-spark in all forms—from the creator down to the ant- He alone is my Guru, be he a Chandala, be he a Brahmin." The author of Vivekachudamani, essence of the divine nector, could not have done otherwise.

Like that there are four other verses one of these is engraved at Laxmi Narayan Temple (Birla Mandir) Delhi. The Acharya immediately realized that the untouchable was no one other than the Lord of his heart, Lord Shiva himself, who disappeared from the scene after this reply and giving his d*arshan* to

Shankracharya. It was the first of life-time experience for Shankracharya to directly come in contact with God, who came down on earth in the form of an 'untouchable', with four dogs as Vedas with him.

Composer of Rig Veda

Kavash Ailush, a Shudra, was the composer of Mantras in Rig Veda (X- Mandla Sukta 30-34). Aiterya Brahmin Contains the story of this Kavash Ailush whose presence in the midst of Rishis performing 'Yagna' on the bank of Saraswati was initially resented but later reconciled discovering that he is a great learned man whom even the Gods honour.

Position of Bhagwad Geeta

Says Lord Krishna :

"Even if you are the most sinful of all sinners, yet you shall verily cross all sins by the raft of knowledge". (IV: 36)

"As the blazing fire reduces fuel to ashes, O Arjuna, so does the fire of knowledge reduces all actions(sins) to ashes". (IV: 37)

How does the worst sinner acquire the knowledge? He is not only sinful but the 'most sinful'. Obviously, a Shudra will not be worse than the 'most sinful' one. One of the great commentators on Bhagwad Geeta, Swami Chinmayanada (Founder of Chinmaya Mission,Bombay), who has held hundreds of National and International discourses on Geeta, comments on the above first sloka: "Such a clear charter of man's right to be divine has never been so far written in any other existing scripture of the world".

This is in Geeta, the essence of Upanishads. Right to knowledge is thus to everyone with no holds barred.

This is clear mandate from the God himself, on the knowledge about one's own-self.

Lord Krishna further says:

"Neither by study of Vedas, nor by penance, nor by charity, nor by ritual can I be seen in the form (Cosmic Vision) as you have seen Me". (XI: 53)

"Through single minded devotion, however, I can be seen in this form and known in essence and even entered into, O valiant Arjuna". (XI: 54)

Universality of Truth Revealed in Upanishads

- This is the truth- As from a blazing fire thousands of spark similar to it in nature, issue forth, so O my young friend manifold beings are produced from the imperishable and they verily go back to it again.

- Self-resplendent, formless, unoriginated and pure, that all-pervading being is both within and without. Anterior both to life and mind, He transcends even the unmanifested causal state of the universe.

  Mundakopanishad

- This self is beyond all expressions or words, beyond all acts of mind. It is all peace, ever effulgent, free from activity and fear. It is attainable through concentrated intellect.

  Mandukya Upanishad

- He who constantly sees everywhere all existence in the self and self in all beings and forms, thereafter shrinks not from anything.

Isavasyoparishad

- This Atman subtler than the subtle, greater than the great is seated in the heart of each living being. He who is free from willing and wishing with his mind and senses composed, beholds the majesty of the self and become free from sorrow.

  Kathopanisd

The universal knowledge of Upanishads as above can not be limited by any cosideration of high or low, caste or religion.

4
Aryan Gods Versus Caste

"Beginning from Buddha down to Ram Mohan Roy, everyone made the mistake of holding caste to be a religious institution and tried to pull down religion and caste all together, and failed. But in spite of all the ravings of the priests, caste is simply a crystallized social institution, which after doing its service is now filling the atmosphere of India with its stench"

- Swami Vivekananda
Complete works Vol.-V P.22-23

The concept of one God is basically opposed to the system of caste which is only a social institution, as said by Swami Vivekananda. While God is unifying factor, the caste is a divisive one. If we assert one caste the another is denied. "But caste-by-birth is an essential part of Hindu religion" one can say. No, it is not. All achievements in this country including the attainment of Independence itself can be directly traced to the liberalization of Hindu thoughts on caste system. Similarly, all evils of strifes and conflicts, poverty and ignorance, slavery and deep agonies through foreign rules, can be directly linked to the rigidness in caste system.

"When, in what period of history your rich men, noblemen, your priests and potentates took any thought for the poor-the grinding of whose faces is the very life-blood of their power?

But the Lord is the great, the vengeance came sooner or later, and they who sucked the life-blood of the poor, whose very education was at their expense, whose very power was built on their poverty, were in their turn sold as slaves by hundreds and thousands, their wives and daughters dishonored; their property robbed for last 1000 years, and do you think it was for no cause?"

Complete works Vol.VIII P. 330

And who is the author of above quoted words "He is more learned than all the learned professors of United States put together" said the professor Wright of USA. His simple words "Sisters and Brothers of America" electrifies the largest ever gathering of World Parliament of Religions and there is non-stop thunderous standing applause for more than two minutes by all Delegates ! In the very first speech. He is the hero of the conference, Messiah of the New World. But at the moment of highest honour to him by the world, he weeps during the night, the pillow becoming wet with tears. 'O, Mother, what do I care for name and fame when my motherland remains sunk in utmost poverty ; To what a sad pass have we poor Indians come when millions of us die for want of a handful of rice.... who will give them bread? Show me, O Mother, How I can help them' groaned Swami Vivekananda. That was in Sept. 1893.

How do Aryan Gods look at the caste system, let us see in the following pages (God is one, but He manifests differently according to time and place, God is above being Aryan and un-Aryan).

Lord Krishna

In his divine form as universal God, Shri Krishna gave immortal teachings in Bhagwad Geeta on the

Kurukshetra battle-field, which have come to be regarded as the most sacred revelations in Hindu religion. In one of the verses, Shri Krishna says that he created four castes i.e Brahmin, Khastriya, Vaisya and Shudras on the basis of worth i.e. gunas and karmas, as contained in sloka 13 of chapter IV. This is brought out in detail in Geeta on the basis of three gunas, i.e., Sattva, Rajas and Tamas operating in different acts of human beings, as given in its different chapters (produced in Appendix-1 of this book).

Shri Krishna is one of the greatest champions of Universal Equality, as preached in Bhagwad Geeta (excerpts follow). He spent his childhood amongst the cowherd boys of village and practiced one of the lowliest professions of that time. Just as Krishna spent his whole of childhood in the company of cowherd boys, his son Pradyumana spent his entire childhood in the house of a maid-servant of king Sambara. In fact considering facts like above from the life of Shri Krishna, Sishupala, the adversary of Krishna, when objecting to his first honour ceremony being performed by Yudhister in Raj-suya sacrifice, brought out all such 'disqualifications' to arouse public anger of assembled kings against him. Sishupala charged that Krishna does not belong to any caste and dharma and does not possess nobility of birth, acts always against Vedic injunctions and established usages, and that the father of Krishna was only a servant of King Ugrasena (one can notice here the complete absence of charge against Krishna out of one hundred, on matters of gopies – the females of Vrindavan village, which could easily move the princes against Krishna had it contained any word on it in the manner of present day presentations). Indra is the chief Vedic God of Aryans, but Krishna stops his worship in childhood and lifts Goverdhan mountain to protect the villagers against his wrath of pouring devastating rains on them. When on a peace mission to Hastinapur, He preferred to stay and dine with a Shudra (Vidur) after rejecting the invitation of the king for royal palace and food. Al-Beruni, a great Muslim scholar who came to India during the period of attacks of Mahmud of Ghazani (1000-1026 AD), gives an impartial scholarly and detailed account of India of that period in his book ' Tarikhul Hind'. In chapter (IXth) on Vasudeva, he describes him as belonging to a cattle owning low Shudra family. Yadavas of that period may not be exactly the low Shudras of present times, but in the medieval period of 1000-1030 AD, Al-Beruni might have got such perception though interaction with the Indian society which accepted liberation of all castes based on the philosophy of Krishna (he called him Vasudeva), though hearing words of Vedas was barred to Shudras even at that time. A news items in Times of India (dated 1st March 2004) mentions "In 1935 five Yadavas were killed by upper caste Bhumihars when they insisted on the right to wear sacred thread" and also "The consolidation came about gradually with the first attempt dating back to 1912 when some castes notables got together to launch Gope, Jatiya Mahasabha (GJM) a caste body patterned after formation launched by upper castes". It is to be noted here that only Shudras are denied to wear the scared thread, as *dwija*- the upper three castes- are allowed to wear it in Hindu Shastras and prevalent tradition. It will be in order to mention here the classification of Yadava clan as given in the Other Backward Castes (OBC) Report of Mandal Commission (1990) for the purpose of reservations in services, accepted by the Government of India vide office Memorandum dated 13 August 1990. For the state of Uttar Pradesh, it states the OBC names as:

1. Agri 2. Aheria, Aheriya 3. Ahir, Ghosi, Gwala, Yadhuvanshi/ Yadav 4 ...etc....

The 'Aheriya Caste' and 'Gaul caste' is also mentioned as the scheduled caste under the castes of Uttar Pradesh in the schedule attached to the Government of India Act 1935. Presently (May 2005), there is Bill pending with standing Committee of Parliament to club the reservation of SC's (Scheduled Castes) with OBC, though it is being resented by some SC leaders so that the safeguards for them are not diluted (The *Pionner* report dated 11.5.2005). The purpose to mention the above facts is not anything except to show the closeness of Krishna's worldly caste (as God he was free from any caste) to the present day low castes in India.

The famous Greek, Magesthene, an ambassador to Chandragupta Maurya's court and the contemporary of Kautilya (300 BC) in the book. 'Indaika' writes that there were seven categories of Indian Society in Maurya's period. The category as 'Ahirs and Herdsman' who were to keep on moving from place to place very much resemble the life of Yadavas (also called Ahirs in Mandal Commission Report) in Krishna's period. Krishna himself says "There are neither cities nor territories nor villages nor houses in our possession. We have ever had our abode in the forest dwelling as we do in woodlands and on mountain" (X/25: Srimad Bhagwata Purana) pleading before his father to worship mountain (Goverdhan) and not Indra. The other two categories given by Meghesthene somewhat nearer to the present day low castes were 'Agriculturist' who formed bulk of population and 'traders and artisans'. These categories of society in Maurya's period do not even remotely resemble later day Manu's period outcastes bordering on untouchability. Kautilya's Arthshastra has called Shudras an Aryan stating that he can not be made a slave (3/13). Yajnavalakya Smriti calls shudras as 'Gopa' (2/

48) and Mrichhakatika as 'Gopala'. According to Yajnavalkya, the Shudras of good conduct could perform 'Shradh-Karma' like *Dwija* (1/121). Referring to the confusion of Kshatriya and Shudra writes Dr. B.R. Ambedkar "The Yadava community to which Krishna belonged is popularly believed to be Kshatriyas. But according to Madras Hight Court the Yadvas are Shudras !!". (Dr. Babasahib Ambedkar writings and speeches Vo.-7 P. 164). Actually such situation arises because of imposition of caste-by-birth on the individual's true *Varna*. We do not accept that supermen can be born in any 'caste-by-birth.'

What have these 'herdsman' become today in 20th century AD will be described by the following episode which was reported in Indian Express through an article "Futile untouchability Law" (17th March 1984). The instance relates to a person of scheduled caste of Ajmer district who owned some 150 animals in herd together with a little land in the village. He happened to drink water from a community well besides the road while on his way to a place outside village. The upper caste persons caught him and brought before the *Panchayat*. He was threatened with life but left at a penalty of Rs. 51. He complained to all authorities in the state including District Magistrate and Police, who completed some formalities, but ultimately allowed the matter to go without any action against the culprits, making a mockery of untouchability law.

In his book, 'Chamars' (first published in 1920), which term refers to 1156 sub-castes or its different names of 1891 census, synonymous with present day 'Scheduled Castes', Mr. G.W. Briggs, a British Writer, gives accurate details of the life of 'Chamars' (outcastes). On question of religious practice of these people he writes "On the birth day of Krishna people fast and no one begins to eat until about mid might when the moon rises". Further, he writes (about Chamars):

"Nesfield suggests that they may be an occupational ofshoot from the Yadavas tribe from which Krishna came". It appears that after the creation of Manusmriti in around 200 AD, the distance between then-Yadavas the 'herdsman' and present day 'Chamars' (90 % of whom are linked to agriculture, as per the above book of Briggs) increased to this level of higher Shudras or intermediary caste, and lower Shudras. The former are even exploiting and suppressing the latter in rural areas today. Details have been given in the chapter "Shudras to Ati-Shudras"of this book showing how bulk of Shudras became untouchables-the lower Shudras.

Swami Vivekananda has to say the following on Krishna :

"Go now this minute to the temple of Partha sarthi and before him who was friend to the poor and lowly cowherds of Gokula, who never shrank to embrace the Pariah Guhaka". *Compete works Vol. V P.17*

"The other Incarnations were but parts of the Lord. He, Krishna was the Lord Himself.——— He was the most wonderful sanyasin and the most wonderful house holder in one —— Krishna can never be understood until you have studied Geeta ——(on play with Gopies) none ought to attempt to understand until he has become perfectly chaste and pure".

Compete works Vol. III P.256

"He from his childhood was against snake-worship and Indra worship. Indra worships is a Vedic ritual.

Throughout the Geeta, he is not favorable to Vedic ritual. This is the period of his love to Gopies. He was 11 years of age".

Compete works Vol. V P.321

It is, however, true that a lot of pleasure-seeking poetry has developed around Krishna later in some literatures and other books, without realizing that description would not reconcile with the age of Krishna as 11 years before leaving Varindavan (never to return back). Whatever the might and powers of Krishna may be as a divine person, his age factor would always remain relevant while speaking on social morals of the world, because if one speaks of his divine powers and philosophy, he has repeatedly said that all beings are his own expressions.

Mahabharta contains the story of a Brahmin sage Utanga. Krishna after the war departs to Dwarka. While on the way, he meets Utanga, who on learning about the death of Kaurva and others got angry with Krishna. But Krishna shows the whole events through his cosmic form and cools down the sage. Krishna asked Utanga for a boon. Initially hesitated, utang requested for water to be available whenever he wishes for it (the sage was living in a desert area). After some time Utanga felt thirsty and prayed for the water boon to materialize. A Chandala appeared with water skin, but Utanga will not accept water from the hands of an untouchable. He remembers Krishna to find out why his boon is not becoming effective. Krishna appears and tells him that not mere water but 'Amrita' (nectar) was being offered to him by Indra, disguised as Chandals, which is not given even to the gods, but the sage failed in the test of maintaining equality between high and low in the worldly plane.

Krishna can not be understood fully except by deep reflections. Take the case of killing of Daronacharya in Mahabharta war. One can notice a sort of divine humour in the act. Daronacharya was the commander-in-chief of Kaurva army when Abhimanu, the illustrious son of Arjuna was killed weaponless against all rules of war by a combination of all major warriors of Kaurva force including Drona himself. And here is the situation that Drona on mere half-hearted mention of the news of his son Aswathama's death ceases fighting in grief and sits down in meditation. Was not Darona aware that those whom he had been slaughtering with weapons of mass destruction, are also sons of some one who are equally grieved by their death.

Who can understand him, the infinite might of this universe, as shown to Arjuna is cosmic form? "If there be the effulgence of a thousand suns bursting forth all at once in the heavens, even that would hardly approach the splendor of the mighty Lord" (Geeta XI : 12).

Universal Equality in Bhagwad Geeta

Whole of Bhagwad Geeta contains the message of universal equality as given below:

— "A wise looks with the same eye on a Brahmin endowed with learning and culture, a cow, an elephant, a dog and a pariah". (V :18)

— "Having known me as the disinterested friend of all beings, my devotee attains peace". (V:29)

— "He who sees me present in all beings, and sees all beings existing in Me, I am never out of sight for him, nor is he ever out of sight of me". (VI:30)

— "He who looks on all as one, on the analogy of his own self, and looks on the pleasure and pains of all with a similar eye, such a yogi is regarded as supreme". (VI:32)

— "I am equally present in all beings, there is none hateful to me or dear to me". (IX:29)

— "I am the self seated in the hearts of all beings". (X:29)

— "He who is devoted to me and free from malice towards all beings, reaches me". (X1:55)

— "Those even minded towards all and devoted to doing good to all creature, ——— come to me". (XII:3,4)

— "He who is free from malice towards all beings, who is friendly as well as compassionate—— that devotee is dear to me". (XII :13,14)

— "Sublimity, forgiveness, absence of malice and self importance, are marks of the one who is endowed with divine virtues". (XVI:3)

— "Hypocrisy, arrogance, pride, anger—— are the marks of one born with demoniacal properties". (XVI:4)

Lord Rama

Lord Rama is the hero of epic Ramayana. He is also called Maryada Purushotam, i.e., an ideal human being, associated with supreme human qualities. Valmiki, the author of Ramayana, had precisely enquired as to who is the person of noble qualities in that era, when he was told by sage Narada that Rama, the son of Dasaratha, is that person of such greatness. Valmiki Ramayana is the only authentic account of Rama's deeds, as he witnessed in person all that is said about him and participated in the end scene of Rama's court where Lav and Kush (Rama's sons) through songs narrated the Ramayana story which Valmiki had composed. Valmiki thus was an author as well as a character of Ramayana. Tulsidas's *Ramachatrita Manas* is a recent creation, about 500 years back composed during the rule of Mughal emperor Akhbar. Its historicity of Rama therefore, is not as authentic as that of Valmiki Ramayana's where there is any difference between the two on any point. There are other floating sources of dubious credibility, which even refer to Sita as Rama's Sister, forgetting that Rama won

Sita after performing the impossible task of lifting and breaking Shiva's bow *(Dhanush),* **which chance came to Rama in the last when all other Kings had tried it.** Janaka, Sita's father, had cried in anguish that alas, no Kshatriya are now left in the world to fulfill the condition for Sita's marriage. Had any other Prince succeeded in breaking the bow, Sita's marriage to Rama would not have taken place. Rama's greatness is sought to be diluted by another event of Bali's killing. Valmiki Ramayana gives the reasons for this killing. But not going into its details suffice it to say that Bali was told how he had captured the wife of his younger brother Sugriva alongwith the Kingdom. While breathing his last, Bali realized the totality of situation and placed his son Angad at the service of Rama. Dying declarations are honoured even today in court of law as truth. Later, Angad challenged Ravana in his court that if any of his men can move his foot, Rama shall return back to Ayodhya without Sita. He could not have done so if there was even a trace of ill-will in his heart towards Rama.

Lord Rama when he was about 16 years of age felt greatly dejected seeing the nature of the world. This was about the time when Vishavamitra had come to Dasaratha to take Rama and Laxmana with him to forest to fight devils (Ashuras). Sage Vashista gave the immortal teachings to Rama through Philosophical discourses as contained in the master-piece scripture 'Yoga-Vashist', in the presence of Valmiki. Finally Rama had realized his nature as Brihm, the supreme self (some excerpts in chapter 11).

While Rama just enters the forest for his exile of 14 years, he meets Nishad Raj Guha- a low caste person. Both liked each other so intensely that Lord Rama after completion of exile period and winning over Ravana remembers Guha first, even before Bharta who was about to die as per his oath if Rama was to return late by one day. This was the moment of highest achievement and happiness for Rama in his life time. Bharta is waiting for 14 years to see Rama. Despite this, Rama asks Hanumana to meet first the Nishad Raj and inform him of his arrival, and then go to Bharta to likewise inform him of his arrival. Valmiki Ramayana records the message of Rama for Nishad Raj as :

"Meet Nishad Raj Guha and convey that all is well at this end"

"Finding we well, in good health and free from worry, Nishad Raj Guha will be very happy, because he is my friend and is like my own soul for me"

श्रुत्वा तु कुशलिनमरोगं विगतज्वर म् ।
भवि यति गुहंः प्रतिः स ममात्मसमः सखा ।।

On return from Lanka Rama meets and embraces first Nishad Raj and then proceeds to Ayodhya.

In Tulsi Das's *Ramcharitmanas* we have a description of Nishad Raj and love of Rama for him, when Nishad Raj comes to encounter Bharta, mistakenly thinking that Bharta has come to fight Rama.

'Who in this world and Vedas both has been considered low in all respect, whose shadow touch causes one to take bath, embarrassing the same Nishad, Bharta is feeling so happy in love and affection".

लोक बेद सब भाँति नीचा ।
जासु घाँह घुइ लेइअ सींचा ।।
तेहि भरि अंक राम लघु भ्राता ।
मिलत पुलक परिपूरित गाता ।।

Tulsi Das further Says:

'A low person from all considerations and still the God embarrassed him like his own brother Bharata' (on return from Lanka)

While describing the above happening of Ramayana period, which is said to be more than 1000 BC, Tulsi Das, incidentally, is also touching upon the prevailing social attitude of a caste Brahmin towards a Shudra during the period of medieval India- 16th century A.D. A Shudra of this medieval period is one whose touch of shadow itself causes pollution to a caste Hindu. These adjectives of lowliness of Nishad Raj caste have been added by Tulsi Das taking them from his own period of 16th century A.D. Contrast this with the condition of Rama's period. Nishad Raj is a low caste person, but he is being addressed as friend and brother in deep affection by Rama and Bharata. There is no relationship of master and servant.

There was no concept of social differentiation attached to Shudras and they were freely honoured on all important sacred occasions. What can be a more sacred occasion than the sacrificial ceremony arranged by Dasaratha to obtain the blessings to beget children, as Dasaratha was childless even in advance age. The sacrificial horse (Asavmedha) was finally touched by three women, one being a Shudra woman by name 'Priviratti' (Valmiki Ramayan-'Balkanda' 14/35). Rama alongwith his three brothers, was born as a result of this ceremony.

The same Rama fights Ravana with the army consisting of monkeys (Vanaras) and bears, developed to human consciousness. His most ardent devotee is Hanumana, one amongst this race. This only shows that to Rama the races not observing the Aryan caste system were equally acceptable. These fighting vanaras and bears were not Kshatriyas of Aryan caste.

After the end of war, Rama thanked the vanara forces for their sacrifices. In reply to this, the vanara said :

"O, Raghunatha, you are the lord of three world. Considering us vanaras the lowly ones, you have favored us".

In a way Rama has proved that he needs no Kshatriya-by-caste to fight the fieriest epic battle with as great an adversary as Ravana. On a worldly plane, it is no agreement to dilute the above position saying that these monkeys etc. were certain deities in previous birth, even if that be true.

Rama's love for Low Castes

Nishad Raj Guha: Rama's heart was of universal love and affection towards all unaffected by worldly traces of castes and religions. The friendly love of Rama for the low caste Guha has been described in detail above, where Rama meets him first even before Bharata, on return to Ayodhya after the victory over Ravana.

Sabari: This story is already popular, in which Rama eats her tasted berries when he alongwith Laxmana came to her cottage in the forest. Though belonging to a low caste, she was engaged in great *'tapasaya'* (austerities) as a disciple of Rishi Matang who had left for his heavenly abode entrusting the charge of Ashram to her alongwth 'Akhand Jyoti' (eternal light) burning in the campus. While showing this light to Rama, she meditated and alighted herself on fire with it in the presence of Rama. She appeared as a great deity in heavenly cloths and ornaments to head towards Divya-Dham, the Divine Abode. It is said to be a place above the heaven. The heaven is meant for enjoying the merits of good deeds of an individual soul, on exhaustion of which it again takes birth on the earth. Entry to Divya-Dham, however, liberates a soul form the cycle of birth and death for ever.

Justice to a Dog: As a daily routine, Rama is seated on his throne alongwith Rishs and other counselors. There comes a call from some complainant. Rama sends Laxmana out to fetch the aggrieved. He finds a dog at the gate, curiously enough. Assured that the dog has a complaint, Laxmana asks it is to come to the assembly and narrate it before Lord Rama. Dog hesitates, considering itself a low animal to face such an august assembly. Laxman reports matter to Rama, who orders Laxmana to bring the dog immediately to his presence. The dog comes to hall and Rama ask it to bring forth its grievance. The dog states that it was just standing in the street when a Brahmin hit it with a rod out of anger. The Brahmin is brought to the *'Darbar'*. He admits his guilt, pleading that he hit the dog out of anger as it was found in his way when he was trying to fetch some food for hungry stomach, by bagging after the time for food was over. Rama asks the counselors to suggest appropriate punishment. No answer comes forth readily. The dog ask Rama to permit it to suggest punishment for the Brahmin, if the Lord be so pleased. Rama agrees. The dog suggests that the Brahmin be made the head of monastery. Everybody is amused, including Rama. He asks the dog to explain the reasons for this punishment which looks more like a reward. The dog states that he was the Brahmin, head of a monastery, in his previous life. Due to some minor slips on his part, he was thrown to this birth (as a dog). If a Brahmin be so ill-tempered as the present one and he be made to head a monastery, the serious consequences for him in the future can only be imagined.

Inferences: One that even a dog, the lowest creature could expect justice against a Brahmin-supposedly the highest creature. Second, the life of strict austerity which a Brahmin was required to live to claim high status in society, makes this a matter of hard duty and not of privileges, punishment being sever for any deviation.

Sambuka Episode

In this story Rama kills Sambuk- a Shudra, while the latter was practicing sever penances by hanging from the tree with head downwards, to enter into heaven with physical body and rule over it. As a consequence of this act, the son of a Brahmin had died while in the Kingdom of Rama there were no untimely deaths, the people were prosperous and free from miseries, the trees were laden with fruits, the cows etc. gave plenty of milk, the soil gave enough crops, there were no thefts and crimes. An impression is sought to be given in this event as if Rama kills a Shudra for showing the audacity by the latter to imitate a Brahmin who alone are entitled to such *tapasyas*. Such a view is in direct contradiction of Sabari, who performed tapasya and ascended to Divya Dham right in the presence of Rama. It seems the tapasya being referred to Sambuka is 'Hat-Yoga' which is not considered desirable for any normal person. Bhagwad Geeta Says "The penances done under a deluded understanding with torture to the mind, senses and body, or with the object of causing injury to others, is said to be Tamasic" (XVII/19). Rama's own ancestor 'Trisankhu' (earlier called satyavarta, the father of

Harish Chandra) had this desire of going to heaven with body, for which he got performed a great yagna through the sage Visvamitra. As soon as Trisankhu enters the gate of heaven, Indra pushes him down to earth. Vishavamitra halts his downfall, thus Trisankhu remains hanging mid air ,head downwards, between heaven and earth. This punishment was worse than death. There is, however, a parallel case of Sambuka mentioned in Valmiki Ramayan just after the event of Sambuka killing. This is in fact narrated by Laxman to Rama to purge himself of sin by performing the same Asvamedha Sacrifice as performed by Indra after he killed a Brahmin, Vritasur, who was engaged in the sever penance, thus shaking Indra's Kingdom (as the presiding deity of mind Indra's kingdom is always shaken as soon as some one tries to transcend the mind). A Brihm-hatya (killing of a Brahmin) was attached to Indra which was removed after the Ashavmedha yagna was performed by Indra with the blessing of Lord Vishnu. Rama performed this Ashawmedha yagna on the advice of Laxmana.

Lord Shiva

There is a Parvati- Maheswara dialogue on caste system, as given in Anushasan Parv of Mahabharta (Chapter 143). Reference to this dialogue has been given by Swami Vivekananda also when saying 'But seeing that we find clear proof about caste being based on qualification both in Bhism Parva of the Mahabaharta and in the stories of Ajagar and Uma and Maheshwara——' (quoted in Chapter 3 of this book). Says Mahaeswara :

"Brahmin, Kshatriya, Vaishya and Shudra are according to nature (savabhav) of an individual, in my opinion".

"Even a Shudra by controlling senses and making his inner thinking pure, becomes respectable like a twice-born, as said so by Brahma himself."

"In my opinion if a Shudra possesses good Karma and Savabhav (good nature) he becomes more respectably than the twice born" It is given so in the following sloka (49):

स्वभावः कर्म च भुभयत्र भूद्रेडपि तिश्ठति ।
विशिवटः स द्विजातेवै विक्षेय इति मे मति ।।

"Attainment of Brahminhood is neither through birth (Yoni), nor through past impressions (*Sanskars*), nor through learning. Good conduct (*Sadachar*) is the main cause for becoming a Brahmin" (50)

We have already seen how Maheswara corrected the caste tendency in his devotee-Adi Sankracharya and in ancient times cursed Brahmin race for their arrogance (Chapter III of this book). Is it a coincidence that Lord Shiva appeared on this earth in human form before the two great historical personalities either as a tribal (*Bheel*) before Arjuna while he had set out to acquire divine weapons or as an untouchable before Adi Sankracharya when he was coming to Kashi temple after a bath in Ganges (detailed in chapter 3 of this book)?

Realised Souls

There is a galaxy of divine personalities in this land who raised their voice against the caste system. It is difficult to give all names, but some of these are; Lord Buddha, Ramanuj, Swami Ramananda, Chaitanya, Guru Nanak, Sant Ravidas, Kabir, Eknath, Tukaram, Namdev, Narayana Guru, Saibaba of Shirdi, Swami Vivekananda, Swmai Dayananda, Swami Shivananda etc. Swami

Dayananda started Arya Samaj's movement against untouchability. Their's was the first attempt to loosen the caste barrier in present times, but they could not succeed beyond a point as the basis of caste remained in books like Manusmriti.

Sages and Personalities of Mahabharta

Practically the whole of Mahabharta contains the instances of caste system in flexible form that was prevalent at that time though later day tampering in Brahmanic period can not be ruled out. Before touching upon various episodes and instances, first let us focus our attention on the author of Mahabharta himself. This author of the greatest epic of the world, containing Bhagwad Geeta in it, is also the compiler of Vedas and Puranas. He is therefore, one of the most important personalities around which revolves the ancient and present Hinduism or Sanatam Dharma. "As a character Buddha was the greatest the world has ever seen, next to him Christ. But the teachings of Krishna as taught by the Geeta are the grandest the world has ever known. He who wrote that wonderful poem was one of those rare souls whose lives send a wave of regeneration through the world. The human race will never again see such a brain as his who wrote Geeta" Said Swami Vivekananda

Complete works Vol. VII P.22.

This author is Krishna Dvaipayana Ved Vyasa. He was born of a Shudra woman (fisher women). His father a Brahmin sage Parasara had only a few hours living together with this woman, never to meet her again throughout life. Vyasa was brought up by her in her own company and environment. Even otherwise, in terms of chapter 47 and 48 of 'Anushasan Parv' of Mahabharta, the son born of a Shudra mother, is Shudra himself, as given below:

"A son born of a Brahman from a Brahmin or Kstriya woman is Brahmin himself but the sons born of a Brahmin from Vaishya and Shudra woman are considered to be of the caste of the mother herself". (4)

Likewise Manusmriti Says

"From a Brahmin with the daughter of a Vaishya is born a son called an Ambashtha, with the daughter of a Shudra a Nishda, who is also called Parsava (body of shudra woman considered as corpse)" (Manu X:8)

In this case of Vyasa, he did not live in the social company of his father in his early life and went to forest straight at a tender age for performing tapas. Sudrahood of Ved Vyasa is a matter of general acceptance with the scholars.

A very brief history of the origin of Pandaves and Kaurvas will be in order in this context. Satyavati, the mother of Ved Vyasa was married again to the King Santnu on the terms dictated by her father, a boatman. Though she got two sons from Santnu her further progeny came in grave peril due to the untimely death of both of them. By the grace of Ved Vyasa, she was blessed with two grand children Dhritrastra and Pandu through the two widows Ambika and Ambalika. Vidur was born to the maid servant. Vidur the God of Justice in previous life was cursed by sage Mandavya for awarding disproportionate punishment for crime committed in childhood through innocence. Five sons were born to Pandu while one hundred were born to Dhirtrastra. The main characters of Mahabharta were, thus, a mix of Shudrahood.

There are well known episodes in Mahabharta where the caste of an individual has been established to be by his merit. When banished for 12 years forest life, the Pandvas were roaming about in jungle. One day, an heavy snake (said to be a cursed Rishi Nahusa) caught hold of Bhima. Not reaching home, other brothers got perturbed. Yudhister went around and saw Bhima in the clutches of the Python. Yudhister requested it to release Bhima and instead take him for its food but to no avail. Ultimately the Python asked Yudhister to answer his questions and if answered correctly it shall release Bhima, otherwise eat him up.

> Python said "who is a Brahmin and what is worth Knowing"
>
> Yudhister answered, "Any person who possesses truth, forgiveness, gentleness lack of cruelty, austerity and mercy is a Brahmin. The element worth knowing is par-Brahm".
>
> Python Said "The above mentioned qualities can be found in Shudras also, and according to you, they also are Brahmin?".
>
> Yudhister Said "If above qualities are in a Shudra, then he is not a Shudra and if these qualities are not in a Brahmin, then he is not a Brahmin".

On the above answer of Yudhister, Bhima got released. The point to note is that these words have come out of the mouth of a person who never told lie in his life time except one half lie in battle field under grave situation. The fact that Bhima was released also testifies to the truth of above statement.

Similar instance occurs at the end of their forest life when a Daksha (Spirit) had killed four brothers of

Yudhister in a pond. Among several other questions Daksh asked the similar question as to what makes one the Brahmin. Yudhister gave similar answer as mentioned above and the four brothers became alive. A wrong answer could have resulted into the death of all five brothers. There is therefore, no element of doubt on Yudhister's definition of Brahmins, the same being death-tested, uttered by the most truthful person in the history of mankind.

There is another story of a Kaushik Brahmin in Mahabharta. After becoming learned in Vedas and other disciplines, he one day set meditating under a tree. A bird sitting on the tree threw some leaf on the head of this Pandit. He grew so angry that he burnt the bird just by his mere look. He had achieved great 'Sidhi' indeed. One day he went to a town to beg for alms. A lady came out near the door of house and said 'please wait', and went back. Just then her husband had come tired from days work. She got busy in attending to him by serving food, and came out for giving alms to the Brahmin after a bit of delay. The Brahmin got angry on this negligence. She bagged apology but to no avail. Ultimately she said, look, O learned Brahmin, I am not a bird that you can burn with your eyes. Listening this, the Brahmin was extremely surprised and asked her as to how she knew the incident. She told that as the one serving her husband and house hold selflessly, she has acquired great merit only on this account. You do not know the central point of Dharma still, despite your learning. Please contact Dharam-Vyadh at Mithalapuri. The Brahmin went to this place and was shocked to find that Dharm-Vyadh is selling meat(of animals killed by others). He got another shock when Vyadh told him the purpose of his visit and as to who has sent him here. He prostrated to Vyadh and asked for the real meaning of Dharma. The teachings of Vyadh are given quite in detail in Mahabharta. After being satisfied, Kaushik left Mithlapuri, realizing that a person engaged in whatsoever a profession can reach the highest perfection and acquire knowledge which is superior to that acquired through formal education in Vedas, etc., by virtue of birth. Kaushik Said:

> "Against this, he who is called Shudra if follows sense control, the truthfulness and Dharma, I call him a Brahmin, because man becomes *Dwija* (twice born) only by his good conduct". (Van Parv 216/14)

There are innumerable verses in 'Van Parv', 'Bhism Parv', 'Shanti Parv' and 'Anushasan Parv' of Mahabharta where system of caste has been brought out to be in above spirit. There could be other verses against Shudras in it, but overwhelming indications of the time are those which prevail in the above major instances.

5
Worship of God-Impersonal, Personal and Social

"Science knows now that there is no such thing as empty space, but rather a vast hidden universe of Living Energy which is the secret root of matter. In short, the Overself encompasses us all and lack of a acquaintance must be laid to our own fault"

- Dr. Paul Brunton

What is God

When some of his disciples asked about the existence of God, Lord Buddha kept quite but pointed him out to a tree, meaning thereby that sit under a tree, meditate and realize Nirvana, which is state of enlightenment.

God can not be said as existing, nor as non-existing. It simply can not described in words, as this is human language and can not capture the transcendental entity. Let us see how those souls who have a concept or experience of God, attempted to describe it in our language:

> "It is the complete dissolution of thought in simple existence which is the mightiest nothing. It is an immediate here and now of spaclessness and timelessness, the inexpressible, beyond joy and sorrow, beyond knowledge and ignorance,

> beyond life and death, beyond all that is beyond ! It is the fullest reality, the completest consciousness, the imensest power, intensest Bliss. Truth, knowledge, power, happiness and immortality are its shadows. Unseen, transcendent, uninferable, unthinkable, ununderstandable, indescribable, imperishable, the loftiest, the deepest, the Truth, the Great-That is the Absolute. The light of limitless number of suns is darkness in its presence. It oversteps the boundaries of being and nullifies all ideas of existence. It is Giant-Spirit which swallows up the mind and the ego and wipes off the individual consciousness to the very extreme. It is the Thunder that breaks the heart of the universe; the Lightening that fuses all senses of empirical reality...
>
> Nothing is beyond That. It is neither form nor content nor existent. The soul sinks into it by an experience of all fullness, neither essence nor kingdom, nor wisdom, neither equal nor unequal, neither static nor moving, neither sitting nor resting, neither one nor two, neither true nor false. It has no name, there is no definition of it. It is that which is. It is not love, nor grace, nor world, nor soul, nor God, nor freedom, nor light, for all these are relative concepts. Sachidananda is only the logical highest..... Sun moon and stars are dissolved in it. Brahma, Vishnu and Shiva vanish into it. It is the Life of life.............. It is not existent but existence.
>
> From 'Spiritual Experiences'
> by Swami Sivananda.

Brihman is existence, knowledge, Infinity, Pure, Supreme, Self-existent, Eternal and indivisible Bliss, not different from the individual soul and devoid of interior and exterior. It is ever triumphant.

From Vivek Chudamani of
Adi Sankara Charya

Fools, not knowing My Supreme nature, think low of Me, the Lord of creation who have put on the Human body. - Geeta IX/11

These are the representative concepts of God or Brahm in Vedanta Philosophy. "It is an amazing yet universal paradox that the overself (God), which is nowhere visible, is everywhere present" says Dr. Paul Brunton. Till date the human beings are still skeptical on the question of existence of God, because it is not visible, though this argument does not go far, as there are so many things and beings like micro organism that exist but not visible. That which eye can not see but due to which the eye sees, is Brihm and not that which people do worship here, is an Upanishadic statement. Eyes are mere instrument, the medium of expression. It is not the seer. The eyes of a dead person may be physically absolutely in fit condition, but the same can not register any experience of the world around. Of course, when these are transplanted after being taken out of such a dead person, 'these again start seeing'. So much for the proof of existence of God with actual seeing. It is an highly materialistic view. We have not seen the mind, but everyone except a lunatic knows that it is there in his body. "We see the world piece by piece, as the sun, the moon the animal, the tree, but the whole of which these are shining parts, is the soul" says Emerson. Millions of waves are present in a room which can not be seen or felt in anyway but these can be seen on TV and heard on radio through proper equipments and tunings.

Says Dr. Paul Brunton, a great scientific-philosopher of West;

"But descending to unphilosophical level it may be affirmed that we shall find God at the end of this quest, but it shall be God as he really is. It shall be neither the glorified man of religion nor the attenuated gas of metaphysics. Yet it shall still be the God whom men rightly but remotely revere in oriental temples and occidental churches; but whom they tread underfoot and try to torture with their ignorant hatreds and intolerant persecutions of other men. We shall find the God whose caricatured image scornful rationalists or bitter atheists rightly reject and against whose cruelty they justly rebel, but whom they wrongly deny, for he is none other than their own ultimate self. We shall find God whom lean ascetics seek but do not find in gloomy caves and starved bodies and upon whom satiated sensualists shut the door in night clubs and jazz halls, yet who paradoxically dwells in both cave and club unseen, unnoticed and unknown".

We admit creation, but not the creator. We admit laws, but not the law-giver. The scientists have discovered laws of this physical universe, but not created these. He has discovered law of gravitation, but not created it. It was existing since the time of creation of universe and will exist till the universe remains, even it we forget this law, once again. Now if we see the conditions of life on earth, e.g., just the required distance from sun, the rotation of earth creating seasons etc. we should be able to infer the existence of some intelligence, which has created this arrangement and is in its background.

Father of the modern science, Isaac Newton, himself believed that the solar system appeared too contrived to have arisen solely from the action of blind forces. He writes in his 'Philosophiae Naturalis Principia Mathematica (1687), book III, general scholium' as:

"The most beautiful system of the sun, planets and comets, could only proceed from the counsel and dominion of an intelligent and powerful Being".

Quoted from the book
'Mind of God' by Paul Devies

Albert Einstein, one of the greatest, if not the greatest scientist of 20th centuary says:

"But on the other hand, everyone who is seriously involved in the pursuit of science becomes convinced that a spirit is manifest in the laws of the Universe-a spirit vastly superior to that of man, and one in the face of which we with our modest powers must feel humble. In this way the pursuit of science leads to a religious feeling of a special sort which is indeed quite different from the religiosity of someone more naïve" (Albert Einstein: A short Biography- Rupa-Co.)

Similarly, says James Jeans- the great astronomer and Philosopher "The universe appears to have been designed by a pure mathematician".

The concept of God in absolute sense is beyond the human mind. It is only a concentrated mind, converged at one point that can penetrate into the mysteries of God. Says Mundaka Upanishad "Taking as bow the mightily weapon furnished by the Upanishad, fix on it the arrow (Jiva) rendered sharp by constant meditation. And having drawn it with the mind absorbed in his thought, penetrate the mark-Imperishable Brahm".

Worship of God-Impersonal

We can not worship God in its unmanifested form, we can only mediate upon it. Barring a few, the generality of human beings are left outside this concept of God. The human beings with whatever limitations of mind and intelligence they are born with are also to be catered for. Ishavasya Upanishad says "He who worships the impersonal God-head and the personal God together, overcomes death through the worship of the personal and obtains immortality through the worship of the impersonal". Yoga Vashistha containing the (Vedantic) teachings given to Lord Rama by Rishi Vashistha, in his childhood, lays stress on meditation. It says that God is infinite consciousness of which divinities like Brahma, Vishnu and Shiva are parts, sharing its true nature like red-hot iron which shares the nature of fire. According to Yoga Vashistha meditation alone is true worship of God and even meditating for thirteen seconds is equivalent to giving away one cow in charity.

Meditation on impersonal is to transcend thoughts and realize that from which the thoughts arise. It is to reach a state of 'thoughtlessness'. Says the Bible "Be still and know that I am God".

Worship of God-Personal

As said earlier a mind can not hold on to the concept of impersonal except in deep meditation. Worship of personal God is thus a psychological requirement. Even in meditation, it helps him to concentrate his mind at one point and then take off to the impersonal. Since time immemorial the human race had been worshiping God in personal form and in fact for the majority this is the only concept of God in mind. There is no devotion without the concept of duality. This is the reason why even Ramakrishna Pramahans-a realized soul-used to worship Goddess Kali. It is a prop for the mind. It is through different expressions of the divine in different time and place, that the humanity is helped to move towards Good-head.

There is galaxy of such divine personalities in India and outside. Each prophet appears at one age and leaves some eternal values to be followed by the generations to come. As time passes, the modification takes place in the original teachings due to the interpretations by human mind. It is for this reason that the grand truths of Upanishads were lost in the sacrificial and ritualistic ceremonies by the time Buddha appeared on the scene. Even the Buddhistic teachings of great rationality, gave birth to *tantras* and other gorgeous ceremonies of image worship after some centuries. The teachings of universalism given by Adi Sankaracharya were lost within a period of about two hundred years into the religion of bind faith and superstitions meant to sustain a small sect of Hindus. It is for this reason that the divine comes to help the humanity lost in the darkness from time to time. The Lord will listen the prayers so long there is some purity, some sincerity in it.

This worship of personal God is an affairs between the individual and his '*Ishta*'. That is why Lord Krishna says in Geeta :

> "Whosoever offers to Me with love a leaf, a flower, a fruit or even water, I appear in person before that disinterested devotee of purified intellect, and delightfully, partake of that article offered by him with love" Geeta IX/26

So far as God is concerned this is all the requirement for the worship of him.

Worship of God-Social

The three stages of worship, i.e., Impersonal, Personal and Social come according to the inner development of an individual. The first one is the spiritual worship, the second the mental and the third the physical. It is in the third stage that the worship appears at physical level, involving temples, idol-worship, groups and communities. And it is at this level that distance becomes maximum between various groups and communities. If we picturise a ball or a sphere, we can see that at the center there is no difference between two radii converging on it. This is so at spiritual level too. As the distance from center increases, the difference between two successive line of radius becomes more. This is at devotional level. But when the distance from center reaches the surface, the difference becomes maximum. We can also say that when we are at surface (i.e. not possessing depth), we are at maximum distance from each other. The differences narrow down as we go into the depth (of the matter). The difference of course reach the level of nullity when we are at the center – one with the God. Talking on idol worship, Al-Beruni the Muslim traveler of 11th century A.D. writes "For those who march on the path of liberation, or those who study philosophy and theology, and who desire abstract truth which they call 'Sara' , are entirely free from worshiping anything but God alone and would never dream of worshiping an image manufactured to represent him"

But while on earth, we have to live on its surface. In our earthly existence physical appearness are more real to us, be it an illusion in absolute sense.

A particular form of worship gives a particular identity to the group of worshipers. In fact the identities are so strong that this itself has become the basis of classification of the human beings. On the basis of form of worship we have Hindus, Muslim, Jews, Christians, Sikhs, and Parsees etc. on the earth. Separate Identity of a particular faith while it creates distance with respect to other faiths, unites and emotionally integrates its followers. So far God is concerned, it is reached by any one of these faiths traveling vertically as said by Ram Krishna Paramahamsa. Horizontally jumping from one faith to another makes no difference to the God. Says Lord Krishna in Geeta :

> "Whatsoever form any devotee desires to worship with faith that very faith of him I make firm and inflinching". Geeta VII/21.

With such a wonderful Philosophy of toleration born out of enlightenment, no doubt we have in India the faiths of the world co-exiting. Even non-believers like *charvka* have been given the status of a philosophy (*Darshan*). We had the freedom of thinking in India which gave rise to the universal philosophy of Vedanta. We had the restricted view on society and we see a totally stagnated and distorted society put in watertight compartments.

There is no denying the fact that worship of symbols like temples, churches, mosques and Gurdwars is important part of any religion. This is to catch the common people engaged in worldly activities who have not yet reached high stage of spirituality. Such people will always be in majority compared to those who are either highly evolved or outside the human civilization in lower stage. The sacred should be left as sacred and secular as secular. The secularism with fundamental rights like freedom of thoughts, equality, justice and fraternity, protection of life and liberty, etc., as enshrined in our constitution is important in the life of individuals whether he believes in God or not. These rights can not be allowed to be encroached by any amount of religious fanaticism. But pseudo-secularism is equally dangerous, as it defeats and narrows down the true meaning of secularism and is thus a companion of religious bigotry either by fault or by design.

Worship by Shudras and Low Castes

Lower Shudras or what is classed as 'Outcastes' had deep roots in the worship of gods and goddesses of Hinduism. Those who have converted to Buddhism, of course, do not have any such belief in them now. They (low caste) visited and still vist the pilgrimage places of Hindus like Haridwar, Varansi, Prayag, Badrinath, Kedarnath, Kanniyakumari, Triputi, Kali temples, Dwarka and Mathura and all such sacred centers in India. They observe all Hindu festivals like Ramnavami, Shivrati, Janmastami, Onam, Rakshbandhan, Dussera, Goverdhan Puja, Deepavali and Holi etc. Particularly the festival of Holi is celebrated by them for a long period of about a fortnight in some rural part of North India. They perform the birth, marriage and death events like any other Hindu, though limited to the financial capacity and social bindings. In rural India, the *bani* of Sant Ravidas and Kabir is sung and listened by them, alongwith the tales of Hindu Kshatriyas and local heroes. Particularly the celebration of Janamastmi had been seen by this auther being performed in real hard ways in some areas, by keeping fast throughout the day, even while working in agricultural field, breaking it only at midnight amidst ladies devotional songs. They do have followers in Aryasamaj, Radha Swami sect, Nanak Panth and Kabir's Satnami sect.

Descending down to lower forms of belief these people worshiped stones, trees, rivers and *matas* (female spirits) of various diseases, in rural India. The underworld king of snakes was worshiped in the annual fairs held in his name, to secure his protection. The belief in lower spirits was common and these were appeased through offerings and prostrations. Being illiterate, it was easy to inject superstition in them, leading to their exploitation by *Tantriks* and *Ozas*. Interestingly a few of them were seen worshipping Muslim *pirs* and *sayyads* apart from sufi saints.

Temple entry was earlier banned to them (some instances even now occur of denial of entry to them) and therefore, they constructed their own low cost temples or platforms. Barring of such entries to them by high caste Hindus in their temples was more a racial act than the religious one, as they considered the low castes to be some inferior beings not fit for equality in the God's house. Who can say that high caste Hindus do not suffer from superstition considering their belief in the image of Somnath Temple while it was being attacked and destroyed by Mahmud of Gazni. The myth of superior race is exposed by their slavery of last 1000 years to foreign rule, but human mind has a fency for illusion. No race has ever become superior through selfishness, cruelty and ignorance. To become super power they have to be like liberating and embracing Negroes as did so by Abraham Lincoln of America, even by paying price for it.For non-entry in temples if the question was only of maintaining physical cleanness, even then this argument does not hold ground, as the low castes are responsible enough in this regard which can be seen now in all temples of free entry.

The temple-going is the social or psychological requirement for an individual till he grows up beyond and above it's need. It is not essentially a part of spiritual practice and therefore, highly evolved souls were generally in no need of it.

The educated elite of low caste now hardly care to be a blind believer of religious dogmas. He is not alone in this attitude, as his 'higher caste' colleagues have similar mind. The fast developments around the world, of high interconnectivity etc., are bound to change the orthodox attitude and for good reasons and higher cause. But if taken to the extreme, they will become rootless and consequently hollow as if in a vacuum. President George W. Bush of America invokes God now and then on formal occasions (without its excessive show, of course), but our elites hesitate in doing so. Bush is not the ideal for humanity and even said to tilted (naturally) towards Christianity but the point to note is that the Head of world's most powerful and secular democracy does not feel guilty in acknowledging the existence of God. On the occasion of his second term as Present of America in March 1865, which was a month before he won the war against the South, liberating the Negroes and uniting the states, Lincoln spoke:

"The judgements of the Lord are true and righteousness altogether. With malice towards none; with charity for all; with firmness in the right, as God gives us to see the light, let us strive on to finish the work we are in, to bind up the nation's wounds......to do all which may achieve and cherish a just and lasting peace among ourselves, and with all nations"

6
Shudra's Concept of Indian History- Glorious Spots are their's or the Periods of Social Homogeneity

If we see the Indian history with unbiased and a focused mind, a different picture emerges out of Shudras role in it than is commonly understood. This is because the nature is working independently of the Brahmanic laws in human affairs. The nature's law work in harmony only with those teachings which are imparted by the God or his true messengers for the welfare of all humanity. The hereditary caste system of Hindus did produce some persons of high integrity and spiritual depth touching the highest in divinity. But at the same time it produced a large number of those who betrayed their people and nation for their selfish ends. Brigadier J.P. Dalvi who fought Chinese aggression of 1962, describes the true position in this regard in his book 'The Himalayan Blunder' as:

> "India has a near unbroken record of military failures through the ages. Our peasantry has always fought gallantly; but it is an undisputable fact that seldom has this bravery been utilized to win battlefield victories and thus to attain our

> political objectives, due to inept political or military leadership or both. Need we follow the tragic path interminably".[1]

Shudras in Indian history were the persons of very high caliber and of great achievements, touching the divine aura in their wisdom and military might. The impartial nature could not but have done otherwise than produce persons of exalted character in all castes based on their guna and Karma. That Brahmanic social system calls them as Shudras etc. is a different matter.

Different periods of Indian history briefly described below will support the above fact about Shudras. Those events which have been described in detail elsewhere in this book, have been mentioned briefly to put up them in a thread of history(important dates of Indian history are given in Appendix-2 of this book).

Vedic Period

This was the period of Aryans in which the caste was by occupation and not by birth. The famous mantra of Rig Veda, IX:112 (3), mention "I am a singer, father is the physician, mummy throws corn upon the grinding stones. Having various occupations and seeking riches, we remain in the family like cattle in a common stall. May you follow, O elixir of bliss, for the sake of aspirant self".

This is the reason why modern exponent of this philosophy, Swami Dayanada Saraswati, the founder of Arya Samaj, consider the caste system to be based on guna and karma. There were Shudras like kavasha Ailush who composed several mantras of Xth Mandla of Rig Vedas, described in Chapter-1 of this Book.

Epics Age (Mahabharta Period)
Ved Vyasa

The author of Ramayana Rishi Valmiki and of Mahabharta Maharishi Ved Vyasa are linked to shudrahood. Though there are different opinions on the origin of Valmiki, one view is that he was from low origin. In case of Ved Vyasa all recorded proofs are available to establish him to be a Shudra. He was the son of rishi Prasar (Brahmin) and mother Satyavati who was a fisherwomen. The son born by this combination of castes is described in Mahabharta as well as in Manusmriti as a Shudra (details given in chapter IV of this book). There is, therefore, no doubt about one of the greatest personalities of Hinduism, Ved Vyasa as belonging to shudra caste. He is the compiler of Vedas and author of Mahabharta (including Bhagwad Geeta) and some Puranas.

Lord Krishna

Full incarnation of God, who showed his infinite cosmic form to Arjuna in the battlefield, belonged to the whole of humanity without any distinction of caste, class and religion. Still on the worldly plane, he came from Shudra caste (now forming upper Shudras or intermediary castes) as detailed in chapter 4 of this book.

Vidur-the Prime Minister/Adviser of Pandvas-Kaurvas

He was the son of a maid-servant from Vyasa. He is said to be the reincarnation of God of Justice (Dharma-Raja) who due to curse of a rishi to whom excessive punishment was given for the fault of childhood, took birth in a maid's house. He was considered the most forthright and wise advisor, taking side of truth, even by offending king Dhirtrastra at times. He objected to the game of dice and saved Pandavas from burning in a house of inflammable material which was planned by their cousins. The mother of Pandavas, Kunti, stayed in his house for 13 years when Pandvas were banished to forest for this period. Krishna preferred to stay in his house while on peace mission to Hastinapur before war, declining the royal hostage.

Mahabharta Heroes

Brief history of the dynasty of Kaurva-Pandava race has been described in chapter-IV of this book. This, in brief, is that the mother of Ved Vyasa is a Shudra fisherwomen Satyavati and through Ved Vyasa are born Dhritrastra and Pandu. Dhritrastra is the father of 100 sons of Kaurvas, eldest being Duryodhana and Pandu the father of five pandavas, i.e., Yudhister, Bhima, Arjuna, Nakul and Sahadeva. Either on account of Satyavati or Ved Vyasa the great sage, the race of Mahabharta heroes can be said to be a mix of Shudrahood.

Dharma-Vyadha

To briefly state what has been written elsewhere in the book, there was once a learned Brahmin by name Kaushik. Once his was sitting under a tree when a bird dropped leaf on his head. Enraged by this, this Brahmin looked at the bird and burnt it through his power of learning. He goes to bag alms to a nearby habitation, where a lady reads his mind of bird episode and directs him to go to Dharm-Vyadha at Mithilapuri to complete his education. At Mithilapuri, Kaushik is shocked, to find that Dharm-Vyadha is a meat-seller Shudra. Still he goes to him and gets further shock to know that this meat-seller already knows his purpose of visit. He then imparts lesson to Kaushik for several days. Kaushik finally parts by considering Dharam-Vyadha as his preceptor and thanks him for completing his education about the true meaning of a Brahmin and Shudra. This teaching is given in good details in Mahabharta, the central point being that it is not the profession as such but the dedication and selflessness with which it is performed, which gives merit to an individual.

Buddhist Period

The enlightened society of Veda and epic period seems to have come in the grip of ritualistic Brahaminism, gradually. Brahmana portion of Vedas concerning itself with sacrifices and ritualism, found its further expansion in Dharam Sutras and Dharam Shastras, which were materialistic in concept and easily caught the fancies of weak-minded kings, who found it more difficult to live upto higher values of life enshrined in Upanishad etc. The karma-kand had an upper hand over the Jnana-kand. By the time of birth of Buddha (563 BC) animal sacrifice was made in thousands and the slaughtering was too large to come within the grasp of words, the animal agony being lost in the chants of mantras by the Brahmins. The compassionate Buddha could not tolerate such inhuman practices, and offered himself a sacrifice if that could brighten the prospects of the sacrificer to the entry in heaven. This had an effect and the mass animal killings was reduced greatly. The period of awakening came again with the teachings of Lord Buddha the enlightened one and of Lord Mahavira the 24th and last Tirthankara of Jains. But the old habits and customs die hard. The caste system though shaken by Buddha, could not disappear altogether and we have instance of Virudhak, a king from low caste mother being discriminated against by the very of clan of Sakyas to which Buddha belonged, even while Lord Buddha was living on earth. The story goes that king Prasendi who was a follower of Buddha, once invited Sakayas to dine at his palace. To his surprise he found that Sakayas are not eating their food (later discovered to be due to their superiority over Prasendi's people). To close this gap, Presendi proposed to marry a girl of Sakya clan, who devised means to marry a low caste girl secretly to him. Virudhak was born of this marriage. He, on a visit to his maternal relatives in Sakyas, in childhood, found himself being treated indifferently, to the extent that furniture and places of his visit were washed with water after his departure. Virudhak come to know of all this later, to be due to his low status. He attacked Sakyas and conquered them to merge their kingdom into his own.

Maurya Empire

However, the effect of Buddha's teaching on masses was felt gradually and by the time of 322 BC, Chandragupta Maurya, a Shudra, was able to establish the first great empire in India after the epic period, extending upto Afganishtan, by defeating the Alexander's General Seleucos. As a youth the Maurya had challenged Alexandra while the latter was camping near Texila in Sindh Region and made a daring escape all alone despite the resistance by Alexandra's forces. Except in later period's Buddhist *Mahavansa* which links Maurya to 'Khattiya' clan all other vital sources, viz. the ancient Greek author, the Puranas and Gupta Period's famous play 'Mudraraksasa', etc., hold Chandragupta Maurya to be a Shudra, as given below, popular view being that he was from Shudra mother named 'Mura' with father as the last Nanda king, who himself is said to be a Shudra.

Justin : The Roman author says; Chandragupta Maurya is from 'humble birth'.

Vishnu Purana:

It records as below:-

"In future there will be a king called Mahapadmananda. Like a second Parashurama, he will destroy all Kstriyas. The Shudra will then become king.

Mahapadama will have eight sons and he and his sons will rule the earth for hundred years But a Brahmin named Kautilya will kill all of them and the Shudra king known as Maurya will rule. Kautilya will make Chandragupta King".[2]

Mudraraksasa

It is play written by Visakha-Dutta, a courtier of Chandragupta-II (380-413 AD), which contains the life and instances of Chandragupta Maurya in detail, establishing him to be from low caste. The play calls Chandragupta Maurya a '*Vrashala*', i.e., the offspring of an inferior birth. The play exhibits in detail the establishment of Maurya Empire. Chandragupta with the help of North-West tribal king Pravataka attacks Nandas at Patilputra and ascends the throne with the help of master-piece in state-craft, the great Chanakya. But somehow Pravataka is killed in the city due to which his son Malayaketu with the help of wise and able Rakshasa (a Brahmin), the Minister of Nanda who had escaped from capital, plan to avenge his death. The play contains the modern day tricks and diplomacy of how the opponent is removed from the scene or converted to his side. Finally, Rakshasa turns to Chandragupta Maurya and becomes his Prime Minister. Chandragupta has been addressed as 'Vrashala' at several places and ACT-II and ACT VI in particular hints at the low birth of Chandragupta through the mutterings of Rakshasa to himself in anguish, comparing Vrashala to a women of low birth in scene –II of ACT VI.

Dhundiraja

A famous commentator on Mudraraksasa, Dhundiraja gives the dynastic history of Chandragupta Maurya, as below:-

At the beginning of Kalayuga, Nandas were rulers of the whole earth in which Sarvarthasidhi was famous for his prowess. He had two wives , sunanda and Mura. Once a sage came as a guest to the king and blessed the two ladies after they washed his feet. He threw this water '*Charnamrita*' over the two queens. Nine drops fell on the elder Sunanda and one on the younger Mura. Sunananda begot nine sons called Nandas and Mura, the Shudra, only one called Maurya. Maurya, the father of Chandragupta was made the Army Chief ignoring the nine sons of Sunanda. Enraged by this Nandas killed Maurya and his sons other than Chandragupta who escaped to safety. Later, Chandragupta killed all Nandas with the help of a Brahmin Chanakya and ascended to the throne.

Brahmin Kautalya ie Chanakya, the Prime Minster and Maghasthenes the Greek ambassador posted by Seleucos, are the two great personalities of Maurya period. Kautaliya's *Arthshastra* is the great work on administrative, economic, social and political matters of running a state and is relevant even for modern day world with some modifications. It describes the administration of centre with '*Manri Prishad*', states under Governorship of Kumars, districts i.e. '*Vishya* ' under Visyapati and local levels controlled by *Panchayats*. There were several heads of departments at the centre called *Amatyas*, *Mahamatras* and *Adhyaksas*. The selection to administrative posts was through open competition.

Similarly, Meghasthenes '*Ta Indiaka*' gives an insight into the social, cultural and political system prevalent in Chandragupta's time. 'Buildings of exceptional magnificence were created in the time of first Maurya Empire' says Vincent Smith. According to Meghasthene Indian Society was divided into seven classes (already described in detail in chapter IV of this book). Kautilya's *Arthsastra* conclusively says Shudras are Aryans (III 13.1) and can not be made slaves (III 13.182). *Arthsastra* further says that though the army of Kstriya is the best, the army of Shudras and Vaishya is preferable, because they are in large numbers (IX:2), the army of Brahmins not likable (IX:2). In this period the Shudras were allowed agriculture work in addition to the labour work (*Karamkars*) where they were to give half the produce to the king (II.24). There were Varna-Samkar (mixed-castes) like those described by Manu in later period born through *anuloma* (father higher, mother of lower varna) and *Prtiloma* (reverse of above) order (III.7). According to *Arthsastra,* villages were to be constructed at a distance of 2 to 4 miles, with Shudras and agriculturists as its main inhabitants (II.1). Meghasthene says that inter-marriage between two classes was not permissible but the list of mixed castes shown in *Arthsastra* indicates that inter-mixing of castes continued in that period also even though by losing status.

Ashoka the great as successor to Chandragupta Maurya (his grandson) embraced Buddhism and became more benevolent to the people converting the kingdom as entirely a welfare-state. The fame of this rule is known the world over till now. H.G. Wells calls him as amongst the six great personalities of the world. The lion capital of Ashoka's pillar at Sarnath is the emblem of Independent India. He honoured all sects and religions equally as mentioned in Rock Edict No. XII 'there should not be honour of one's own sect at the cost of honour of other's sect'. He honoured Brahmins, though it appears that they were not satisfied with the equality of treatment given to all under the judicial system. They were fed so far on the special privileges and superiority over others. Particularly the stoppage of mass scale animal sacrifices, which gave status and riches, made them internally unhappy. It was perhaps on account of such factors that a Brahmin Commander-In-Chief Pushayamitra Sunga killed Brihdratha, the grandson of Ashoka on the prade ground itself in 185 BC. Some historians of course mention other grounds as well for the end of Ashoka dynasty, one amongst which is the policy of non-violence due to which army became alienated.

Era of Manusmriti

After the usurping of Maurya empire by Pusymitra Sunga, the Brahminism which was hitherto subdued during Maurya period, got a fresh lease of life. After the downfall of Kanishak in 160 AD, history of India is mostly enveloped in darkness till the veil lifts up in Gupta period in about 320 AD. This period (of darkness) is fixed for the creation of Manusmriti and some other Smirities where there was none to question the wisdom of these authors. When Manu was keeping the four castes in water-tight compartments and thus not allowing a cohesive society, foreign hordes from central Asia, were invading India and did not allow formation of stable Governments. The two exceptions are the Gupta empire (320-413 AD) and Harshvardhan rule (580-647 AD). Gupta rulers were Kshatriyas (Vaishyas according to some). Chinese traveler Fa-Hien visited India in the reign of the Gupta period and Yuan-Chwang in the rule of Hrshvardhan. They describe the rules as benevolent to the people, the Buddism and Hinduism existing in cordial relationship, infact Buddha having been declared as 9th Avtara of Vishnu in Gupta period. The condition of Shudra in these two periods improved by assigning them agriculture trade and artisanship in addition to their service duties. Shudra king in Sindh has been mentioned in the records of Yuan-Chwang. Almost in all fields like literature (author Kalidas), science (scientist like Arybhata), Arts, administration, military powers etc. the Gupta rule excelled and the same has been described in all praise by Fa-Hien.

After the above rules, the chaotic political conditions prevailed, with increasing invasions from Huns, Turks, Muslims and Britishers. India remained slave for about two thousand years till 1947 AD excepting for the two intervening periods of Gupta empire and Harshvardhan rule described above. And this period of slavery coincides with the period of Manusmriti in which the social conditions of Shudras greatly deteriorated. The nature does not permit its laws to be twisted without consequences, as rightly said by James Allen :

"Remember that there is the eternal Law which is absolutely just and that he who oppresses today must himself be oppressed tomorrow and from this there is no escape". But James Allen also says "Despondency irritability, anxiety, complaining, condemning and grumbling- all these are thought cankers, mind disease, they are indicative of a wrong mental condition, and those who suffer there from would do well to remedy their thinking and conduct".

So, not by condemning but by learning lessons from the past, we have to look to the future.

Medieval India- of Defeat and Disaster for Hindus

After the death of Harshavardhan in 647 AD, the empire and alongwith it the Buddhism came to sharp decline. It was broken into innumerable kingdoms and principalities. It is a dry and dull exercise to collect various names of the kings in this historically dark period. When the scene opens up during 1000 AD on the attacks by Mahmud of Ghazni, some light is thrown on the conditions then prevailing. It was a bad situation, the kings constantly fighting with each other on flimsy grounds, indulging in all types of treacheries to acquire powers, unashamedly helping the foreign powers against their own kind, having no concept of belonging to a nation or society overall, perpetrating cruelties on the people, particularly of lower castes, living in superstitions and practicing *tantras*.

Manusmriti and other smritis were being strictly followed in social matters as described by Al-Beruni, a Muslim scholar and traveler to India (1000-1030 AD). He has brought out whatever was great and likable about India, for example on the teachings of Lord Krishna in Bhagwad Geeta. He in disgust asks the question "why should the people be led on poison in a land where the nectar stream of an ancient and life-giving religion flows perennially". Al-Beruni also did not fail to point out whatever was not so glorious about India and its people. He writes "We can only say, folly is an illness for which there is no medicine, and the Hindus believe that there is no country but their's, no nation like theirs, no king like their's. They are haughty foolishly vain, self-conceited and stolid. They are by nature niggardly in communicating that which they know, and they take the greatest possible care to withhold it from men of another caste among their own people..... their ancestors were not as narrow-minded as present generation is ———".

In the period after Harshavardhan's death (647 AD) till the occupation of the country by Muslim invader Mohammad Ghori in 1192 AD, mostly Rajputs were the ruling class. They were in various names like Gurjar Pratihars, Chalukyas, Chauhans, Chandels, Parmars, Gahadwals. The Pratihars acquired Kannauj, Parmars the capital of Ujjain, Chalukyas Annihwara and South,

Chauhans Ajmer, Delhi and Chandels the region of Bundel Khand.

There is a controversy on the origin of Rajputs. General perception amongst historian is that they were the tribes of Sakas and Huns who got absorbed in Hindu religion through the fire ceremony performed by Brahmins (and they are called as *Angnikulas*). They exhibited two extreme characteristics; one; of exemplary courage, general truthfulness, simplicity, man of words and honour, second; of treacherous conduct, violence for the sake of petty reasons and selfishness even at the cost of nation. Speaking on social condition of this period Swami Vivekananda said, "When the greater part of their number sank into ignorance, and another portion mixed their blood with savages from central Asia and lent their sword to establish the rule of priest in India, her cup become full to the brim and down sank the land of Bharta not to rise again until Kstriya rouses himself and making himself free strikes the chain from the feet of the rest" Complete Works Vol. IV, P. 326.

The post-Harshavardhan Indian history is one of defeat and disaster for Hindus. In very brief are given below the important events of Medieval India, mainly for the purpose of learning lessons from the same that nature and its laws do not act as per dictates of the ignorant priests, be they Hindus or Muslims (because after all Muslim empire also collapsed after the death of Aurangzeb).

712 AD: Sindh was ruled by a Shudra Sahiras a contemporary of Harsha. His son and successor Rai Sahasi-II had a Brahmin Minister called Chah. On the death of Shashi, Chah usurped the kingdom and married the widowed queen. His rule was oppressive hence unpopular. Dahir a son of Chah ascended the throne in 708 AD. He faced the Arabs invasion of Mohammad Bin-Kasim in 712 AD and perished due to superstitious belief in a talisman tied to a red flag. Majority of male members were killed and others converted to Islam.

Attack of Mahmud of Ghazni

Mahmud of Ghazni attacked India 17 times during 1000-1027 AD and totally plundered it, looting its wealth, massacring or enslaving its people and converting them, as much as possible, to Islam. Al-Beruni writes "by these exploits Hindus became like atom of dust...." In the Arab countries, there was tradition of selling and purchasing of slaves, and Mahmud supplied Indian slaves in such numbers that it flooded their market. Only important invasions are described below:

2nd expedition (1001 AD) : This was against the Hindu Shahi ruler Jaipal. On defeating Jaipal, Mahmud collected huge booty of Gold with lakhs of slaves including women and children.

7th Invasion (1009 AD) : During this invasion Mahmud attacked Nagerkot. He with big army marched towards Kangra. After some resistance he conquered the fort with booty which was so enormous that procurements of camels to carry it become a problem.

9th expedition (1012 AD) : In this expedition he plundered Thaneswar and returned with huge wealth and slaves.

11th expedition (1015-16 AD) : He invaded Kashmir with the similar results of loot and plunder.

12th expedition (1018-19 AD) : He attacked Kannauj which was ruled by Rajaypal Gurjar Pratihar. On way,

Haridutt, the king of Bulandsahar surrendered without fight and embraced Islam with his soldiers. Mahmud destroyed Mathura and its temples and carried uncountable gold and large number of slaves. When Mahmud reached Kannauj during 1919, Rajaypal fled from there but was put to death by Chandela king Ganda of Kalinjar for showing cowardice.

13th expedition (1020 AD) : Mahmud directed his next expedition against Kalinjar on learning about the death of Rajaypal. Ganda faced him with his army supported by other Hindu rulers. Ganda fled in the night having come to know of his allies going on the side of Mahmud. Mahmud returned with huge booty as a prize of his victory.

16th expedition (1025-26 AD) : His next attack was on Somnath Temple in Gujrat. The Hindus of Somnath were fed on the belief that other kings in India are falling before Mahmud because they have lost the blessing of Lord Somnath. This reached Mahmud's ear and he set towards Somnath to settle this question about the deity, himself. The Hindus organized no resistance to Mahmud considering that Lord Somnath himself would take care of it (the temple). Mahmud destroyed the idol by his own hands. The massacre of priests and others was on a large scale, the booty was enormous consisting of immense Gold and slaves.

Mohammed Ghori's Invasion (1192 AD)

In between 1026 AD and 1192 AD, the Hindu kings learnt nothing and forgot nothing. While any fighting must involve all sections of society to render all helps whatever they can, in India the caste system laid duty only on one section, i.e., Rajputs in this case. They were not helped even by Rajputs of neighbouring kingdom what to say of other castes. They had to face their enemy all alone. In 1191 AD Prithivi Raj Chauhan defeated Shahab-ud-din Mohammed Ghori at Trai and left him free after a little chase. In 1192 AD, Ghori again attacked Prithivi Raj Chauhan with the help of Jai Chand, Hindu King of Kanauj. In the sudden attack of early morning Prithivi Raj lost after a day's long fight and was killed. Ghori established Muslim rule at Delhi.

Slave of Slave as Ruler of Delhi

Mohammad Ghori returned to Ghazni after appointing his slave general Qutb-ud-din Aibak as ruler of Delhi. Aibak in turn appointed his own slave. Iltutmish as ruler of Gwalior, who later occupied Delhi on the death of Aibak. What a spectacle displayed by the Providence that Manu's caste Hindus had to be ruled by the slave of slave. Daughter of this 'slave of slave' Razia Begam further ruled Delhi from 1236 to 1240 AD.

Other important events of Medieval Histroy are as below:-

1194 AD : Qutb-ud-din Aibak defeated and killed Jai Chand of Kannauj and returned with massive wealth. After all, a person not loyal to his people can not be trusted by others.

1197 AD : Bakhtiyar Khilji plundered Bihar and killed many Buddhists and destroyed Nalanda university.

1199 AD : Bakhtiyar attacked Bengal and Palas fled without fight.

1290-1320 AD : Jalal-ud-din Khilji ascended throne after defeating the slave dynasty. His son-in-law Ala-ud-din Khilji captured the throne after killing Jalal-ud-din Khilji and his other family members in 1296 AD.

Conquest of Gujrat 1297 AD : Ala-ud-din marched to Gujrat, which was ruled by Rai Karan Deva Baghella. Karan Deva fled to south with his daughter. His treasure and the queen fell into the hands of invader.

Conquest of Ranthambore 1300 AD : Ala-ud-din laid seize of the fort which was occupied by Rajputs under the king Hamir Deva. The seize lasted for one year. The fort was ultimately conquered due to treachery of Ranmal, a minister of Hamir Deva. Rajputs died fighting to a man, but no one else came to their support for the whole one year.

Conquest of Chittor 1303 AD : The aim in this invasion was to capture India's famous beauty, Padmini. The seize lasted for 8 months, Ala-ud-din resorted to stratagem by making the king captive after offering the hand of friendship. King Ratan Singh died fighting alongwith their last soldier. Padmini performed *Jauhar* alongwith thousands other women. Desperated, Ala-ud-din ordered mass killing of population. This is a story of exemplary courage of Rajputs and their women who died fighting rather than compromising their honour. None else came to their rescue during such a long seize.

Conquest of Madura 1311 AD : Malik Kafur a general of Khilji, defeated first Raja Karan Deva who had fled from Gujrat compelling him to take shelter of Khilji. He later defeated king Ram Chander Deva who afterwards collaborated in the design of conquest of south by Kafur. At this time there was a quarrel between two Pandaya brothers of Madura, Sunder Pandya and Vir Pandaya. Malik Kafur joined Sunder Pandya and defeated Vir

Pandya. The booty captured was so enormous that all the wealth looted by Mahmud of Ghazni hardly compared with it.

Attack of Timur Lung 1398-99 AD : Timur Lung marched to Delhi and camped about 6 miles from it, alongwith a lakh of Hindu prisoners. Mohammad Tugluq put some resistance but he was defeated. The leading citizens of Delhi sought mercy from Timur which was granted, but his soldiers were in no mood to let the opportunity of loot go just like that. They picked up some quarrel with citizens in which some of these soldiers were killed. Infuriated by this happening, Timur ordered mass slaughter of Delhi population (excluding muslims) alongwith the prisoners he had brought. The scene of destruction was so terrible that no one was left to rule at Delhi for several days, as the Tugluqs had already fled Delhi. Timur returned to Lahore with massive wealth and a large number of slaves for each of his soldier. He destroyed Meerut, Haridwar and Jammu while returning back to Lahore.

1398 to 1857 AD : The above period includes the rule of Mughal empire (from 1527 to 1857 AD). Further description of historical events is not considered necessary, as the invasions given from 712 AD to 1398 AD are enough to show that the Hindu caste system, throwing all responsibilities of defence on a particular caste and making others as if the spectators, could not but lead to these depressing situation of all-round disasters. The last of invasion was by Nadir Shah from Persia in 1739 AD, who marched upto Delhi to loot the huge treasury of Delhi emperor (Mohammed Shah) worth Rs. 70 crores alongwith famous Kohinoor diamond and massacred thousands of Delhi citizens.

Maharana Pratap — The True Kshatriya

Limitless courage, love for freedom, sacrificing or suffering for honour and noble cause, protecting and even associating with low (caste) people, were the marks of a true Kshatriya. Maharana Pratap fits into all these characteristics. A myth was spread by the vested interests in India that real Kshatriyas have ceased to exist in these times. This is not possible in the human affairs. Who was American Eisenhower Dwight D, the Supreme Commander of Allied forces and Marshall Zhukov of Russia in second World War to force Fuehrer, i.e., Hitler of Germany to commit suicide by shooting himself on April 30, 1945?. At home, who were the fighters of Indian Independence?.

Maharana Pratap on his famous horse Chetak faced the might of Mughal Empire of 80,000 Men with guns at Haldighati on June 18, 1576 AD. Pratap had only 20000 men without guns[3],* which included *Bheels* (the tribals) with bows and arrows and a commander Hakim Sur Afgan. His very daring to challenge the well-equipped imperial army with limited resources, for the sake of protecting his freedom, has placed Maharana Pratap on the glorious spot of Indian History This war also contains universal message in it; If you do not protect your honour and freedom, when threatened, the only alternative is to accept slavery through compromises, first mentally then physically. Man Singh the commander of Mughal army narrowly escaped his death (and therefore defeat) when the spear of Pratap hit his *Mahout* instead of him on elephant while Chetak had placed its forelegs on the head of Man Singh's elephant. Pratap had to leave the field due to his injured Chetak.With the help of these tribals, Pratap could not be captured for next 10 years by the Mughal emperor and died a natural death as a free man after recovering large part of his lost kingdom.

Akabar when at Lahore, did concede this victory as he heard the news of Partap's death. It has been said elsewhere in this book that Pratap's grand father Rana Sanga himself a great warrior, had honoured Guru Ravidas, a 'chamar' sant at Chittorgarh, whose memory still exists in the fort in the form of 'Chhattri' and footprints engraved in stone inside the temple. Pratap's father Udai Singh was saved by a maid-servant *Panna Dhya* by sacrificing her son. When king Banvir Singh, illegitimate cousin of Udai Singh came to kill the latter in childhood, Panna put her son on bed in place of Udai Singh was thus saved who fled the fort in disguise.

End of Aurangzeb's Theocracy-By Shudra's Rising

As opposed to the liberal rule of Mughal emperor-Akbar the great, the rule of Aurangzebs is considered as the one of religious fanaticisms. He persued the policy of religious persecution against the non-muslims, i.e., Hindus and Sikhs. He imposed 'Jazya' on Hindus-a tax burden on them only for being Hindus. Forced conversions to Islam was his policy to resist which Sikh Guru Teg Bahadur sacrificed his life. Earlier, Hindus from Kashmir had approached the Guru to save them from forced conversion. Poet Bhusna who lived in that period wrote a poem which means "Kashi has lost its splendor, Mathura has become a mosque; if shivaji had not been, all would have been circumcised (converted)". Almost the whole of India was suffering from this communal rule. Some resistance was offered by Rathore and Sisodia Rajputs (of Maharana Pratap's dynasty) when Aurangzeb was preparing to leave for south, never to return back for next 25 years. For him the Marhattas under Shivaji, a Shudra, had posed enough challenge which went on for 25 years ending in the supremacy of Marhattas power in most of India including Northern areas. Jats of district Mathura had also revolted against Aurangzeb in 1669.

Satnami Chamar's Revolt (1672 AD)

The low caste Satnams revolted against Aurangzeb empire in 1672 AD at Narnaul, a place between Delhi and Jaipur, presently located in Haryana. Against the might of Mughal empire, such a revolt was bound to be quelled ultimately, but it left a message to Aurangzeb after giving him a tough time 'your tyranny shall not go unchallenged'. Writes GW Briggs in his book 'Chamar' on Satnamis, "These Chamars, who made up the largest and oldest Chamar group in this part of India, have given up leather work entirely and have become cultivators. Many of them have tenent rights and a number of them have obtained village (p. 27)...... The Satnami movements have their rise in teachings of Kabir. The word means 'the True Name' and indicates that they worship the one reality under this title (p. 219) .... They came into conflict with the Government of Aurangzeb (p. 220)" (Page numbers added). Writes Dr. Ishwari Prasad in his book The Mughal Empire[3] (p. 594-95) "The immediate cause of the revolt was a dispute between a Satnami cultivator and a foot-soldier, who was keeping watch over a field. The solider broke the Satnami's head and thus stirred the fanaticism of the whole tribe. They belabored the soldier who very nearly died. When the local shiqdar tried to arrest the culprits, the Satnami assembled in large numbers and broke out into open rebellion. The faujdar of Narnol marched against them, but he was repulsed and compelled to seek refuse in flight. When the emperor heard of this out break, he sent forces, but they were all beaten 'by the Zealous sectaries'. So helpless was the Mughal army against them that it began to credit the rebels with magic and witchcraft and incredible stories about them became current in the country. The emperor who was known as a living saint *(Zinda Pir)* tried to beat them with their own weapons. He wrote some prayers and incantations with this own hand and had them sewn in the imperial banners. A terrible battle followed in which about 2000 Satnamis were slain, and the rest fled from the field of battle. The rebellion was quelled with ruthless violence, and the country was "Cleaned of infidels".

Chhatrapati Shivaji and Guru Gobind Singh challenge Mughal Empire:

The greatest resistance to Aurangazab's theocratic rule was offered by Shivaji, the leader of Marhattas, though he treated with respect the mosques, women and prisoners when captured. His army consisted of Mavalis, Peasants, Cobblers etc. Guru Gobind Singh in North did the same. With the heroic deeds of these two fighters, the Aurangzeb's empire virtually came to end. This release to Hindus was brought by Shivaji who was declared as Shudra by the Brahmins and by Guru Gobind Singh who promulgated a new code for Sikhs, one item of which was to do away with caste distinctions and adopt inter-marriage and inter-dining. First let us talk about Guru Gobind Singh. *"Mark me, every one of you will have to be a Gobind Singh, if you want to do good to your country" said Swami Vivekananda.*

Complete works Vol.III, p.378-80.

This great Guru established Khalsa on Baisakhi day of 1699 AD at Anandpur after being baptized by five-beloveds (*panj pyare*), most of whom were Shudras. The event goes like as follows. A great gathering was announced for Baisakhi day at Anandpur in 1699 AD. On the day before Baisakhi, Gobind Singh stood before a pitched tent, nacked sword in hand, thundering like a lion and asking for the head of persons for the sake of Dharma. None comes forward, but when repeated third time Daya Ram, a *khatri* of Lahore moves towards death. He is taken inside the tent and people hear the sound of sword cutting some one. Gobind Singh comes out with sword dripped in blood and repeats the call for second head. Seeing the reality of death, it is met with silence. But next comes Dharam Das, a Jat from Delhi. Third one to offer his head was Muhkam Chand a washerman of Dwarika. The fourth to do so was Sahib Chand, a barber of Bidar and the fifth Himmat Rai, a water-carrier of Jagannath. The Guru stops at five and finally appears before the public with all the five 'beheaded' as alive. They were called *panj pyare* and given the baptism through double-edged sword. Next day, i.e., on Baisakhi Gobind Singh himself got baptized from these *panj pyare* and he alongwith others who tasted *pahul* were given the epithet 'Singh'. The Shudras, who made the supreme sacrifice of their heads thus were honoured by Guru Gobind Singh by the name of *panj pyare*. They formed the core of Khalsa to give active resistance to the tyrannies of Aurangzab. Earlier it was a low caste, person by name Jaita, who had brought the head of Guru Teg Bahadur from Delhi against all odds, to perform proper rites at Anandpur for the martyred Guru. "His head was carried off by another low caste Sikh to Anandpur where his son was. Here it was cremated with full honours".[4] The book further quotes Guru Gobind Singh on Shudras and low Caste people as;

"True service is the service of these people. I am not inclined to serve others of higher castes. Charity will bear fruit in this and even in the next world if given to such worthy people as these. All other sacrifices and charities are profitless".

Shivaji

It will be worth going into bit details about Shivaji, one of the bravest fighters of medieval India. Dr. B.R. Ambedkar in his book 'who were the Shudras' writes in the context of coronation ceremony of Shivaji as Chhatrapati during 1674 AD as, "Shivaji's claim that he was a Kshatriya was opposed by many. His principal opponents were Brahmins who were led by his own Prime Minister Moro Pant Pingle. Unfortunately for Shivaji even his Maratha Sardar had refused to give him social precedence and had ranged himself against him. In their view, he was a shudra". Shivaji had not undergone sacred thread (*upanayana*) ceremony in childhood, "This was taken to be evidence of his being a shudra. He was, however, fortunate in securing the service of one Gagabhat, a renowned Brahmin, resident of Benaras". Writes Dr. Ambedkar about declaring Shivaji as Kshatriya, "That the decision of Gagabhat was not an honest decision is obvious from the amount of money which Gagabhat and other Brahmins received as officiating priests". Initially on his arrival from Benaras Gagabhat had examined records and felt convinced that Shivaji was a Shudra. Again,writes Dr. Ambedkar "what did Gagabhat do on his arrival ?. He said that he had re-examined the evidence and had come to the conclusion that Shivaji was a Shudra and was therefore, unfit for coronation."

In his book 'History of India (1000 to 1707 AD)' Dr. A.L. Srivastava writes "Orthodox Brahmins in Maharastra were averse to recognizing him as Kshatriya .... At his initiation into the rites of the twice-born (D*wija*) Kshatriya, Shivaji's Guru and other Brahmins uttered Vedic mantras, but the king was not allowed to utter or repeat them...." Coming to position of descendants of Shivaji, Dr. Ambedkar in the same above book writes, referring to aversions of Brahmins, "They could do nothing to the two sons of Shivaji, Sambhaji and Rajaram. Shivaji had their upanayan performed in his life-time by Brahmins with Vedic rites. They could do nothing to his grandson, Shahu because the Brahmin had no ruling power in their hands. The moment Shahu transferred his sovereign power to his Brahmins Peshwa their road to repudiation became clear..... There is definite evidence that upenayana ceremony of his successor, Shahu-II, who was adopted in 1777 AD had been performed with Pauranic rites and by the direction of Peshwas. The performance of upanayan of Shahu-II with Pauranic rites was tantamount to his being regarded by the Peshwas as a Shudra".

Dr. S.V. Ketkar in his book "History of caste in India"[5] writes similarly (p. 60) as, "even today I know of a Brahamana of character sufficiently independent to give up all his Jahagir of 40,000 rupees a year and refuse to perform Vedokta ceremonies in the family of Shivaji".

As an ideal king and able administrator Shivaji helped the poor peasants by distributing Zamidar's land and taking minimum revenue.He ensured that justice is given to all and never favored his family at the cost of others. He did not have blind belief in orthodoxy and superstitions and undertook sea journeys. He practiced secularism by placing Muslims in his army in good position.

It is the might and greatness of Shivaji that confronted Aurangzeb and his theocratic rule, and ensured that this oppressive rule goes into oblivion from this land. He exhibited unimpeachable character throughout with a broad outlook even while defending the Hinduism. His Deecan fight with Aurangzeb went on for 25 years. Local wars suited Shivaji in the hilly terrain but in bigger confrontation also he exhibited great courage. His daring escape from Agra where he was imprisoned by Aurangzeb reveals the element which Shivaji was made of.

The important dates of Indian history have been given in Appendix-2 of this book. There is no full-scale war after the period of Chandragupta Maurya which Hindus have won decisively against foreigners. After the defeat of Seleukos, the general of Alexander, by Chandragupta Maurya in 306 BC, the only great war won with glory is the Bangladesh war fought against Pakistan in 1971. Earlier, 1965 war was indecisive and Chinese aggression of 1962 was all disgraceful due to political failures though soldiers fought gallantly, as detailed by Brig. J.P. Dalvi in his book 'Himalayan Blunder'. The then Defense Minister, Sh. V.K. Krishna Menon resigned accepting responsibility for the defeat on Chinese aggression. In 1971 war of victory for India, Babu Jagjivan Ram was the Defense Minister, coming from the same stock of Shudras and 'untouchables' as Dr. Ambedkar (This is not to deny the role played by Smt. Indira Gandhi as Prime Minister). Perhaps there was some hidden message in it given by the Almighty; the only two wars won were under the leadership of Shudras. Babu Jagjivan Ram was a very capable Minister in the Govt. of India and handing of Bangladesh war was not mere luck for him. Earlier, the Ministry of Agriculture, known then as 'Minister eating Ministry' was handled by him when India was importing wheat from America and other countries. Since then despite population growth, there had been no shortage of food grain, rather India is even in a position to export its food grains to other countries. In an article on Babu

Jagjivan Ram (The Pioneer dated 11.4.2005) Mr. Kishore Gandhi concludes "He is reckoned as the father of our Green Revolution and the liberator of Bangladesh; these breakthroughs occurred during his stints as Minister of Agriculture and as Minister of Defence".

But what is the situation he had to face as Dy. Prime Minster in Janta Party regime. After the fall of Morarji Desai Govt. in 1979 leader of oppositon Sh. Y.B. Chavan was asked to form Govt. who declined the offer due to lack of numbers with him. Discussions were held by the President of India Shri Neelam Sanjiva Reddy with Sh. Desai and Chaudhary Charan Singh, finally asking the latter to form Govt. and prove majority on the floor of house. The Congress, however, withdrew support from Sh. Charan Singh who recommended dissolution of house instead of resigning. Discussions were again held by the President with Sh. Jagjivan Ram who was now the leader of opposition, who told the President that he possesses requisite number of MPs necessary to form the Govt. and that the President may satisfy himself on this in the manner he likes. The President, however, ignored the plea completely and went by the advice of Ch. Charan Singh who not even once faced the House. Ch. Charan Singh was made the caretaker Prime Minister for next six months after the dissolution of house. So, we have the laws of Manu submerged but not dissolved fully as yet.

References

1. 'Himalayan Blunder' by Brig. J.P. Dalvi, Natraj Publishers Dehradun, 1969.
2 'The Vishnu Purana' , Books for All. New Delhi
3. Not the exect figures but only proportion is meant here.

4. The Mughal Empire by Dr. Ishwari Prasad M.A. D. Lit Chugh publications Allahbad
5. *"Evolution of the Sikh Faith"* by H.N. Raj, Unity Book Service, New Delhi
6. *"History of caste in India"* by Dr. S.V. Ketkar, (1909) Low Price Publication, Delhi.

7
Real Merits and Demerits

The caste-by-birth does not recognize merit as basis of an individual's excellence for Shudras or Ati-Shudras. Even if one is as great a fighter and man of character and abilities as Shivaji, he will not be recognized as Kshatriya, except through a long and circuitous route of doling out money to a Brahmin (details in chapter 6). The thoughts of inferiority enter the brain of Shudra child right from the day the comes in contact with society and these keep on impinging upon it throughout his life, hindering the growth of his positive thoughts and self-confidence.

Merit

Any job in hand well performed through diligence, selflessness and application of mind, should be considered as an act of merit even if it be a job of mending shoes or as high as commanding an administration. Says Dr. Paul Brunton, "Destiny has given you a part to play. Play your part, do your duty, even as others have their duties. Whether you are a maker of shoes or a stenographer in a business, or a general in an army, do what your place calls for at the time. Do not make the error, however, of confusing this counsel with the notion that you are to do it all time. That is entirely different. What is right for you this year may be wrong for you next".[1] This is what Krishna did. He was a cowherd boy in childhood, then a king-maker, later a charioteer and finally a king. His role as charioteer is specially to be noted as Karna was often chided as the son of charioteer, *'Sut Putra'* by the princes to make him aware of his low origin. Several other great personalities in the world like Socrates who was a mason to begin will prove this point. The changing duties is in accordance with the evolutionary law of growth. A person may be recruited in a job at low level requiring physical work, but he need not stay there all the time if he works efficiently through dedication, and earn promotions. Like Robert Clive a clerk in East India Company, he may rise to the position of commander-in-chief of the company and even Governor General of Bengal. The system of promotions in India and world over, whether in public or private sector, recognize this basic law of human growth, due to which variety of talents in the same individual's personality keep on coming up to meet different job requirements. Abraham Lincoln was a poor wood cutter, then a lawyer, and finally a President of America fighting civil war to unite North and South America and to liberate Negroes of Slavery. He laid the foundation of the mightiest empire on earth in present times. He fulfilled the evolutionary needs of his being as a man in a single life. The Brahmanic caste system fixed the profession of an individual for a life time with only a rebirth capable of changing it.

The initial merit would no doubt consist of a combination of Intelligent Quotient, formal education and analytical abilities with required physical fitness. A really meritorious person is an asset to the society and the nation, as in his jobs he wades through the known and unknown problems of life. After all mind controls matter; as we see that a labourer despite full day's hard work is paid lesser wages than say an engineer who installs the machines or prepares a building complex design and then executes it. However, we have to be cautious in one aspect, which has been stated by Dr. Paul Brunton as "People are duped into believing that because a man is famous for his keen capacity in one field, or is doing his public work in an efficient manner, his opinion about matters outside the sphere of his professional work have the same value".

But there are limitations even to this professional merit. Higher calls of life, life and death struggle for survival and tenet of social justice, etc., go outside the circle of normal merit as we understand it. A Bhagat Singh will strike at the heart of British empire, even by sacrificing his life for it, even if the Britishers were meritorious to rule over India. A Subhash Chandra Bose will throw away his appointment to ICS for the sake of achieving freedom for his country. Even an 'Illiterate' politician shall rule the state, controlling IAS, IPS and Technocrats, as such a politician represents the will of the people. So, there is an higher realm of merit corresponding to the higher place and value of life. Ramakrishna Pramahansa and Ramana Maharishi did not have any formal education and were 'Illiterate' in our conception. In their view of higher wisdom, however, we educated are such illiterate and ignorant people not knowing the very basis of facing vital questions of graceful life and death. Even T.S. Iliot said "where is the wisdom we have lost in knowledge".

Therefore, both the higher merit of wisdom and lower merit of knowledge and information, serve their respective fields. The merit as we know it, thus, can not claim to be real merit for itself unless it contain some element of higher wisdom in it. In the absence of higher sense, such merit become only the efficient killing machine. Thus you have two principals of Govt. schools,

Delhi raping a Class X girl student at knife point (main news item on print and electronic media Feb. 17-18, 2005).

Higher Merit

Good conscience, fairness in public dealings, positive and helping attitude towards all, firmness against false and low values, dedication for the job in hand, having broader vision on the problem in hand than merely a technical view of it, etc. are the constituents of higher merit. Some essence of these, if not all, must filter down to the normal plane of merit, otherwise, Swami Chimayananda, the great commentator on Bhagwad Geeta will roar, "A pure intellect devoid of the qualities of heart is considered not only in the East, but in the West too, as villainous and killing instrument. Such a pure intellect, a data-mongering, fact-hunting intellect, negative and uncultured intellect in all its brutal violence is a soul-killing self poison". He is not alone to say it as a religious and saintly person. Albert Einstein considered to be the greatest scientist of 20th Century has to say this:

> "It is the moral qualities of its personalities that are perhaps of even greater significance for a generation and for the course of history than purely intellectual accomplishments. Even these latter are, to a far degree than is commonly credited, depend on the stature of character"[2]

Einstein is one case of exemplary merit in Germany. Adolf Hitler is another case of 'merit' in the same Germany who set out to conquer the world and used all weapons and means to destroy even innocent people in the world war-II. Einstein was all out for peace and progress and he felt great sorrow when the atom-bomb based on his theory of matter and energy wiped out two big cities of Japan, an ally of Hitler.

The same above book on six scientists contains the observations of Charles Darwin as:

> "In his Desent of Man, he said that he fully subscribed to the judgment of those writers who maintain that of all the differences between man and the lower animals the moral sense or conscience is far the most important".

Bhagwad Geeta accordingly says "Absence of pride, freedom from hypocrisy, non-violence, forgiveness, straight forwardness, service of the preceptor, purity of mind and body, steadfastness, self-control .... All this is declared to be knowledge (wisdom); what is contrary to this is called ignorance" –XIII/11.

Dimensionless corruption, sycophancy, criminal indifference to public interest, utter selfishness, moral decadence, arrogance in public dealings are the hallmarks of today's public administration. To the extent there is good administration and sound development visible anywhere, it must be on account of higher merit operating into the background of it. If a magistrate in Gujarat blindly signs warrant against the President of India and Chief Justice of Supreme Court (year 2004), it is not because he lacks in normal merit, but that he has no concept of higher merit which requires resistance to temptation for such tainted money. Sometime back there was a complaint in newspaper (Hindustan Times 8 Feb. 1993) from a widow of a sweeper, whose husband in Railways died 35 years ago as class-IV employees while in service. No Provident Fund, Gratuity, Family Pension and last two months salary due before death, was released to this women for 35 years though she approached all concerned authorities during this period. This may be an extreme and exceptional case. But well known legal personality N.A. Palkiwala is not wrong when he writes, "To India nature has given immense intelligence and skill but no sense of public duty, discipline or dedication" (We The People of India). This is no place to give details of all horrifying cases of atrocities being committed on poor and low caste people, as published in national dailies, like killing of a *dalit* for wearing shoes in the presence of high caste people in M.P.(1993). But some excerpts shall be quoted here in brief from the book 'Dr. Ambedkar and Dalit Future'.[3] by Sh. V.R. Krishna Iyer, former Justice of Supreme Court, to bring out lack of higher merit in our governing system. 'Even if in spite of all these odds the complainant does succeed in securing a conviction, the penalties imposed are so ludicrously light as to have very little deterrent effect. An analysis of 22 cases resulting in conviction by Elayaperumal Committee revealed that the median penalty was a fine of Rs. 10/-, the minimum and maximum fines were Rs. 1/- and Rs. 100/- respectively... In such a high level of judicial lenience it is not difficult to see why few untouchables would feel that there is anything to be gained by instituting cases under untouchability (offence) Act". This is not to treat low caste people as holy cows, always blameless. They have good and bad elements in them like any society of the world. But the point here to make is that Brahmanic consciousness operating at the back of the mind does not allow fair and impartial treatment to the helpless low caste person who goes with a complaint. The compassion is missing in this superirority which is followed by loss of conscience, as said so by the God in 'Conversations with God – Book 2' by Neale Donald Walsch (P-51): "A group consciousness which speaks constantly of separation and superiority produces loss of compassion on a massive scale, and loss of compassion is inevitably followed by loss of conscience".

It is extremely difficult to judge elements of higher merit in a candidate during recruitment process. Being a corrupt, petty-minded with little element of impartiality in his character and ever ready to compromise his duties attached to the post for the sake of his personal interests, are becoming the common features of functioning of today's bureaucrats or technocrats (with honourable exceptions, of course). This is despite high degree of merit in competitive examination. A 'Zee' news item 'inside story' on 13 feb. 2005 holds the above picture as true, where it was shown that an highly efficient and honest class A Railway Engineer (from lower strata of society) had to face the entire might of Railway's administration of Engineers only for pointing out the visible glaring irregularities in track constructions, for the purpose of ensuring public safety. He was shown as running for his life while the whole set-up above him was acting like a monolithic block to protect the culprits of grossest impropriety, involving several crores of rupees. In the same period we had the case of an IAS officer who held the highest post of state government and made so many properties in varios cities of India that even CBI found it difficult to account for them. Later, we saw another IAS officer on TV calling Press Conference to malign Election Commission at the behest of a political party which had moved his case for three year's extension after retirement. Another IAS officer swalled huge money in flood relief work as per FIR lodged against him and others. All these are examples of a few months of the year 2005 and they were high on merit list of the competitive examination. Other services are also not lagging behind in this regard. Where is the case against reservations for low castes in this situation? The deprived of any section of the society however, also need financial support from the government. The purpose here is not to pull down the hard-won merit, which has also given gems of persons, but to assert that the state's interest is served best whenever a public servant acts sincerely and wisely to perform his duties, paying some price of his self—interests if required, whether he be from reservation or general side.

The Meritorious State

But do we have any example of merit and higher merit being combined to produce good governance, efficient developmental works for the welfare of people and justice saturated society with strong army to protect it from any invader? Yes, it was the first great empire in the recorded history of India, ruled by a Shudra, Chandragupta Maurya, (details given in Chapter 6 of this book). This is the shining example of a really meritorious person rising from low level to the crown of a glorious empire, after matching his courage with the forces of world conqueror, Alexandra the great, in the latter's own camp.

Negative thoughts weaken merit

Pulling down of caste-system altogether though desirable, is a negative idea in Indian context. It is like blocking a river by constructing a dam without providing for overflow. Such damming can give only devastating results by its bursting. The positive approach is to change the course of this river slowly through protective works and by diluting the caste consciousness in the light of higher wisdom while living in the developmental mode of today's scientific age. Election use of caste through appeal to baser sentiments strengths this Manu's system rather then loosening it.

The negative thoughts do not create any positive form. It is of limited value. As any psychiatrist would tell, the interior thoughts are like software source which finally emerge on the world scene in material form. Said Swami Vivekananda:

"I feel as if thunderbolt strikes me on the head when I have people dwell on negative thoughts. That sort of self depreciating attitude is another name for disease-do you call that humility? It is vanity in disguise"

–Complete works Vol.VI, p. 273

Dr. Paul Brunton has similarly said:

"The ordinary man who surrenders to negative thoughts courts and strengthens the very trouble he wishes to avoid"

And Lord Buddha preached;

"I am being hated, mistrusted, misunderstood and deceived by others—he who harbours such thoughts in his mind can never become free from the causes which inflict their destructiveness upon himself."

Materialism Taints Merit

The new socio-economic changes brought about during last 58 years in this country have set certain trends in general masses. The most evident of all these is the materialistic attitude of society, Shudra caste not being an exception. There is some misconception in the word 'materialism'. It is not a term coined to be against prosperity as some people preach it. It only denotes attitude of mind. When one sets aside all morals, scruples, sincere efforts and hard work to achieve material gains, and thinks he is justified to achieve it through means that are unfair, crooked and cruel, he then is a materialist. In a religion where one worships God directly or indirectly, consciously or unconsciously, willingly or unwillingly, there is still possibility of some check on his thoughts. But think of the havoc such an attitude will play in a society that finds pleasure and justification in denouncing God or the Super Intelligence or moral laws. This is not, of course about those who act honestly in the belief that there is no God. It is about those who neither believe in ethical laws, nor in God, nor in laws of nature governed by higher intelligence. In the absence of such checks, there is inflated ego in every matter rather than the humility born out of power and enlightenment.

Positive Software Bbrings about Results

Therefore, it is only the positive thought that can result into social harmony, developments and power. James Allen says in 'From Poverty to Power':

> "Listen, and let may words burn themselves in your heart, for that which I say to you is truth: You may bring about that improved condition in your outward life, which you desire, if you will unswervingly resolve to improve your inner life. I know this pathway looks barren at its commencement (truth always does, it is only error and illusion which are at first inviting and fascinating) but if you undertake to walk it, if you deservingly discipline your mind, eradicating your weaknesses and allowing your soul-forces and spiritual powers to unfold themselves, you will be astonished at the magical changes which will be brought about in your outward life".

References

1. *"The Inner Reality"* by Dr. Paul Brunton, B.I. Publication Pvt. Ltd.
2. *"Six Great Scientist "* by J.G. Growther U.K.
3. *"Dr. Ambedkar and Dalit Future"* by Sh. V.R. Krishna Iyer, B.R. Publishing House, Delhi.

8
Shudras to Ati-Shudras

Shudras before Manusmriti (322-185 BC)

In the Maurya period major population amongst Shudras was *'Karmkars'* who were either the Kishans, working on the land for the king or the agricultural labourers working on wages. According to Kautalya, they were to get ½ amount of share of crop if working with their own seeds, oxen's and implements and at ¼ part if these were provided to them by the king. Others were agriculture labour working on wages or payment or in kind of food grains. The Shudras continued to work on the land as above with some modifications in different periods till the independence in 1947. In addition to agriculture, Kautilya further mentions the trading, artisanship and animal-keeping as the means of livilihood for Shudras. In Manu's period their above occupation of agriculture continued with them which could not have been altered drastically for economic sustenance of the society. Attempt was, however, made in this (Manu's) period to degrade Shudras and many of them were made to turn up to the house-hold service of the Brahmins and other castes, and to other lowly occupations.

1. Shudras after Manusmriti

The Smrities like Narada smriti, Vishnu Smriti, Manu Smriti, Brahaspati Smriti and Dharama Shastras like Gautam Dharam Sutra, Vasishta Dharam Sutra,

Apastamba Dharam Sutra place Shudra not only the lowest in social hierarchy but also outside all symptoms of human civilization. There is a very sever punishment (not fit to be recorded) if a Shudra hears the words of Vedas or gives words of advice to higher castes etc. Even Manu Smiriti says "As nothing belong to a Shudra, a Brahmin may take possession of the property of a Shudra with perfect case" – Manu VIII/417. If this is where Shudras are placed in the Brahmanic society, one wonders if there can be still castes below them. Manu mentions them as Chandala, Antayavasayin and Svapakas. But before coming to castes below and besides Shudras, let us see the position of Shudras in more detail which obtained in the period of Smritis and Sutras, after the fall of Maurya Empire. Obviously, there was an attempt to put them in low and degrading position. They continued to remain connected to the agriculture occupation either as the tillers or the labourers, alongwith house-hold service of the Brahmins and other castes, and doing miscellaneous jobs as required in different seasons of the year which were added in this period. In the period of Smritis, Shudras can be said to be just existing and not living with dignity, except for a small section of them who were able to get into better vocations of artisans or direct holding of lands. The Smritis (except Yajnavalkya Smriti) do not give them (to Shudras) human rights of advancement and evolution as shown below :

No Education

"One should never recite the Vedas in the presence of Shudras" *Manu IV : 99*

No Property

"As nothing belongs to a Shudra, Brahmin may take possession of the property of Shudra with perfect ease" *Manu VIII : 417*

"No collection of wealth may be made by a Shudra even if he is capable of doing so, for a Shudra who acquires wealth gives pain to Brahmin"

Manu X : 129

No Self-Defence

"The slayer of a Shudra should practice all observations for six months or he may give to a priest ten white cows and a bull" *Manu XI : 127*

"Shudras are the servant of another, to be expelled at will and to be slain at will" *"Aitaterya Brahmana"*

No Dharma

Shudras have no right to the work of Dharma"

Manu X : 126

No Good Name

"The last part of shudra's name should mean service" (like Dasa) *Manu II : 32*

No Food and Clothes

"Shudra should be given food as left-overs and old cloths and beddings" *Manu X : 125*

It will be in order to contrast the above position of Shudras with that of Brahmins, to highlight the big difference between the two.

Bramin is Above Gods

"By his origin alone he (Brahmin) is a deity even for gods and his word is authoritative for men"

Manu XI : 83-85

"———— Whatever exists in the world is the property of Brahmins" *Manu I : 100*

"King should get up early morning and serve Brahmins and work according to their directions"

Manu VII : 37

2. Catagories of Caste in Manusmriti

Broadly speaking, there are three categories of castes in the Manusmriti, given as below:

First is the category of Chaturvarnya, the castes in the four Varnas of Brahmin, Kstriya, Vaishya and Shudras in their original form as given by the creator from his mouth, arms, thighs and feet. Let us say it as category 'A'. Second is the Varna-Samkar i.e. the mixed-castes. Manu says there are only four varnas and not the fifth (X:4). Obviously so, other than the four varnas, the different mix of them can not fall in any of original four varnas. It shall be dealt with in detail later, but presently let it be stated that mixed-caste form the occupational guilds and not castes, according to Manu. Different occupations have been assigned to different mixed-castes, depending upon the grading of *Anuloma* and *Pritiloma* orders. *Anulomas* are those where father is of higher varna and mothers of lower one. *Pritilomas* are progeny of mothers of higher varna and fathers of lower varna. *Paritilomas* are considered to be *hinas* i.e. the inferior ones to the *Anulomas.* Manu says that Mixed-caste can also be identified from its occupation (X:40). Let us call the second as category 'B'. It seems that over a period of time the guilds were converted into castes. The third category is of the outcastes, who were despised even by the lower castes. These are the Chandalas, Svapakas and Antayavasyin. Most degraded treatment is given to these castes by Manu, putting them practically as untouchables. Let us call this as category 'C'. It will be found that even in later period of Indian history, these basic three categories of castes have been observed by the foreign travelers though there had been decrease in their numbers in category 'B', as the occupation changed with time, like Sutas as charioteers no longer required in later periods. Manu seems to have discovered a deadly combination of some mixed-castes which gives rise to the three sub-human groups, given above in category 'C'. The category 'A' castes lived in the village or town together, the category 'B' occupational castes on the boundary of village(Manu X:50) and category 'C' outside the village(Manu X:52). There was no feeling of segregation or untouchability in respect of category 'B' castes; how could it be for professionals like charioteers, who came in touch with higher castes all the time. The foundation of untouchability had been laid with the three 'C' castes, which thought grew in big proportion in subsequently period. Amongst these, of course, Chandalas, the progenies of undesirable births (of all kinds), had always been a shunned caste even before the period of Manu. It seems that Manu did not mean untouchability to these castes, but only their segregation from the free contact with others (Manu X: 53- by day they shall go about for the purpose of their work distinguished by marks).

3. Mixed-Castes Of Manu:

Brahmin father to Vaishya mother is born Ambastha	Manu X:5
Brahmin father to Shudra mother Nishada	X:8
Kshtriya fathertoShudra mother Ugra	X:9
Kstriya father to Brahmin mother Suta	X:11
Vaishya father to Brahmin mother Vaideha	X:11

Shudra father to Kshtriya mother Khattri X:12

Shudra father to Vaishya mother Ayogava X:12

Shudra father to Brahmin mother Chandala (most despised) X:12

Dasyu father to Ayogava mother Sairandhra X: 32

Nishad father to Margava or Dasa mother Kaivarta (boatman) X:34

Nishad father to Vaideha mother Karavara (Charmakar) X:36

Chandala father to Pukkasa mother Svapaka (the sinful) X:38

Chandala father to Nishad mother Antyavasin (who works in burial ground) X:39

Their occupations are:

Killing fish to Nishad, carpenter work to Ayogava and to Medas, Andlras, Madguos the killing of wild animals. X:48

To Khattaris, Ugras, Pukhasas the caching and killing of animals living in holes; to Dhigvanas working in leather and to Venas the playing of drums X:49

The dwellings of Chandalas and Svapakas shall be outside the village, they must be made apapatras, and their wealth shall be dogs and donkeys. X:51

Their dress shall be the cloths of dead and the ornaments made of black iron and they shall move from place to place. X:52

Their food shall be in broken dish, at night they shall not walk about in village and towns. X:54

4. Vrityas

Manusmriti says;

"But in consequence of the omissions of the sacred rites and their not consulting Brahmins, the following tribes of Kshatriyas gradually sunk in this world to the condition of Shudras"

Viz: the Pundraka, the Kodas, the Dravidas, the Kambogas, the Yavanas, the Sakas, the Paradas, the Palhavas, the Kinas, the Kiratas and Dradas: X:44

The Kshatriya tribes mentioned above were degraded to Shudra castes simply because they did not care to observe rites and ceremonies as ordained by Brahmins.

5. Shudras Brought Down

As already brought out, the period of Manusmirti is given by the historians after the fall of Maurya empire. The latter having the element of Shudra ancestry, it was but natural that Shudras shall be brought down low socially in Brahmnic Smritis of a subsequent period. But despite all such efforts, the Shudras and below- Shudras were not untouchables though some of them were considered impure. To the ancient culture of India, whether Buddhist or Brahmanic, the untouchability was a foreign concept. Even if we take the three castes of category 'C' in Manu's period as bordering on untouchability, about 430 castes of untouchables as obtained at the time of Independence of India in 1947, is not explained by that existing in Manusmirti. Something entirely different had happed to bring about mass untouchability in India after the Smritis period. This will be dealt in detail in this chapter, different from the reasons of beaf-eating and their adherence to Buddism etc.

6. Caste-by-Worth

The caste-by-birth of Manu is in direct opposition to the castes-by-worth of Krishna as given in Bhagwad Geeta (I.V:13). There is a merit in Manu's castes wherever it coincides with caste-by-worth like the case of Adi Sankracharya, Ramanand, Ramakrishna Pramahansa etc. But wherever there is a contrast between the two, we obtain the position like in the case of sant Ravidas, who is a person of great spiritual insight by worth but remains a Shudra by birth. The Astrologer fixes the caste of an individual by worth, based on his past karmas as reflected in the position of planets at the time of birth. But social castes can not be fixed according to this classification, as it is going to create lot of confusion, so this caste in an horoscope remains only for judging temperament/ character of an individual. The nature's caste-by-worth, however, shall ultimately reveal itself and it is going to dilute or modify the Manu's castes, as the society gets enlightened, keeping it only in loose form and not in the sharply divided water-tight compartments.

7. Constituents of Caste

Despite impact of teachings of great saints, the Hindu caste system retains the following elements in its constitution;

1. *Heredity*: The castes are based on heredity with no scope of modification or its termination. It goes on endlessly on the basis of some good deeds of Brahmin ancestors or the evil deeds of Shudra

forefathers. Human mind can not conceive of that meritorious deed or the sinful act which is capable of giving eternal award or eternal condemnation to the progenies of such doers.

2. *Marriage*: The castes are endogamous but the *Gotras* within are exogamous. The marriages are within ones own caste and any transgression being looked down upon by the society. How the person born from the face of the cosmic person shall have blood different from him who is born from the feet, only the Brahmins who perpetuate such differences will be able to tell. But Swami Vivekananda says, perhaps considering the blood to be same in the above cosmic person "There is for example a good reason for intermarriage in India (within the same religion) in the absence of which the race is becoming physically weaker day by day"

   Complete works Vol.V P.334

3. Occupation: The higher castes take higher occupation like those of teachings, temple worships etc. while the lower castes take the lower and despised jobs of scavenging and skinning works. Middle castes take up job in between. The Gods however do not have such inhibitions and a Krishna can do the job of a village cowherd or the driving of chariots like a Suta and be a king later.

4. Hierarchy: It is an essential element of caste system due to which a Brahmin has to be placed on top and a Shudra at the bottom, other varnas occupying position in between. It is like an army command structure but devoid of fraternity elements so necessary for cohesive working. Different layers in the caste system run dry over each other creating frictions and sparks occasionally.

5. Purity: Purity of food in particular is the essential ingredient of Hindu caste. The food gets impure even by a look of wicked or low person. The physical purity is understandable or desirable but what about the internal purity of intentions and desires. The latter is even more desirable. Yudhishtra said so while defining a true Brahmin to the Yaksha.

Change in caste system can be effected by the change in any or all of the above constituents.

8. Period of Guptas(320-413AD) & Harshvardhan's (629-647 AD)

This was the period when two famous Chinese travelers Fa-Hien and Yuan-Chwang visited India and gave detailed account of this country on those periods, mentioning about the cordial relations between Buddhists and Hindus of Vaisanavism and Shivism sects.

Gupta Period: A number of literatures came up during this period, including the work 'Amarkosh' by Amar Simha, who was one of the nine jewels of Chandragupta-II. The position of Shudras in it is given as below:

The artisans were in Shudra class numbering 30 as gardeners, watermans, masons, weavers, painters, charmkars and blacksmith etc...... (Amarkosh 11.10.5-10).

Brahspati and Narad smritis consider landless agriculture labour as Shudras (Narad 5/23). Trading is also considered as the duty of Shudras according to Yaganvalkya. All mixed-castes(varna-samkar) were considered to be in Shudra category according to Amarkhosh.

Harsha Period: The Chinese traveler Yuan-Chwang (or Huen-Tsang) visited India between 629 AD and 645 AD during the reign of Harsh Vardhan. He has described the condition of Shudras by recording that agriculture was the normal profession of Shudras, who were of 3 types viz: (i) Independent Kishans who were paying a little part to the king (ii) Kishans working on share-cropping *(batai)* who were getting about 1/3rd of the produce (iii) Agricultural labour getting about 1/6th part or so as wages. This classification of agricultural occupation for Shudras/untouchables was more or less the same till the independence of India in 1947, as witnessed by this author in the villages. The name of the workers, however, had changed from Karmakaras in Maurya period to Chamaras etc. in present times, engaged in the same profession. In the period of Yuan-Chwang's visit, the Shudras were not considered as untouchable though some castes like Chandala, Swapaka and Badhik were nearly so.

9. Al-Beruni's Records (1000-1030 AD)

Al-Beruni, the famous Muslim traveler during the period of Mahmud of Ghazni's attack on India, gives the details on the position of Shudras and below-Shudras in the book 'Tarikhu'l Hind', as below:

(a) There was not much difference between Vaishyas, and Shudras and they lived together in the same village.

(b) Below-Shudras were eight categories of Antyajas who were outside the caste system but identified on the basis of their profession or guild. They lived near the village but separately from four castes. The guilds were; (i) Shoe-maker (Charmkar), (ii) Fuller (Washerman), (iii) Juggler, (iv) the basket and shield maker, (v) the sailor or *Kaivat*, (vi) the Fisherman, (vii) the Weaver and (viii) the hunter of wild animals, who lived together in a separate group.

(c) Below these eight guilds were the persons called Hadi, Domas, Chandalas, and Badhatu, who were neither in any case or guild. They did dirty work and were shunned by the society.

The above classification is more or less the same as given by Manu and described in 2 above, in (A), (B) and (C) categories. The eight professions of category (b) above, mentioned by Al-Beruni were not untouchables, as no body could afford to be untouchable with a person like sailor nor his profession has any impurity. Almost all of them are covered in the Shudra list of artisans given in *Amarkosla.* These professionals were in very small numbers compared to the bulk population of Shudras in the villagers, simply because no bigger employment was possible in them. The worker in hides or shoe-making even in present day village of large population is only one or two families. The last category 'C' of course, bordered on untouchability, like that of category 'C' of Manu's Castes.

10. Period of Sant Ravidas or Rai Das (1411-1527 AD)

Sant Ravi Das was born in 15th Century AD in a village near Varanasi (in present Uttar Pradesh) in the family of a Charmakar (Chamar).

Manu gives the ancestry of this caste as;

"Through Nishada father and Vaidehi mother is born the Karavara' – the leather worker" (X:36)

Now, Nishada is from Brahmin father and Shudra mother (X:8) and Vaidehi is from Vaishya father and Brahmin mother (X:17). The great Ved Vyasa was

Nishada by caste who produced the Kaurva and Pandava race through Kshatriya mothers Ambika and Ambalika. How much different is Charmakara of Manu from the above racial mix of Pandvas can be a matter of hair-splitting argument, but certainly it is not the difference of heaven and hell which is made out in the Smritis against them.

In his life he performed the job of a cobbler throughout. He became the disciple of the famous saint Ramananda who was preaching the greatness and universality of Shri Rama and Sita. Through selfless devotion, Ravi Das rose to great height of spirituality and many wonders are attributed to him. He was the contemporary of Sant Kabir and Guru Nanak, in fact the latter visited him during his pilgrimage to Varanasi. The saying (*Bani*) of Ravi Das find place in the sacred book of Sikhs 'Guru Granth Sahib'. Several spiritual deeds are narrated in various books on Sant Ravi Das. In one legend, a rich man of high caste went to see the renowned Ravi Das and found him busy in mending shoes. After the discourse, a chamar brought water in a pot in which shoes were wetted. The water drops were thrown over the visitor as part of blessings. On returning home the rich man found that the stains of this water thrown on his clothes are not being removed, as a result of which he gave the cloths to a sweeper. After some time, it was noticed that the sweeper had become better and happy, while this rich man became a leper. Realising his folly, he sought mercy of Ravi Das and was cured of the leprosy.

In another event, a Brahmin came to Ravi Das and paid a small coin to him for the services of repairing shoes. Ravi Das asked the Brahmin to give this coin to *Gangaji* after his offerings. As he was about to throw the coin in the river, *Gangaji* came out to receive it herself and offered a golden bangle for Ravi Das. But the Brahmin took it to the king to please him with the wonderful item. King gave it to the queen. But the queen demanded another one to make it a pair. The Brahmin having been trapped, disclosed everything to Ravi Das and bagged his pardon. Ravi Das brought another similar bangle from his 'Kathauthi' (a pot for dipping shoes) and placed it in the hands of the Brahmin, who was shaking with wonder.

Mira Bai, the devotee of Lord Krishna, became disciple of Ravi Das. As his spiritual wonders were spreading fast, Jhali Rani, the mother-in-law of Mira and wife of Rana Sanga the great Rajput emperor of Chittorgarh, also became his disciple and brought Ravi Das to her fort of Chittorgarh. The queen arranged a feast and invited Ravi Das to it. But the Brahmins refused to sit alongwith him and formed a separate group to take the food. As the food was being served, they saw Ravi Das sitting between every two of them (Brahmins). The Brahmins felt ashamed of their conduct. Sant Ravi Das at this time ripped open his skin and showed them under it the golden thread, proving that he is a greater Brahmin.

The Ravi Das *Chhatri* and his foot-prints in stone are still preserved in Kumbh-Shyam Mandir inside the fort of Chittorgarh Rajasthan (Photographs also produced in the book 'Sant Ravi Das' – Hindi -, Govt. of India, Ministry of Information and Broadcasting).

So, in the period of Ravi Das i.e. 15th century AD, there was no general untouchability of low caste masses, though there was segregation on the basis of professional impurity.

In his *Bani*, Sant Ravi Das has called himself Chamara in various couplets. It is difficult to read the mind of spiritual saints, but even as a worldly persons we have to make our assessment in the social context of such facts of low appellation being retained by them. It seems that in that period it was just a professional name and the feeling of repulsion against it grew later when masses of Shudras were also covered in this name, as will be shown in the end of this chapter. Ravi Das only tried to remove the inferiority concept attached to the caste by his own example of spiritual attainments in this very caste. There was no good reason for him to leave the profession on which his community survived. It had money in it, though Ravi Das used to give free pair of shoes to the saints and the needy, due to which he was expelled from the house by his father. If not chamars, somebody else could take it over, as is being done today with skinning on contract basis in India. The animals will keep on dying and their skin yielding leather shall remain a permanent requirement of society the world over. What Ravi Das did to remove the inferiority complexity of the profession through his spiritual achievements, the industrialization of the leather industry today is doing that with the profession slipping out of their (Chamars) hands.

11. Medieval Saints Against Caste

As pointed out by Justice M.G. Ranadey, the political effects though visible at a later stage, is preceded by religious and social pioneering work. There were other great saints in the medieval India, some of them contemporary of sant Ravi Das, preaching against the caste system, as mentioned below. It is their teachings which finally produced great warrior like Shivaji and Guru Gobind Singh.

Ramanuja (1017-1137 AD): A Brahmin, who hailed from a place near Madras(Chennai) in South India. He preached Vaisnavism i.e. devotion to Lord Vishnu. He was dualist in Philosophy and therefore preached *Bhakti Marg* to attain the Lord. He also preached forcefully against casteism prevailing then in South.

Namdeva (1270-1350 AD) : He was born in Maharastra in a family of washer -man. He strongly denounced idol worship ritualism and superstitions in the society. Ek Nath and Tukaram in Maharastra similarly led movements for *Bhakti* but against the casteism.

Swami Ramananda: (15th Century AD (1410-1510 AD): Born in *Prayag* (Allahabad in U.P.) in a Brahmin family, he preached devotion to Rama and Sita. Amongst his disciples were the famous two who belonged to the low castes i.e, Ravi Das a Cobbler and Kabir a weaver. He strongly preached against casteism.

Sant Kabir (1440-1510 AD): Kabir preached for one God and for the unity of Hindu and Muslims. His D*ohas* are still popular, rather on the lips of public, being simple but of direct and deeper impact. He attacked blind faith and ignorance in Hindus as well Muslims, not sparing Hindus for rigid casteism.

Guru Nanak (1469-1538 AD) : He was born in Talwandi (now in Pakistan) in a Khatri family. He laid emphasis on one God and strongly opposed the differences of caste and even religion. His followers ate together without observing any distinction amongst themselves. He was opposed to ritualism and believed in the usefulness of devout life of a householder.

Chaitanya Mahaprabhu (1486-1533 AD): Born in the family of Brahmins of Bengal, he developed *Bhakti* movement around the worship of Shri Krishna and deadly opposed the caste system and segregation of human beings.

Mira Bai (1502-1546 AD): A Rajput princes who married in the family of Chittor King Rana Sanga. She became a widow and thereafter a disciple of Sant Ravi Das. Her songs and couplets in praise of Lord Shri Krishna are sung even today.

Sant Tuka Ram (1601-1649 AD): Born in a low caste family of Maharastra, he was strongly opposed to casteism. He by his saintly qualities earned the gratitude of Shivaji.

Samaratha Ram Das (1608-1681 AD): He was Guru of Chatrapati Shivaji, hailing from a Brahmin family of Maharastra. He performed sever *tapsya* near the bank of *Godavari* through *Japa* of 'Shri Rama'. Though he attained *Siddhis*, but he rarely used them. Because of his desires coming true, he was called 'Samaratha'- the competent. He gave a copy of his work 'Dasa Bodha' to Shivaji and praised the coconut to signify purity from inside and hard and rugged on outside. Shivaji lived up to this concept. As it has been shown elsewhere, Shivaji, was a Shudra and a Brahmin's teachings to him shows the large heartedness of Ram Das.

12. Chhatrapati Shivaji's Period (1627-1680 AD)

How a Shudra became the Chhatrapati and the mightiest soldier of that period to challenge the great Mughal Empire of Aurangzeb, has been described in detail in Chapter 6 of this book. But suffice to mention here that untouchability against general mass of Shudras and low castes did not prevail in this period. The high castes Hindus themselves had lost honour and other privileges of society and they some how were existing under the *Jazia* taxation and frequent humiliations with little thought and luxury for tyrannizing others below them. They had no command structure of a king to enforce the injections of Smritis. The untouchability however, increased against low castes later during the period of Brahmin Peshwas.

13. Era of Starvations, Foreigner's Loot, Famine Deaths and Mass Untouchability (1707- 1947 AD):

In this book 'The Chamars' (1920 edition), the British writer G.W. Briggs quotes the Census Report of 1911 (Page 57) to state "The figures from the United Province show that only five percent of the Chamars are leather workers; that seventy eight percent of them exploit the earth's surface (e.g. are cultivators, agriculturists and labourers); that four percent are engaged in other industries; that two percent are occupied with transport and trade; and the nine percent are general labourers". The term 'Chamar' includes 1156 sub-castes as per Briggs (figure could be less as some names are only different words) and can be said to include majority of scheduled castes of today. Briggs ponders over as to how 95% of agriculturists came to be associated with the name while he writes, "It is as a tanner and worker in leather that the Chamar obtains his name". He states 150 grades of *mochis* to be working in leather from skinning, tanning to manufacturing sophisticated products. So the numbers working with baser jobs of initial work of skinning and tanning in leather shall reduce to about one percent from the five of Census Report. Thus the bulk of Chamars i.e. 99% of them do not associate with the profession from which their name derives. This is also witnessed by this author in the villages of Northern India. Briggs answers this question as, "Chamars very name connects him with the carcasses of cattle. Besides, he not only removes the skins from the cattle that have died but also he eats the flesh. The defilement and degradation resulting from these acts are insurmountable. The fact that the Chamar is habitually associated in thought with these practices may partially explain why the large non-leather working sections of the caste are still rated as untouchable". Why the bulk of agriculturist and labourer Shudras became untouchable is because of their association with the dead body of cattles, which was until now the job of below-Shudras. Facing the starvation death he had no option left but to turn to this occupation and food when crores of such people died during famine in the 18th and 19th Century AD in various parts of the country. Deaths numbering so high have been reported by the Britishers in their period. Sage Vishavamitra could get away by eating a dog in hunger during famine but the Shudras did not. Manu Smriti records, "The knower of dharma and adharma rishi Vishavamitra had prepared to eat from the hands of Chandala the haunch of a dog when dying of hunger (during famine)" (X:108).

Conditions After the Break-up of Mughal Empire

When an empire breaks up, it has an adverse effect on the political, social and economical conditions of its people. After the death of Aurangzeb in 1707 AD, the war of succession began and continued till there remained nothing to succeed to. The country was almost in a state of civil war, the nobles were shifting their loyalty frequently, even claiming independence for themselves at times. Intrigues, treacheries, jealousies, cruelty were orders of the day. To add to the trouble, foreign invaders like Nadirshah and Ahmedshah Abdali freely looted the population and even the emperor himself. Nadirshah is said to have parted from Delhi after emptying the royal treasury of Mughals worth 70 crores of that time (1739 AD). The impoverished rulers and nobles began to squeeze and oppress the peasantry to subsist and recover their lost fortune. The concept of revenue-farming was introduced under which instead of collecting land revenue at the given rate, a contractor or a middle man was introduced who would pay a fixed amount to the government but afterwards shall remain free to extract the revenue from the peasants as he liked. There was nothing left with the small farmer except his existence for the purpose of feeding every one else above him. It was a strange sight of everyone looting everyone under him. Foreigners plundering the kings, king demanding from nobles, nobles extracting from peasants, and peasants squeezing themselves with half-meals. The money lender *(Bania)* in the village or town would complete the exploitation process by lending money in hard times(which were in plenty) at such exorbitant rates that they will never be able to pay it back and thus lose the lands and remain only landless labourers. After the release from Muslim rule of about 600 years, the high caste Hindus felt free to exploit the lower castes, themselves. Caste councils were formed and the Hindu society was getting divided into innumerable castes on slight pretence of superiority or difference of occupation. Evils like sati and untouchability were promoted by the crafty and superstitious priestly class. Being selfish to the core, the latter easily shed their social responsibility in favour of their personal gains and power.

British Entry:

As if the conditions at the downfall of Mughal empire were not bad enough for the small agriculturalists, the entry of British in India through East India Company added salt to the injury of low castes during 1757 to 1857

AD and even afterwards. India was transformed into a colonial state, meant to serve only the British interest. Rapid industrialization of British and stagnation of India economy with outdated farming and cottage industries, ruined the jobs of millions of artisans, with British factory made products flooding the Indian market at cheaper rates. These jobless artisans had nowhere to go but to fall on agriculture. The cotton weaving and other related handicraft occupations were hit maximum, which provided job even to a farmer in spare or part time. To add to the woe, the Indian export items like silk, wooden garments, pottery, paper, glass, Jute and other Indian products which were traditionally finding place in British market, were made costlier and therefore less acceptable through high import duties there. This further made huge number of Indian workers jobless. The Britishers had introduced local Zamindars or Zagirdars in between them and peasants to feed them with lion's share of crop under the sysem of Permanent Settlement. Other systems of revenue collection like Ryotwari settlement and Mahalwari systems etc. were equally exploitive for British Interest. The Zamindars were left free to exploit the peasants as they liked. There was none to listen to their complaint against Zamindar's atrocities. As said earlier, they (peasants) will also lose their land once they mortgaged it to the moneylender for raising loan in adversity.

With so many agricultural labourers available surplus, they will not but get only the low starvation wages from the landlords and higher peasantry, despite hard works, even in normal times.

Writes Pandit Jawahar Lal Nehru in the 'Discovery of India' about this period:

"The liquidation of the Artisan class led to the unemployment on prodigious scale.... They could die of course; that way of escape from an intolerable situation is always open; They did die in tons of millions...... All these hordes of artisans and craft man had no job no work and all their ancient skill was useless. They drifted to land, for the land was still there. But the land was so fully occupied and could not possible absorb them profitably ... and with it grew the poverty of the country. The number of landless labourers increased by millions..... and made the peasant one of the poorest and most miserable beings on earth".

Visit of Famines and Unrouchability

The agriculture system in India uptil 18th and 19th century was almost wholly based on rains, with little artificial irrigation canals and other alternative source to water the fields, in existence. Earlier kings could help a little during famines either by relaxing revenue or providing some means of subsistence to the peasants. But during the period after the end of Mughal empire and at beginning of British company's rule, no such aid was forthcoming. The Britishers in East India Company were taking only the revenue and not the responsibility for the people, in temporary settlement scheme. It is irony of fate that the Britishers who brought some concept of freshness in Indian thoughts and society at a later period, were totally callous to the pains of the natives in the initial period of about one hundred years. Marginal farmers and agricultural labourers died out of hunger during famine in lakhs and lakhs. Even on present day, the news paper report 'The Pioneer' dated 25 May 2004 puts the farmer's starvation death as 44 in one week in Andhra Pradesh, due to failure of crops, despite all protective measures of modern free Indian Government and there being no famine in the state.

The famines occurred during 18th century, whose details are not available, except for the period 1770 to

1774 AD about which the condition is described by the famous author of Vande Matram, Bankim Chandra Chatterjee in his book 'Anand Math'. The famine occurred in Bengal during this period, as a result of which about 1/3rd of its population was wiped out. The author says that there was nothing to eat and people then ate tree leaves and grass. He gives the story of a landlord, who too had to leave his place due to conditions of starvation. With his wife and a small child they leave towards Calcutta, when on the way the wife and the child get kidnapped by dacoits who take out all her ornaments. Being hungry they (dacoits) are not satisfied with this loot and quarrel with their leader to give them rice instead. They kill this leader in hot arguments and say 'we have so far ate flesh of dogs and jackals, let us roast this dead leader and eat him up'.

But the Britishers did furnish the famine periods in 19th century as; 1802-04, 1806-07, 1812-15, 1819-20, 1823-26, 1830-32, 1837, 1860-61, 1865-66, 1868-70, 1876-78, 1889-90, 1896-97, and 1899-1900. They also furnished the figure of those died of starvation in second half of 19th century as about 3 crores of human beings. With nothing to eat for humans, the animals will die even more. But while dying, they will yield their skins to those who survive upon it traditionally as well as to those who are dying of hunger and now forced to remove the hides and even eat the flesh. This is how the peasants and landless Shudras became untouchable enmass while earlier there were only few in this category. This also explains the curiosity of G.W. Brigs (the author of book 'The Chamars') as to how 95% no-leather workers, mostly working as agriculturists, came to be associated with this low epithet which was earlier meant for 5% of Shudras. The Shudras were thus got divided into two categories, the upper and lower one. The upper Shudras were those who escaped hard times and could not be classed as untouchables. This also explains how there are common Gotras likes Kataryas, Ahirs, Gothwals, Huddas, Gangwals etc. (a long list in all parts of India) in the higher and lower Shudras both. Perhaps it is for this reason that Briggs in this book has said "Furthermore, there are good reasons for believing that the caste has received large recruitments from above" (Page 17). Barring a few, nearly all of the lower Shudras left this occupation of skinning and eating of such flesh after the famine about a century ago, but the stigma is not leaving them, though it is thinning out by the passage of time. Almost all races in the world did face tough times, but they recovered by the healing touch of this time itself. In India the victim of time fell into the pre-classified category of low birth as per Smritis and therefore, taking time to recover back. There is need to remind the Sankracharyas of society of what Lord Shiva as 'Untouchable' said to them "what should I remove from your path, the universal Atman or the body made of five elements, which are common to all beings". Nature has already proved the above words of Lord Shiva to be true through shining examples of low caste personalities glorifying Indian history in varios periods. To restore some dignity, why can't 'Chamar' be spoken as Kamar on the analogy of the word chemistry (in writing it continuing to be chamar only as per the Schedule) which also covers in short form their ancient professional name as Karamkar.

Swami Vivekananda lived himself in the part period of this hard times and seeing the conditions of low caste people around, cried out;

"A country whose millions of people live on flowers of Mahua Plant, and a million or two of sadhus and

Brahmins suck the blood out of these poor people, without even the least efforts for their amelioration-is that a country or hell? Is that a religion or devil's dance? The Hindu, the Mohammedan the Christian all have trampled them under foot"

Complete works Vol. VI p. 254

But such difficult times toughened his spirit, and he said;

"A man who has met starvation face to face for fourteen years of life, who has not known where he will get meal the next day and where to sleep, can not be intimidated so easily. A man almost without cloths, who dared to live where the thermometer registered thirty degree below zero, without knowing where the next day meal was to come from, can not to be so easily intimidated in India"

Complete works Vol. III P.213

Shall we imbibe some element of this spirit and look toward future saying "we shall not be so easily intimidated in India" rather than mentally dragging the negative load of our past, all the time.

"There is no practice more degrading, debasing and soul-destroying than that of self-pity. Cast if out from you" says James Allen.

9
Working of Nature's Laws

External World

Through devices or through ignorance or unwittingly, the universal concept of Varna was mixed-up with the hierarchical concept of caste, the two being similar in appearance only. Once having tasted the fruits of social privileges, the Brahminism was interested only to perpetuate itself by all means, including the promise of passport to heavens etc. But what had been the final results of this system? 'By their fruits ye shall know them' said Jesus Christ. So let us see the fruit this tree of rigid caste system has produced. But before this, let me quote Dr. Paul Brunton, the great English author on metaphysics and spirituality.

- 'Nature never excuses ignorance'
- 'The world which you do not see, the unseen world of thought and feeling, is the real world of causes; the world you see is the world of effects'.

Whenever free ideas and social harmony prevailed in India, we had great achievements even in physical plane. The great work of Art and science on Ashoka's Lion capital (still intact at Sarnath, Varanasi), the rust-free 1500 years old exposed iron pillar at Quitub Minar Delhi, art work of Ajanta caves, Arya Bhata's astronomy and a host of such achievements on physical plane are to the credit of ancient Indians. But when the free creativity or learning of the society got restricted to a particular group and thus stagnated in that pool, there had been practically no progress towards such development of human endeavor. The modern growth of science and technology, by which the whole of human race is deriving utility and sustenance, is mostly the creation of those who are outside our caste system. Comfort and relief has been provided to human life and thus reduced its suffering to some extent by such discoveries. For this, the humanity should be grateful to these scientists/discoverers. I am not trying to enrich the general knowledge of the readers, but only to show the physical reality of how the important discoveries in the field of science, as given below, had been ordained by the nature from the minds of persons outside our social system, barring a few names like J.C. Bose and C.V. Raman.

- **Electricity,** discovered by Edison, USA, 1879
- **Aeroplane,** discovered by Writ Brothers, USA, 1903
- **Rail Engine,** discovered by James Watt, U.K., 1765
- **Motor Car,** discovered by Karl Benz, Germany, 1885
- **Bicycle,** discovered by Macmillan, U.K., 1839
- **Telephone,** discovered by A.G. Bell, USA, 1876
- **Telegraph,** discovered by F B Morse of, USA and Lammond of France, 1837
- **Television,** discovered by J.L. Baird of Scotland and P.T. Farnsworth of USA, 1926
- **Radio,** discovered by G. Marconni, Italy, 1901

- **Computer,** discovered by Van Neumann, USA, 1947
- **Cinema,** discovered by Nicolas and Jean Lumiere, France, 1895
- **Cement,** discovered by Joseph Aspdin, U.K, 1824
- **Atom Bomb,** discovered by Otto Hahn, Germany (atomic theory can be used for peaceful purpose, by generating power), 1941
- **Motor Cycle,** discovered by G. Dajmler, Germany, 1885
- **Photography,** discovered by John Carbutt, USA, 1888
- **Revolver,** discovered by Colt, U.K., 1835
- **Telescope,** discovered by Hans Lippershay, Netherland, 1608

Above are just a few items out of thousands, which concerns us in everyday life, leaving out innumerable ones in almost all fields like medicine, engineerings, atomic theories, quantum, relativity, space, astronomy, etc., where discoveries have been made by foreign minds (mostly of West). Through near perfection of computer and missile technology, the first man to land on moon was from outside our country and society. Even if such landing be doubted by some, the probe of solar system by NASA space vehicles provide occasional thrill and visual knowledge of the planets and their moons located deep in the solar system, even today. The two military and economic superpowers (now only one), is also outside India. In fact military might, the Kshatriya power, belongs to several other countries also, who are way ahead of us. In international games we seldom find place in the list, and if at all, we see it in the end. It was 65th rank in Olympics 2004 with only one silver medal to us.

The foreign countries have produced great poets like William Shakespeare and great philosophers like Immanuel Kant, Rene Descartes, J. Rousseau, Johan Locke, Bertrant Russal etc. The richest man and richest country of the world are not from our society.

Such scientific discoveries are the common property of human race, the laws of Newton and Theory of Relativity of Einstein etc. being freely taught all over the world. Compare it with our past society where the learning will not go beyond one caste. Wherever there is universality, it is all expansion and life; Wherever it is a limitation or narrowness, it is stagnation and death.

Internal Universe

Tremendous achievements as the above are, still these relate to the external world of human life. The inner side of human beings is equally important, if not more. The purpose of life is only to find its core, its relationship with the Infinite Life and other mysteries connected with it. Ancient sages in India concentrated on this 'inside' and made priceless discoveries of one cosmic spirit, Eternal and Infinite, enveloping the whole of creation. The sharpness of mind in deep concentration was far greater than that which discovered physical laws, because the subject in this case was too subtle to come to the grasp of thoughts and words. The latter, had to be transcended to reach beyond and find the Infinite Life pulsating in every atom of the universe. It is only now that modern science has discovered the core of matter as energy, going beyond the constituents of atom as neutron, electron and proton. Says Raja Yoga 'Wherever there is life, the store house of infinite energy is behind'. There is no opposition to the discoveries of external world, as there also the aim is to find the ultimate source of matter. There is some stream of thought in India which decries above materialism and wants to live content with its inner life. The discoverers of higher Truth in India never entertained such narrow interpretation of life for householders, though a *Sanyasi* could live this inner life. Just as there are laws which govern the physical world, there are laws which govern the spiritual world. In both cases, these have to relate to universal application, and not to any limited concept of particular people of the human race.

Wider Circulation of Blood for Healthy Progeny

Even in matters like marriage, the blood should circulate wider for healthy growth says Swami Vivekananda:

"Don't you see how in our society, marriage being restricted for several hundreds of years within the same Sub-Divisions of each caste, has come to such a pass nowadays as virtually to mean marital alliance between cousins and near relations; and how for this very reason the race is getting deteriorated physically; and consequently all sorts of disease and other evils are finding a ready entrance to it? The blood having had to circulate within the narrow circle of a limited number of individuals, has become vitiated; so the new-born children inherit from their very birth the constitutional disease of their fathers..... It is only by widening the circle of marriage that we can infuse a new and a different kind of blood into our progeny". Complete works Vol. V Page 340-41

'...It is the intermarriage, between people of same religion that I advocate'. (ibid P.340)

These are the views of an inner scientist, let us listen to the views of physical scientist, Charles Darwin.

"With animals and plants a cross between different varieties or between individuals of the same variety but of another strain, gives vigor and fertility to the off spring: on the other hand close interbreeding diminishes vigor and fertility. These facts also incline me to believe that it is a general law of nature that no organic being fertilizes itself for a perpetuity of generations: but that a cross with another individual is occasionally indispensable" Origin of species.

Cause and Effect

The whole of this universe is governed by the nature's law of cause and effect. If Newton has discovered it in physical plane, there is no reason why it should not apply in mental world which is only its finer form. James Allen says 'Man is a growth by law, and not a creation by artifice, and cause and effect is as absolute and undeviating in the hidden realm of thought as in the world of visible and material things'.[1] If we do not follow the basic ethics of work or management, the consequences will sooner or later visit upon us, either as individual, or society or the country. Again, says James Allen (in this very book):

"Here is a man who is wretchedly poor. He is extremely anxious that his surroundings and home comforts should be improved, yet all the time he shirks his work, and considers he is justified in trying to deceive his employer on ground of insufficiency of his wages. Such a man does not understand the simplest rudiments of those principles which are the basis of true prosperity, and is not only totally unfitted to rise out of his wretchedness, but is actually attracting to himself a still deeper wretchedness by dwelling in, and acting out, indolent, deceptive, and unmanly thoughts".

Consider the opposite side, the case of an unscrupulous employer:

"Here is an employer of labour who adopts crooked measures to avoid paying the regulation wages, and, in the hope of making larger profits, reduces the wages of his work people. Such a man is altogether unfitted for prosperity, and when he finds himself bankrupt, both as regards reputation and riches, he blames circumstances, not knowing that he is the sole author of his conditions".

The above two cases of nature's law can be seen operating in our society, explaining the condition on which we are placed. There is always an element of hard work and sacrifice behind every healthy condition of happiness and development, wherever it is seen in the world.

References

1. *'As a man Thinketh'* The Peter Pauper Press New York.

10
Modern India-Background Personalities of its Universal Constitution

The Nineteenth and Twentieth centuries of India is the period of general awakening of its masses in religious, social and political fields. It is through the dedicated and combined efforts of so many eminent persons in various fields that an environment was created where positive and creative energies of people found its full potential, which ultimately led to the freedom of India. The dead load of past was so enormous that only mult-pronged attack on variety of evils or dogmas by various personalities could have led to a state of light from darkness, answering to some degree the prayer of Gyatri Mantra *'Tamso ma joytir gamya'* (lead me to light from darkness).

The period nearly starts with the advent of Brithisers on the Indian horizon. It is they who, through the act of providence, as it appears, brought fresh air into the governance, laws and customs and even modern education to this country. However, during the process of entrenching themselves on Indian soil and even aftewards when the rule was passed on to the crown, they used exploitive and ruthless measures to the misery of masses, treating them as breed of inferior beings. The crown like coin thus had two sides. There was mass uprising against their repressive policies and this country had rarely seen such gem of persons fighting together for higher causes. The religious and social leaders acted to loosen the knots of mind to liberate it from the social and religious obscurantism, to the maximum extent possible. Finally India got its freedom in 1947 and a universal constitution in 1950, constituting India into a Sovereign, Socialist and Democratic Republic. The word 'Secular' was added to it during the emergency period in 1976 through 42nd ammendment Act of the Constitution. Not going into all the details of freedom struggle, only the life of personalities whose combined efforts brought about religious, social and political awakening, are briefly described here with reference to their individual contribution. On political side the names are so large that these can be mentioned only by ignoring others. These have therefore, been written very briefly eventhough their contribution was great, because emphasis of this book is on Socio-Religious awakening, particularly that related to Hindu religion. The philosophers and thinkers like Rabinder Nath Tagore were at the core of cultural and political awakening in India, which ultimately led to Indian independence.

Socio-Religious Reformers

Raja Ram Mohan Roy (1772-1833 AD): Born in a Brahmin family of Bengal, he established Brahmo Samaj which believed in the universality of religion with no place for priesthood in it. He was learned in several languages, like English, Persian, French, Greek and Sanskrit etc. He attacked caste system but his main contribution was abolition of Sati practice. He seems to have been greatly influenced by English culture, though he did not abandon the ancient values of India.

Swami Dayananda Saraswati (1824-1883 AD): Swami Dayananda was the founder of Arya Samaj which generated a great social and political movement in the country. He was against idolatry, superstitions and strongly preached against untouchability. He considered the *varna Vyastha* in Hindu castes to be based on Guna and Karma. He preached Vedas and criticised various practices he considered evil in Hindu, Muslim, Sikhs, Christiasn, Buddhist and Jain religion, as contained in his most important book *'Satyartha Prakash'*. In the Nineteenth Century Arya Samaj became a big movement in North India and number of DAV (Dayananda Anglo-Vedic) schools and colleges were opened, which continue till date as symbol of modernity. Some people of low castes were influenced by Arya Samaj objectives and found in it a door for entry to Hindu Society.

*Swami Vivekananda (1863-1902 AD):*Swami Vivekananda was the disciple of Shri Rama Krishna Parama Hansa (1836-1886 AD) of Darkshineswar Calcutta. Vivekananda till he passed his BA was practically an atheist and won't believe anything until it appealed rational to him. Coming in contact with Rama Krishna Parma Hansa however, he realized the meaning of God and Brihm of Vedanta through direct experience of the highest state. He addressed the World Religion of Parliament in Chicago in September 1893 and so great was his influence on the Americans, particularly on those who were scientifically tampered people, that he at once became the 'greatest figure' in the Parliament of Religions and in India he preached Vedanta - the philosophy of Upanishads, unity centre of all religions thoughts. On return from America, he established Rama Krishna Mission in India and foreign countries, the aim of which was universal brotherhood and selfless service to humanity. He came heavily on the discriminative Indian caste system, though not condemned Hindu Religion for it. Almost all big leaders of independence struggle drew inspiration form the life and teachings of Swami Vivekananda.

Narayana Guru (1854-1928 AD) : Nanu, the name by which Narayana Guru was called in his childhood, was born in a village near Thiruitanantapura (also called Trivendrum-capital of Kerala) in 1854 AD in yezawas caste (falling in shudra category). Though not belonging to a Brahmin family, Nanu became a leaned person in Sanskrit and read epics and Upanishads through his own efforts. After the death of his wife in early age, he went to the nearby forests for meditation and having achieved mental illumination, established Advita Ashram there. He also built a Shiva temple ensuring the presence of untouchables on the inauguration function. He attacked caste system and the attendant discrimination to fellow beings. He wrote a small book *'Jati Mimamsa'* brining out that there is no place for caste differences in human society. He also believed in unity and harmony of all religions. Rabindra Nath Tagoare the noble laureate, and Mahatma Gandhi visited him. The first temple entry of low castes in the country side was permitted by the king of Travancore after a long struggle by the disciples of Narayan Guru alongwith others. Earlier, the untouchables were not allowed to use the road to this temple, which was also the hurdle Naryana Guru got cleared through his efforts, facing the orthodox elements of the society. Narayana Guru, thus adopted the positive and effective path to raise the lower castes and attacked the evils in Hindu society, not abandoning the spiritual needs and rights of low castes.

Spiritual Saints

Shri Sai Baba of Shirdi (1854-1918 AD): Shri Sai Baba was born in 1838 in Aurangabad district of

Maharastra. His disciples called him as an *avtar* (incarnation) of Sant Kabir, as Sai Baba also emphasized the unity of Hindus and Muslims. In all his teachings he preached universalism and disliked casteism. Living a simple life of a *faquir*, he tried to remove the pains of humanity. Being pure at heart, having no labels of caste and religion he was able to bring God's mercy on all the suffering humanity and develop a feeling of fraternity amongst them.

Ramana Maharishi (1879-1950 AD): He was born in 1879 in a village near Madurai, Ramanad district of Tamil Nadu in South India in a lawyer's family. He was not much educated and left his family even while as a boy after the death of his father. After performing sever *tapas,* he settled on the hill 'Arunachal' near Madura, as a saint. People from all places started visiting him for solace, though he was not a preacher. The Main mantra of his teachings was to question one self "who am I", which will astonishingly lead to deeper knowledge, gradually. Most important visiter was Dr. Paul Bruton, a journalist form U.K., a great relationlist, thinker and writer of modern times. Through meditation at this place Dr. Paul Bruton realized his deeper self in the presence of the Maharishi. Bruton wrote world famous books afterwards like, Qucst of the Overself, The Inner Reality, A search in secret India, Hidden Teaching beyond yoga etc., which remains the best sellers till date, as these present spirituality to the taste of a modern person of scientific age away from rites, rituals and superstition of old society.

*Swami Shivanada of Rishikesh (1887-1963 AD):*Swami Shivananda was born in 1887 in the family of a sage who were devoted to the study of Vedanta. A doctor by profession, Shivananda served in Malaysia.

He settled in Rishikesh and practiced intense austerities. He found Divine Life Society in 1936 at Rishikesh and authored several books. The aim of his teachings is salvation for human beings irrespective of caste, creed and religion, in the tradition of Vedanta. He writes "I hold that whatever be one's religion, whoever be the prophet adored, whichever be the language or the country, whatever be one's age or sex, one can be religious provided the true implications of that hallowed term *tapas,* which essentially means any form of self control, is made capable of being practiced in daily life to the extent possible for one in the environment and under the circumstances in which one is placed".

*Baba Sawami Sawan Singh founder of Radha-Soami Satsang, Beas (1858-1948 AD):*Founder of this Satsang is Maharaja Baba Sawan Singh born in 1858 in Ludhiana district of Pubjab in a Jat Sikh family. After passing degree in Engineering from Roorkee, he joined central Government service and retired on 1911. He came in contact with Baba Jaimal Singh who initiated him into the Science of Yoga. Baba Sawan Singh was already well read in Yoga and Vedanta so after this initiation, he started the satsang at Beas in Pubjab, heavily drawing on the teachings of Guru Nanak. By calling Radha Soami, he meant to indicate Radha as the soul of an individual and Swami as its lord-the God, the aim of human life being the union (yoga) of the two. The teachings are of universal nature catering to persons of all castes, religion and natinonalities. There are four stages in his spiritual teachings viz., Karam Kand(doing good deeds), Upasana, Bhakti, and Gyan (spiritual knowledge). There is no place for rites and rituals in the teachings of this great master.

Shri Parama Hansa Yogananda (1893-1952 AD): Mukunda Lal Ghosh (name in childhood) was born in

1893 at Gorakhpur of Utter Pradesh in a Bengali family of Kshatriya caste. His Guru Shri Yuktaswar, gave him an experience of cosmic consciousness in his early life. On becoming a monk of Swami order, he founded a Yoga school at Ranchi. He left for America in 1920 as a delegate to a religious conference in Boston and remained there for 15 years. He propagated *kriya yoga* in India and abroad. In India he founded Yogoda Satsang society of India, at Ranchi and other places. The aims of the society are to teach that the purpose of life is evolution through self efforts and reach God-consciousness as taught by Lord Krishna. He believed in universal brotherhood. Commenting on Indian caste, Yogananda says:

"Serious evils arose when the caste system become hardened through centuries into a hereditary halter. India self-governing since 1947 is making slow but sure progress in restoring the ancient values of caste based solely on natural qualification and not on Birth".

'Autobiography of a Yogi'
P. 388 Jaico Publishing House

Swami Chinmayananda founder of Chinmaya Mission (1916-1993 AD): Swami Chinmayananda was born in 1916 in Kerala, in the family of Menons, with childhood name as Bala Krishnan. He had a brilliant academic career, passed MA (English) and LLM from Lucknow University. In his youth, Swamiji was a revolutionary and hated the rituals and monkhood and wanted to expose these to the people. As a student, he took part in Quit India Movement of 1942 and went to jail. On release he worked as a journalist in the National Herald. Due to some articles on the saints of Himalayas, he came in contact with Swami Shivananda of Rishikesh where he changed his agnostic views and took to deeper contemplation under his Guru Swami Tapovan of Uttarkashi. At the age of 27 he became a *Sanyasi*. He preached Vedanta Philosophy and wrote a number of books. He traveled abroad and had a large following in America who liked his modern approach to religion. Chimaya Mission was established by him at Bombay, ashram being known as Sandhipani Sadhanalya (after the name of Krishna's Guru). Swamiji's greatest work was preaching of Bhagwad Geeta by his commentaries on it through several Gyan Yagnas, which he held in India and abroad. Being a great English orator, his teachings appealed to any modern person having a rational unbiased and scientific outlook, due to which his *Gyan Yagnas* attracted a large gathering of well-educated persons in all cities. He interpreted the scriptures, particularly the Bhagwad Geeta in its true sense, bringing out Krishna's message on caste to be by worth and not by birth. His first discourse at Madras (now Chennai) was frowned upon by orthodox Brahmins who did not like that ancient teachings be given to all irrespective of caste considerations. He could find a place there only in a Muslims estate for his teachings. He met Ramana Maharishi. Dr. Rajendra Prasad, the first President of India inaugurated his Geeta Gyana Yagna in 1956 at Delhi. World over he established Chinmaya centers, hospitals, schools for the service of mankind of all religions. He breathed his last in USA in 1993, when his mortal remains were brought back to Delhi for performing the last rites.

Social Reformers

Joyatiba Phule (1827-1890 AD) : Jyotiba Phule was born in the family of gardener in Maharastra. He got his education in missionary school and therefore was well awakened to political and social environment of the country. The Brahmins however, troubled him constantly. Phule engaged himself in social uplifting of down trodden class by taking up cause of their education and the remarriage of widows. He founded *Satya shodhak Samaj* for above purpose. While fighting various social evils, he became popular in the eyes of people, particularly those of lower castes. He organized agricultural labour and the peasants against the exploitation by zamidars and money-lenders. He forced the British Government to pass ' Agricultral Act' which contained several relief measures for the poor farmers and agricultural labourers.

Justice Mahadeo Govind Ranade (1842-1901 AD) :He was also born in Maharastra in 1842 when the Maratha empire had collapsed. He was a Justice in the High Court. He formed social conference to take up the social causes in the country rather than the political one, as he believed that only a unitied and healthy society can effectively fight the foreign powers. Ranade realized the evil of casteism and raised the voice against all such matters which do not help in the integration of society. According to him such political rights are not of much help which the society at large does not accept. Privileges for some in the society go to counter the fundamental rights of other people in a state. Though he formed Liberal Party for social cause, the same could not sustain for long as social conscience of the people at large was not aroused sufficiently in India. He was the author of "The rise of the Martha Power" where he writes that Maharastra political movement was preceded by religious and social awakening. At its head were saints and poets who sprang from the lower order of society— tailors, carpenters, potters, gardners, shop-keepers, barbers and even outcastes.

Swami Sardha Nanda Saraswati (1856-1926 AD): Swami Sardhananda Saraswati was known by the name

Munshi Ram before he became a Sanyasi. He was born in Jalandhar district of Punjab. He came in contact with Swami Dayananda in 1878, who changed him from an atheist to a believer in God. In 1880 he became a Naib-Teshildar, but resigned from the job when he saw discrimination against Indians. He took up law as his profession in Punjab and entered Arya Samaj in 1885, defending its members who were being prosecuted by Britishers. He became ascetic in 1917. Swamiji was with Gandhiji, and in 1921 Congress formed a committee for upliftment of down- trodens, known as *'Achuto-Uddar Sabha'*. But Swamiji found that there is no real sincerity in this committee for raising the low castes. He, therefore, resigned from it and formed, his own *'Dalito-Uddar Sabha'* admitting children of 'Chamars' etc. in Gurukul, Haridwar. Britishers sent him to jail for supporting Sikh cause. On the question of giving Gayatri Mantra to Dalits, he even resigned at times from Hindu Mahasabha. Swamiji had difference with Gandhiji on Moplaha riots which was a fall out of Khilafat movement, where several Hindus were killed. Swami Sardhnanda fell ill at the end but was being saved by his Musulim friend Dr. Ansari, though another Muslim youth shot him dead at his Delhi residence on 23 Dec. 1926.

Dr. B.R. Ambedkar (1891-1956 AD) : Bhim Rao Ambedkar was born at Mhow in a mahar family of Central Province (now Madhya Pradesh). In his childhood he had direct experience of untouchablity in Indian caste system. Despite being descrimated against everywhere, Ambedkar struggled to study in schools and colleges. Maharaja of Baroda sent him to USA for advance studies. Being brilliant in studies, after MA he passed, PH.D, D.SC., LLD, D. Lit and Bar-at-Law from America and U.K. He led numerous movements for the restoration of Dalit rights, like temple entry and drinking water from common source. He also represented low castes in the Round Table Conference at London alongwith other leaders of India. He did not endorse the social reforms launched by Mahatama Gandhi, as he considered them to be superficial. Concepts of castes of Gandhiji were outdated according to him. Ambedkar was a Member of the Viceroy's council from 1942-1946. Reaching the peak of his career, he was made the chairman of the Drafting Committee of the Constitution of India after Indian Independence in 1947, which job he did very well to the satisfaction of everybody. He was instrumental in providing reservations in services and elective bodies to the member of scheduled castes and scheduled tribes by taking cooperation from other members of higher caste in the Drafting Committee Being not satisfied with the working of Indian caste system, he converted to Buddhism enmass at Nagpur in October 1956, three months before his death. He was award *Bharat Ratan* posthumously.

Philosophers and Thinkers

Shri Aurobindo Ghosh (1872-1950) : Aurobindo Ghosh was brought up in English environment, he studied in St. Pauls School, London. As he grew up, he devoted his life for the cause of Indian nationalism and edited papers like *Bande Mataram.* He started political movements on revolutionary lines for which he was arrested by the Britishers. In the later period, however, he shifted to a Ashram in Pondicherry, for meditation and higher contemplations where his aim was 'to bring the superamental power of that divine consciousness into the ignorance of mind, life and body, to transform them, to manifest the Divine here and create a divine life in matter'. It is a strange coincidence that his date of birth is 15 August (1872), the day India achieved independence.

Rabindra Nath Tagore (1861-1941) : He is a famous author of National Anthem of India *Jana-Gana-Mana* and winner of Noble Prize in Literature 'Gitanjali' in 1913. Tagore was a man of varied interest in arts, literature, drama, music and even science and philosophy. Though he did not have high academic qualifications, but like Einstein (who too was not bright in school education) he was a genius par excellence. In fact Tagore and Einstein met around 1931 and exchanged their views on the nature of consciousness, the truth (whether independent of man) and Cosmic Being. Tagore created Shantiniketan to impart lesson in human advancement, which became an international university by the name Vishwa Bharti. But Rabindra Nath Tagore was not a politically inactive person, particularly where humanity suffered injustices. He renounced his British titles in 1919 when General Dyer fired upon innocent persons, killing thousands of them when they assembled peacefully at Jallianwala Bagh, Amritisar on Baisakhi day.

Mrs. Annie Besant (1847-1933) : Though born in England, she chose to work in India and adopted it as her *Karambhumi.* She was greatly influenced by the ideals of Theosophical Society as it taught the link of soul to the God without the aid of any dogmas. Eventually, she became the President of this society. She was a great nationalist, and launched Home Rule movement alongwith Tilak in 1916. She was elected the President of Indian National Congress in 1917 at its session held at Calcutta. For the purpose of securing Home Rule for Indians she launched the paper 'New India', which was banned later by the Britishers. She had difference of opinion with Mahatma Gandhi on the methods of civil disobedience and the distance between the two kept on growing continuously. She was for taking tough postures in the matter of preserving national harmony and was not happy at the outcome of Round Table Conferences of 1931-32. Due to her failing health she passed away in 1933.

Bankim Chandra Chatterji (1838-1894) : He is the author of famous poem *'Vande Matram'* which forms part of his book 'Anand Math'. Vande Matram was on the lips of every freedom fighters while facing the British forces attack on them. This song was put in Anand Math in the same context, singing it while facing the guns of Britishers. He had however, made the British rule a necessity for future independence in this book. Bankim Chandra was born in a middle class family, his father was a Deputy collector in British Government. He was a brilliant student and after securing high marks in the Presidency College of Calcutta, he worked on the post of a Deputy Magistrate. But his mind was bent towards the literature, and he wrote many books like Kapal Kundala. The Britishers no doubt started suspecting the intentions of Chatterji towards their Government and harassed him in all possible ways like frequent transfers and no promotions. Coming from the family of an autocrat and himself holding the job of a British Magistrate, Chatterji could not take the socially low with him. But there is no doubt that he had created a poem (Vande Matram) which stirred the people of India and even the great Rabindra Nath Ṭagoare who gave a tune to it.

Ishwar Chandra Vidya Sagar (1820-1891) : Ishwar Chandra Vidysagar was a great educationist and social reformer of 19th Century. Though born in a poor family, he rose to the level of a Principle of college. Ishwar chandra propagated the spread of Sanskrit language. He founded a number of high schools and colleges and laid emphasis on the education of women. A number of schools were established for the girls separately.

Most important contribution of Vidysagar was to get legalized the marriage of widows, with the children born of such marriage as the rightful inheritor of the parents.

But alongwith this achievement, he raised the voice against the child marriage as well as the polygamy.

Subramaniam C. Bharti (1882-1921) : He was a famous poet of Tamil renaissance. His name Bharti was conferred on him at the age of 11 years when he was called to recite his poems in the court of Raja of Ettaypuram. As he grew up, he started writing to arouse nationalism, for liberation of the country from British rule. During his stay at Banaras, he learnt Hindi and Sanskrit. On returning back to Madras (Now Tamil Nadu) he started working as Assistant Editor in a Tamil Daily, writing for Indian Independence. He was perused by Britishers, to avoid which he remained in Pondicherry which was a French Territory. He died on 1921, leaving a huge collection of his poetry and folk songs to inspire the generations to come.

Revolutionaries

Before the Independence struggle, there was mutiny of 1857 against Britishers where greatmen and women like Rani Laxmi Bai of Jhansi fought with exceptional courage and whose deeds are still sung by the Indians.

The great revolutionaries of Independence struggle are as below:

Lokmanya Bal Gangadhar Tilak (1856-1920) : Claimed against British resistance 'Swraj is my birth right', sent to Mandalay Jail for 6 years, editor of *Maratha* and *Keshari*, author of several books including commentaries on Bhagwad Geeta.

Lala Lajpat Rai (1865-1928) : Called lion of Punjab, an Arya Samajist who founded school for untouchables, opposed Simon Commission and got fatal injuries leading to his death.

Saheed Bhagat Singh (1907-1931) : One of the greatest revolutionaries whose weight increased after hearing the death sentence, hanged alongwith Rajguru and Sukhdev, threw bomb in Parliament without intention to kill but only 'to make the deaf hear'.

Chandra Shekar Azad (1906-1931) : Formed Socialist Republican Association with Bhagat Singh, courageously opposed British despite tortures, died fighting British with last bullet.

*Ram Prasad Bismil, Roshan Singh, Rajinder Lahiri and Ashafaqullah Khan :*All hanged in 1927 in the cause of freedom of India.

Jatindra Nath Das (1904-1929) : A revolutionary from Calcutta who fasted unto death for 63 continuous days dying day by day against British maltreatment by its Jailer. He was jailed for Lahore conspiracy case.

Khudi Ram Bose (1893-1908) : In 1908 he threw a bomb at a carriage which they thought have the infamous Judge of Muzaffarpur in it. He was tried and hanged in 1908.

Vir Savarkar (1833-1966) : To escape from British arrest, he crossed English Channel by summing, sent thereafter to Andman Nikobar jail. Advocated Hindu Nationalism, was in British Jail for 11 years for freedom of the country. When the jailer remarked that he has to suffer two sentences of 25 years each, he remarked 'will the British rule last that long'.

Netaji Subhash Chandra Bose (1897-1945): A great leader who injected courage into the congress party to fight British, after resigning from ICS in 1920. He was elected President of congress in 1939, but due to differences with Gandhiji, where his candidate for president- ship he had defeated, he resigned from congress, went to Germany and Japan formed INA to fight British and finally killed or went into oblivion in 1945 (some say kept in Siberia), people still remembering his heroic deeds and waiting for his return.The Govt. Commission of Inquiry is working to find out mystery of his disappearance in 1945.

Jai Prakash Narayan (1902-1979) : Freedom fighter of 1942 when he organized mass protest against British in the absence of Gandhiji who was in jail. Resisted emergency in 1975-76 and due to serious ailments in this period breathed his last in 1979.

Other Freedom Fighters

The list of revolutionaries above also fall in the category of freedom fighters.

It is a very long list of Indians who struggled against the British empire. In the early period they were the persons seeking to have some say in the governance for Indians, though reconciled to the British sovereignty. It was in the later period that fight for full independence began and culminated in freedom on 15th August 1947. They were :

Dada Bhai Nauroji, Surendra Nath Banerjee, Gopal Krishan Gokhale, Pt. Moti Lal Nehru, Chittranjan Das Deshbandhu, Abul Kalam Azad, Sarojini Naidu, Dr. Rajindra Prasad (first President of India), Khan Abdul Ghaffar Khan, C. Rajagopalachari and others.

Persons Connected with Destiny of India

The persons who were connected with the destiny of India before and after the Independence were:

Mahtama M.K. Gandhi (1869-1948) : He fought discrimination in South Africa, entered on Indian scene in 1917-18, associated himself with khilfat movement, launched 1942, Quit India movement, made non-violence truth, Satyagraha and Swadeshi as his tool of struggle, raised voice against untouchability, strove to bring about Hindu-Muslim unity but without success resulting into the creation of Pakistan and was shot down by Nathu Ram Godse in 1948.

Pt. Jawahar Lal Nehru (1889-1964) : Person with modern outlook, took active part in independence struggle, was the first Prime Minister of India, laid the foundation of Industrial development and socialism, suffered due to trust in China, ignored realities due to illusion of ideologies, died in 1964.

Sarder Vallabhbhai Patel (1875-1950) : Successfully took up farmers case aganst the British, strong yet rational man who as first Home Minister of India integrated 562 princely states into India by taking practical steps. India is one today because of him, who is also called 'Iron Man'.

Lal Bahadur Shastri (1904-1966) : Belonged to a poor family but never compromised with honesty and self-pride, as a Railway Minister resigned to take moral responsibility of an accident, was Prime Minister of India during 1965 war with Pakistan, showed his grit and determination to face it effectively.

Smritis are Submerged into the Ocean of Human Liberty

In the long history of India, such an era of mighty men of courage, sacrifice and brilliance, all springing up together in about one century, is rare. With all their great deeds pooled together first we got the freedom in

1947 and then the consititution of India in 1950, with its preamble as below:

We the People of India having resolved to consitute India into a Soveriegn, Socialist, Secular, Democratic, Repblic and to secure to all citizen:

Justice	social, economic and political
Liberty	of throught, expression, belief, faith and worship
Equality	of status and of opportunity;and to promote among them all
Fraternity	assuring the dignity of the individual and the unity and Integrity of the Nation.

In Our Constituent Assembly this twenty-seventh day of November 1949, do Hereby Adopt, Enact and Give to Ourselves this Constitution[1].

In the above universal constitution, lofty principles of justice, liberty, equality and fraternity have been provided to all citizens of this nation, with no privileges to anyone on the basis of birth. The end of laws of Manu coincides with the freedom of India and enactment of the universal Constitution for its people. The Providence could not have selected a person as the chairman of its Drafting Committee better than an 'untouchable', Dr. B.R. Ambedkar, who was born on the fringe of social system envisaged by Manu.

1. Dr. Rajendra Prasad was the President of the Constituent Assembly, Dr. B.R. Ambedkar the chairman of Consitituion Drafting Committee with other luminaries like K.M. Munshi, Sir Tej Bhadur Sapru, Sir Alladi, Krishnaswami Ayyar, C. Rajagopalachari, B.N. Rau, Dr. Gadgil and others as its members, whose great contributions merit separate narration.

11
Glimpses of Universal Science of Life

Transcendental life, that is the life beyond worldly material existence, had been the matter of speculation for the ancient saints and philosophers since the very existence of man as a evolved being. The realized ones have said that this life is one in the universe existing since eternity and extending to infinity, beyond the reach of human mind though expressing through it. The philosophy, religion, society and politics are its outer coverings in the order of grossness, the finest being philosophy and grossest the politics. What is called enlightenment or freedom or *Moksha* is the realization (and not mere knowledge) of this life center through philosophic contemplation or religious devotion. Religion tends to develop certain traits or *Samskars* by engaging human beings in certain practices meant to discipline the fluctuating mind. If de-linked with politics and superstitions, the religion prepares a person for higher stage of life, that is, to the philosophical study where one can apply the intellect to probe into the mystery of life and universe. Such a search of higher being is not a dry intellectual gymnastic meant to play with the words or exhibiting one's intellectual superiority over the lesser beings. It is a deep and dedicated drilling through the layers of matter and mind to reach the all-pervading spirit in its transcendental glory-the source of all life, power, wisdom and blessings. To quote Swami Vivekananda again; "Each soul is potentially divine, the goal is to manifest this divinity within by controlling nature external and internal.......".

Some sources of universal teachings of ancient and modern times are given in brief in the following pages, de-linked with any religious practice or dogmas and which are beyond the limitations of any religion, caste, race, time and place. It is said that to be effective the teachings, particularly those based on scriptures, should be learnt through the realized Guru or teacher, who alone is capable of penetrating through the gap between the words. However, the purpose here is to indicate this knowledge to generate interest of the reader, if possible, so as to fall back on the original source. There could be universal teaching of spirituality in other religions as well, but here only the Hindu sources are quoted to show how the grand truths were kept hidden in the religious garbs from the common man. It is now claimed by the real masters that the higher wisdom contained in these teachings is itself capable of remaining unapproachable from the undeserved ones and thus no formal restrictions need be placed by religion on their study.

Qualifications

Just as some basic qualification is needed for taking up any higher course of study in physical science or mathematics, the qualification is also prescribed for taking up study or practice for higher life philosophy. These are stated in Yoga Vashishta as: Contentment-being satisfied with whatever comes unsought, company of good people, Spirit of Inquiry-to go into the depth of matter through intellectual analysis, and self-control-to reign in one's unlimited desires. The purpose is to minimize the agitations of mind and to keep it concentrated for deeper probe into the mystery of life. In addition to the above four-gate keepers (terms used by Yoga Vashishta), Titiksha, i.e., forbearance - to tolerate normal worldly afflictions by resting in higher wisdom or self confidence- is mentioned as one more qualification in Adi Shankrya's Vivekachudmani.

Yoga Vashistha

This is the teaching imparted to Lord Rama by the great Rishi Vashistha, when Rama was of about 16 years of age, in the presence of sage Vishvamitra and Valmiki. Rama, after undertaking a long pilgrimage, was a totally dissatisfied person with life's impermanency and the attendant cycles of death, disease and old age etc. He was feeling least attracted towards the Royal pleasures and had grown pale in disgust.

The teachings imparted by Vashistha in the Court of Dasratha, revolves round the meaning of life, universe and the world. The whole teaching containing the highest philosophy go deeper into all aspects of individual's life *(Jiva)*, universal spirit (Brihm), universal ignorance (Maya) and the means for finding truth (Liberation). It brought Rama to an healthy state of mind and spirit. Some passages (summarized) are produced from this Great Yoga below, which gives the glimpses of the (universal) teaching imparted to Lord Rama.

— In this world whatever is gained is gained only by self-effort.... Self-effort is of two categories: that of past births and that of this birth. The latter effectively counteracts the former. Fate is none other than self-effort of a past incarnation. There is constant conflict between these two in this incarnation, and that which is more powerful triumphs...... There is no power greater than right action n the present.... He who says fate is directing me to do this, is brainless and the goddess of fortune abandons him.

— One may doubt that such unchanging truth may not exist ! If it does not, one comes to no harm by inquiring into the nature of life, seeking the eternal will soften the pain caused by the changes in life. But, if it exists, then by knowing it one is freed. The eternal is not attained by rites and rituals, by pilgrimages or by wealth; it is attained only by conquest of one's mind by cultivation of wisdom. Hence, everyone-gods, demons, men... should seek the conquest of mind.

— Even a young boy's words are to be accepted if they are words of wisdom; else reject it like straw even if uttered by Brahma, the creator. One who studies this scripture and contemplates its meaning has no need to undertake austerities, meditation or repetition of a Mantra; for what is greater than liberation which is granted by a study of this scripture.

— He is the intelligence that supports the entire universe, and every thought that arises in that intelligence gives rise to a form. Though all these forms are of the nature of pure intelligence, on account of self-forgetfulness of this, and of the thought of physical forms, they freeze into the physical forms, even as goblins though formless are seen to have forms on account of perceiver's delusion... the materiality of the creation is like the castle in the air, an illusory projection of one's own mind imaginary.

— Austerity or penance is self-inflicted pain. Of what value is charity performed with wealth earned by deceiving others.... Religious observances add to one's vanity.

- Whether the funeral rites had been duly performed or not, if the departed one believe that thy have been performed, he gets the benefit of the ethereal form.
- In the mirror of infinite consciousness countless reflections are seen, which constitute the appearance of the world. These are the *Jivas*. *Jiva* is like just a little agitation on the surface of the ocean of Brihma.
- In sorrow and in calamity, in dire distress and in pain, remain free from sorrow within yourself, but behave as if in sorrow in accordance with propriety.....

The Upanishads

Upanishad means 'near-below-sit' and contains the knowledge received by the student sitting at the feet of the master. *The Upanishads* discuss the Philosophy of Vedanta. The Upanishads are found in the end of Vedas and therefore, called Vedanta, i.e., end of Vedas or the essence of Vedas. The knowledge of Upanishads is also called '*Brahimvidya*' as its philosophy centers around Brihm- the universal spirit, one life, eternal and infinite. The teachings are universal in nature, not limited by any time and place, like any modern life sciences. The authors of the Upanishads were the transcendental Rishis who did not care to claim authorship of their teachings, far away as they were from the worldly thoughts of name and fame. There are said to be 108 Upanishads, but the major Upanishads are ten only.

The glimpses of knowledge contained in some major Upanishads is given as below:

Isavasya Upanishad

- All this whatsoever moves in this universe, including the universe itself moving, is indwelt or pervaded or enveloped or clothed by the Lord. That renounced thou shouldst enjoy. Covet not any body's wealth.

— He, the Atman, is All-pervading, bright, bodiless,scatheless, without muscles, pure, unpierced by evils, wise, omniscient, transcendent and self-existing....
— He who worships the impersonal God-head and the personal God together over comes death through worship of personal and obtains immortality through the worship of impersonal.

Katho Upanishad

This is the teaching of Lord Death (yama) to Nachiketa who was cursed by an enraged father to go to him (Lord Death). Despite being asked by Lord Death any worldly boon, whatever it be, Nachiketa insisted upon knowing the Atman (self) only, which knowledge was imparted to him as:

— The intelligent Atman is not born, nor does he die; He did not spring from anything and nothing sprang from him; unborn, Eternal, Everlasting, Ancient, He is not slain although the body's slain.
— This Atman subtler than the subtle, greater than the great is seated in the heart of each living being.
— This Atman can not be attained by study of Veda nor by intelligence, nor by much hearing. It is gained by him who chose it alone. To him this Atman reveals its true nature.
— Know the Atman as the Lord of chariot, the body as the chariot; know the intellect as the charioteer and mind again as the reigns, senses the horses and their roads as sense objects.

Mundaka Upanishad

As the name of this Upanishad suggests, mundaka means clean-shaven head, i.e. to rid the student of the veil of ignorance. This is one of the boldest Upanishads, being direct is its attack on orthodoxy and ignorance.

— There are two kinds of knowledge to be acquired- the higher and the lower.

— Of these, the lower comprises the Rig-Veda, Yajur-Veda, Sama-Veda, Atharva Veda, the science of pronunciation etc. the code of rituals, grammar, etymology, meter and astrology. Then there is the higher (knowledge) by which is attained that imperishable.

— As spider spreads out and withdraws (its thread), as on the earth grow the (herb and trees) and as from a living man issues out hair (on the head and body), so out of the imperishable does this universe immerge here (in this phenomenal creation).

— The deluded fools, believing the rites inculcated by the Vedas and Smritis to be the highest, do not understand the other thing (that leads to) liberation.........

— Remaining within the fold of ignorance and thinking 'we are ourselves wise and learned', the fools while being buffeted very much, ramble about like the blind led by the blind alone.

— Truth alone wins and not untruth(*satyamave Jayatey*).

Mandukya Upanishad

Mandukya is a word in Sanskrit meaning frog. Mandukya Upanishad signifies the harsh truth, unpolished and uncut. A deep philosophy is given in this Upanishad which is not easy to understand with surface reading. It covers all the aspects of human life and consciousness, i.e., dream state, deep sleep state, waking state and pure consciousness state as Turiya identical with Self of man. The great grand Guru of Adi Sankracharya, Gaudapada, have given commentaries (Karika) on this Philosophical theme to make it clear to the advance aspirants.

— All this is surely Brahman. The Self is Brahman. The Self, such as it is, is possessed of four quarters.
— The first quarter is the waking state whose consciousness relates to thing external.
— The second quarter is the dream state, whose consciousness is internal.....
— The third quarter is the deep sleep state where everything becomes undifferentiated.
— The fourth state is that which is uninferable, unthinkable, in which all phenomenon cease, which is unchanging, auspicious and non-dual.
— As the dream objects are unreal in a dream, so also, because of that very reason, the objects in the waking state are unreal.
— Just as the space confined within the jars etc. merge completely on disintegration of jars etc, so do the individual souls merge here in this Self.
— Just as all spaces confined within various jars are not darkened when one of the spaces thus confined becomes contaminated by dust, etc., so also is the case with all the individuals in the matter of being affected by happiness etc.
— As the movement of a fire-brand appears to be straight or crooked, so it is the vibration of consciousness that appears to be knower and the known.

Chhandogya Upanishad

The teachings are in the form of many stories, written in ancient lore.

Raikva the Cartman

Once upon a time there lived a benevolent and pious king Jan Sruti, who did lot of public works and in time was filled with a bit of vanity. One night two swans flew over his house, mentioning how great Raikva the cartman is. The king ordered the searching of Raikva, who was ultimately traced by the side of a cart which he used to pull. The king approached him with a lot of wealth, to impart him teaching of supreme knowledge, but Raikva spurned the same saying 'take away all this, O Shudra'. Finally the king approached him in all humility abandoning vanity of a king. Seeing him to be sincere for the knowledge, Raikva imparted the knowledge of Brihm to him.

Satyakama Jabala and Rishi Gautam

Satyakama, the son of maid-servant approached Rishi Gautam to make him his disciple. Gautam asked for his parentage to which satyakama replied 'my mother told me that in her youth she moved about as a maid servant and doest not know to which family I belong to. She gave my name as Satyakama Jabala'. The Guru admitted him as his disciple saying 'No one but a true Brahmin would thus speak the truth' Guru gave him four hundred lean and weak cows and said him to come back only when these have become a thousand. He dwelt a number of years in forest. There he was taught in parts by the Bull, the Fire, the Hansa (Swan) and a water-bird. On reaching back Gautam said to him 'you shine like one who knows Brahman, who taught you'. Satyakama replied 'People other than man taught me, but you should teach me, as only knowledge learnt from teachers is the best'. The teacher Gautam taught him the Brihm Vidya and nothing was left out.

Uddalaka Aruna and Svetaketu

Once there lived Svetaketu, whose father was Uddalaka. He told Svetaketu to go to school and study

Vedas. Svetaketu returned home after several years of study, showing himself as a well read boy. Uddalaka asked him whether he has been given instructions 'by which we hear what can not be heard, by which we perceive what can not be perceived, by which we know what can not be known'. Svetaketu said he does not know such instructions and requested his father to teach him.

Father replied 'as by a single clod of clay all that is made of clay is known, all modifications like pot, jar etc. being only names, truth being that all this is clay'. Just as the subtle portion of curds when churned rises upwards and become butter, so the subtle portion of food, when eaten, rises upwards and become mind..... So there is one conscious being only, others are merely names of it.

Uddalaka asked Sevetaketu to bring a fruit of banyan tree and break it. 'It is broken Sir', what do you see? 'Extremely small seeds, Sir'. Break one of these and tell me what do you see. 'I see nothing sir'. Uddalaka said that subtle essence which you do not perceive is that great banyan tree when grown. Similarly, the subtle essence of all that exists is the Self which you do not see.

Keno-Upanishad

It forms the part of Samaveda and starts with the question of a disciple as below:-

By whom willed and directed does the mind light upon its objects. Commanded by whom does the main vital Air proceed to function. By whose will do men utter speech? what intelligence directs the eyes and ears towards their respective objects !

The teacher answer; 'It is Ear of Ear, the mind of mind, the speech of speech....'. 'The eye does not go there, nor speech, nor mind.....'.

'What one can not feel with mind, but because of which mind feels...., know that alone to be Brahman and not this, which people worship here'.

'What can not be seen by the eye, but by which the eyes are able to see, know that alone to be Brahman and not this, which people do worship here'.

'What can not be heard by the ear, but by which the ears are able to hear...., know that alone to be Brahman and not this, which people do worship here.'

There are other major Upanishads, viz. Brhadaranyaka Upanishad, Aitareya Upanishad, Taittiriya Upanishad and Prasno Upanishad. Their details are not given here, as by now the theme of Upanishads might be clear, though each Upanishad contains a special knowledge and shows the path to the highest from different directions.

Srimad Bhagwad Geeta

'Songs celestials' as called by eminent authors of West, contains the teachings of Lord Krishna given to Arjuna on the battle filed. Warren Hastings the first British Viceroy of India made great prophesy by saying 'this immortal book of East will survive when the British dominion in India shall have long ceased to exist.....'. With the impending war in the background, the knowledge given to Arjuna could not but be practical and of direct application. It is scientific and rational to any mind of modern temperament and can satisfy any inquiry on the existence of higher wisdom in the universe provided one is free of prejudices. It suits all tastes of men be he an intellectual or a practical activists of the world. The teachings in it demand an awakened questioning mind and not the blind believer of divine sermons. Every sloka of Bhagwad Geeta needs detailed commentary to come within the grasp of ordinary mortals and to understand its deeper meanings. In the present days the (English) commentaries of Swami Chinmayanada of Bombay (Powai Sandeepany Sadhanalaya Powai Park Drive Mumbai) and Dr. Paul Brunton a great British Journalist in his 'Inner Reality' are the popular books, amongost others. Below are produced the bare slokas in English translation, which should be able to convey the Geeta essence to any sincere seeker. In fact the problem is to pick up or choose the verses, as all these are saturated with divine knowledge (and inter-connected) and taking up one happens only at the cost of others left out. A few slokas are given here only to show the depth of teaching and their relevance for the modern man of the day.

— Yield not to unmanliness, Arjuna, ill doest it become you. Shaking off this paltry faint heartedness arise, O scorcher of your foes. (II:3)

(It is as if this voice guided our freedom struggle for Independence).

— The unreal has no existence and the real never ceases to be, the reality of both has thus been perceived by the seers of truth. (II:16)

— The soul is never born nor does it die. For it is unborn, eternal, everlasting and primeval; even though the body is slain, the soul is not. (11:20)

— Your right is to work only, but never to the fruit thereof. Let not the fruit of action be your object, nor let your attachment be to inaction. (II:47)

(The idea is to avoid unnecessary worry and consequent loss of efforts while acting in the present for a given purpose, as the future results are directly proportional to the efforts invested in the present).

— ...... Skill in action is Yoga. (II:50)

— From anger arises infatuation; from infatuation confusion of memory; from confusion of memory loss of reason; and from loss of reasons one goes to complete ruin. (II:63)

— Man does not reach perfection..... Merely by renunciation of action. (III:4)

— He who outwardly restraining the organs of sense and action, sits mentally dwelling on objects of senses, that man of deluded intellect is called a hypocrite. (III:6)

— The virtuous, who partake of what is left after sacrifice (giving to others) are absolved of all sins. Those sinful ones who cook food (only) for their own sake verily eat sin. (III:13)

— For whatever a great man does, that very thing other man also do; whatever standard he sets up, the generality of men follow the same. (III:21)

— Arjuna whenever there is decline of righteousness and unrighteousness is in ascendant, than I body myself forth. (IV:7)

— Arjuna, however men approach Me even so do I seek them; for all men follow my path form all sides. (IV:11)

— Even if you are the most sinful of all sinners, you will cross over all sins by the raft of knowledge. (IV:36)

— One should lift oneself by one's own efforts and should not degrade one-self; for one's own self is one's own friend and one's own self is one's animy. (VI:5)

— Arjuna, this Yoga is not for him who eats too much, nor for him who does not eat at all, nor for him who is given to too much sleep, nor for him who is ceaselessly awake. (VI:16)

— Whatever celestial form a devotee seeks to worship with faith, I stabilize the faith of that particular devotee in that very form. (VI:21)

— He who is free from malice towards all beings, who is friendly as well as compassionate,——— that devotee of mine is dear to me. (XII:13,14)

— Sublimity, forgiveness, fortitude, external purity, absence of malice, absence of feeling of self-importance: these are the mark of one who is naturally endowed with divine virtue, O descendent of Bharta. (XVI:3)

— Hypocrisy, arrogance, pride, anger, harshness and ignorance: these are, Arjuna the marks of one who is born with demoniacal properties. (XVI:4)

Patanjali Yoga Sutras

The Sutras (aphorisms) were composed by a sage Patanjali about 2000 years back and contain the essence of spiritual teachings in few words, found to be of interest even to the modern psychologists. A complete study of these sutras provide guidance and help to a seeker of deeper knowledge through meditation. A few sutras are given below to indicate the nature of this yoga system, followed by a brief commentary by Swami Vivekananda in the book 'Raja Yoga' (Advata Ashrama Publication).

The subject is vast, but here only the beginning aphorism has been given to introduce the subject.

"Yoga is restraining the mind-stuff (Chitta) from taking various forms (vrittis)". Chitta is the mind-stuff, and vrittis are the waves and ripples rising in it when external causes Impinge on it. This vrittis are our universe.

The bottom of lake we can not see because its surface is covered with ripples. It is only possible for us to catch a glimpse of the bottom, when ripples have subsided and the water is calm. If the water is muddy or is agitated all the time, the bottom will not be seen. The bottom of lake is our true self; the lake water is Chitta and the waves the vrittis.

"At that time (the time of concentration) the seer (Purusha) rests in his own (unmodified) state".

"The practice is the attempt to restrain the mind in Chitta form, to prevent its going out into waves".

Comments of Swami Vivekananda on some Sutras

Human nature likes to run through the ruts that are already there, because it is easy..... But whenever a new subject comes, new channels have to be made, so it is not understood readily. And that is why the brain refuses unconsciously to be acted upon by new ideas. It resists.. The more thoughtful the man, the more complicated will be the streets in his brain, and more easily he will take to new ideas.

.... That is why we find that the part of religion which deals with the world-side of nature is so widely accepted, while the other fact, the philosophy, or the psychology, which deals with the inner nature of man, is so frequently neglected.

We must remember the definition of this world of ours; it is only the Infinite Existence projected into the plane of consciousness. A little of Infinite is projected into consciousness, and that we call our world. So there is an Infinite beyond; and religion has to deal with both with the little lump we call our world, and with the Infinite beyond.

Raja Yoga (with reference to Patnjali Yoga Sutra)

The science of Raja Yoga provides us the means to observe internal state of the mind. The powers of the mind are like rays of light dissipated; when they are concentrated, they illumine. Raja Yoga is based on Sankhya Philosophy. According to this philosophy, the impressions of external objecs are carried by the outer instruments like eyes, to the mind. The mind put it to the intellect, which in turn places it before Purusha whence the perception arises. Except Purusha all the instruments from intellect, mind and external organ of perception are all matter. Purusha is the spirit, as opposed to the matter. We perceive only those objects to which the mind is attached. It I see a beautiful scene catching mind's fancy, other perceptions like innumerable type of sounds etc. may not be heard by me at all, though these have made impressions on my tympanum.

"In an ocean there are huge waves, like mountains, then smaller waver, and still smaller, down to the little bubbles but back of all there is the infinite ocean. The bubble is connected with the infinite ocean at one end and the huge wave at the other end...... Wherever there is life, the storehouse of infinite energy is behind". The Raja Yoga is the science of meditation to tap this source.

Viveka Chudamani (of Adi Sankracharya)

As its name suggests, Viveka Chudamani means "Crest-Jewel of Discrimination" composed by famous Adi Sankracharya based on the philosophy of Advaita-Vedanta that 'Brahmin alone is real, the world as it appears to be, is unreal'.

— The study of the scriptures is useless so long as the highest truth is unknown, and it is equally useless when the highest truth has already been known. - 59

— In this very body, in the mind full of Sattva (purity), in the secret chamber of the intellect in the Akasa (space) known as the unmanifested, the Atman of charming splendor, shines like the sun aloft, manifesting this universe through its own effulgence. -132

— As layers of clouds generated by Sun's rays cover the sun and alone appear (in the sky) so egoism generated by the self, covers the reality of the self and appear by itself (as if there were not Atman at all). -142

— In dreams when there is no actual contact with the external world, the mind alone creates the whole universe consisting of the experiencer etc. Similarly, in the waking state also, there is no difference. Therefore, all this (phenomenal universe) is the projection of the mind. -170

— Brahman is Existence, knowledge, Infinity, pure, supreme, self-existent, eternal and indivisible bliss, not different (in reality) from the individual soul and devoid of interior or exterior. It is (ever) triumphant. -225

Western Philosophers on the Mystery of Life

There were and are a large number of highly evolved and enlightened persons in the west in the field of Philosophy of life. It is simply not possible to name them all, being large in numbers. However, a few thoughts of some of those who have link with India, are produced below to indicate that these have been given from the level of their deeper-self for the benefit of human beings of all races and religions. Prominent amongst them is Dr. Paul Brunton, a U.K. Journalist who spent quite some time in India from 1930 onward and came in contact with realized saints like Ramana Maharishi. He is the author of several books which are quite popular in learned circles of India and abroad. His book 'The Hidden Teaching Beyond Yoga' gives scientific rendering of spiritual teachings bringing out the latest discovery of science and metaphysics on themes like 'From Things to Thoughts' and 'The secret of space and Time' etc. by raising questions like: How can an image which is said to be internal appear to us as an object which is external and which possesses spatial characteristics? Some thoughts from his books are:-

Dr. Paul Brunton

From 'Quest' of the Overself' (Dr. Paul Brunton) : [1]

— It is not always wise to dictate in advance the manner whereby any difficulty is to be solved, for the fruits of one's desire may be disappointing. The Overself knows and knows best; why not trust it? So long as one does his duty, according to the light vouchsafed him, he may safely leave all questions of ways and means to the Overself. It alone knows how to harmonise one's needs with the fiats of destiny; and to reach solution which are the best in the end.

— The secret of super-personal help is surrender. Not surrender to weakness, lethargy, laziness, hopelessness or short - sighted fatalism, but surrender of the personal power to the central power against the gloomier circumstances which are arrayed against him in the battles of life, he lets this central power get to work on his behalf. Where one fails, it succeeds; where one perceives only impassible brick walls of difficulty, it passes miraculously through. It will work for him and better than him, yet all that one has to do is to open oneself to its expression.

— .... One must have the uncommon sense to say: "I shall interfere no longer. I shall cease this endless calculation of ways and means. I shall put down my load of cares and duties on the ground besides me. I see now what I, in my blindness, refused to see before, that the Overself which supports and carries me can perform all calculations, manage all affairs, bear all burdens in a manner infinitely better than I could ever do, simply because it is itself infinite in power and wisdom".

— No problem is too difficult for the Overself to tackle; it would not be the fortifying atom of almighty God within us if it were so feeble as that. No gloomy cloud of pessimism nor peace-destroying night-mare of fear need descend upon any man's life for ever and ever; the blessed rays of the Overself are with him here and now, ready to shine benignantly down upon his days as soon as he properly invokes them.

— .... Suffering is not always to be shirked; sometimes it is a tutor as excellent as any to be found in the best university. We must look on the troubled side of life as spiritual education and extract the lesson of wisdom from every misfortune.

— Higher powers must take their own time.

— In this way the mental impression is intercepted and one refuses to identify with it.

— The ordinary man who surrenders to negative thoughts courts and strengthens the very trouble he wishes to avoid.

The Hidden Teaching Beyond Yoga (Dr. Paul Brunton):[2]

— The thing and the sensation of the thing live in fundamental and inseparable union, thus there is nothing but awareness.

— The oneness of both idea and object is a discovery to which subtle thinking of the ancient and the sharp observation of the modern inescapably lead, but it emerges only after the hardest and most rigorous reflection.

— A thing can not exist for us when there is no thought of it first.

— Apart from percepts, there is no trace of such a thing as material substance. We pick up no object, whether it be a stick or a stone, which is not picked up in conscious experience i.e mentally.

James Allen

'As a Man thinketh'(James Allen): [3]

James Allen is a great author of the West who realized secrets of the nature through deep meditation. He seems to be having some understanding of Indian spiritual thoughts when he writes in 'From Poverty to Power'

"The divinity of a Krishna, a Gautam, or a Jesus is the crowning glory of self-abnegation, the end of soul's pilgrimage in matter and mortality, and the world will not have finished its long journey until every soul become as these and has entered into the blissful realization of its own divinity".

Some excerpts from the book are;

— Thought and character are one, and as character can only manifest and discover itself through environment and circumstances, the outer conditions of a person's life will always be found to be harmoniously related to his inner state

— Every man is where he is by the law of his being; the thoughts which he has built into his character have brought him there, and in the arrangement of his life there is no element of chance, but all is the result of a law which can not err.

— A man can only rise, conquer, and achieve by lifting up his thoughts. He can only remain weak, and abject, and miserable, by refusing to lift up his thoughts.
— The universe does not favour the greedy, the dishonest, the vicious, although on the mere surface it may sometimes appear to do so; it helps the honest, the magnanimous, the virtuous.

From 'Poverty to Power' (James Allen): [4]
— Remember that there is the Eternal Law which is absolutely just and that he who oppresses today, must himself be oppressed tomorrow; and from this there is no escape.
— The universe grew out of thought. Matter in the last analysis is found to be merely objectivised thought.
— There is no difficulty, however great, but yield before a calm and powerful concentration of thought.

Deepak Chopra
'Seven Spiritual Laws of Success (Deepak Chopra)[5]

Deepak Chpora is a young America-born Indian, who still visits India to give talks on spirituality to its people. The above book is out of many others written by him with depth of experience he possesses in spiritual matters. A few of its contents, summarized, are produce below:-
— Introduce a faint impulse of intention in this field, and the creation of your desires will come about spontaneously. But first you have to experience stillness — In this silence even the faintest intention will ripple across the underlying ground of universal consciousness, which connects everything with everything else.

— ... This turbulence constricts the flow of energy between you and the field of pure potentiality. You literally squeeze the 'gap' between thoughts.
— The gap is your connection to the field of pure potentiality. It is that state of pure awareness, that silent space between thoughts, that inner stillness which connects you to true power.
— The more you give, the more you will receive.
— That which does not multiply through giving is neither worth giving nor worth receiving...... The intention should always be to create happiness for the giver and receiver.

Neale Donald Walsch

'Conversations with God'

Neale Donald Walsch, an American, has produced in 3 books his direct conversation with God around 1992-93, while leading a busy life of an house-holder in Ameriaca, perhaps not linked to any religious or spiritual society. One day, in frustration, he writes an angry letter to God asking some questions. To his surprise, he receives answers to these and in fact he gets into conversation with the impersonal God. No doubt all this appears unbelievable and even blasphemous in the first instance. But, as one goes deeper into the matter, one finds marvellous expressions of the God on various topics of life, society, nations etc. The deepest study of Hindu Philosophy would find the conversations fitting into it. The teachings of Jesus Christ have been placed on high pedastal. Directly upholding of reincarnation of soul, freedom of choice for an individual to evolve, thoughts and its menifestation in the world of reality, emphasis on vegetarianism, non-smoking, non-drinking and host of other topics one can imagine, are covered with the brightness of intelligence which could come only from an higher source. Listen to God just for two questions of Walsch, of vital importance.

Walsch	:	That means that we will no longer exist !
God	:	Not in physical form. But you will always exist. You cannot not exist. You are that which is.
Walsch	:	What will happen after the Universe "collapses" ?
God	:	The whole process will start over again. There will be another so-called Big Bang and another universe will be born. It will expand and contract. And then it will do the same thing all over again. And again. And again. Forever and ever. World without end. This is the breating in and breathing out of God.

References

1. B.I. Publications PVt. Ltd.
2. B.I. Publications PVt. Ltd.
3. The Peter Pauper Press, New York.
4. Wilco Publishing House, Bombay.
5. Excel Books.

12
Towards the Source of Light and Power

The Life-giving Source

Upanishads are the knowledge portion or the end portion of Vedas and that is why these are also known as Vedanta. Teachings of Upanishads are universal in nature, meant for the whole of humanity without any distinction of caste, race and religion. It is a science or philosophy of life above the religion of rites and ceremonies. Bhagwad Geeta is considered to be the essence of Upanishads.

Appreciating the greatness of Upanishads, the famous German Philosopher Schopenhaur says:

> "In the whole world here is no study so beautiful and so elevating as that of the Upanishads. It has been the solace of my life, and it will be solace of my death".

The teachings of Upanishads are opposed to the religion of rites and rituals as propagated by post-Maurya Brahminism. Says Brahdrayanka Upanishad:

"Into blinding darkness (ignorance) enter those who worship ignorance (Rites). Into greater darkness, as it were, than that enter those who are devoted to knowledge (the ceremonial portion of Vedas)".-VI:iv:10

Al-Beruni, a Muslim scholar and traveler to India, (1000 to 1030 AD) wrote after studying the Upanishads "Why should the people be led on poison in a land where the nectar stream of an ancient and life-giving religion flows perennially? "The ancient religion of universality in this land lies co-mingled with the religion of Brahminism together called Hinduism, like milk and water. It is the milk or the 'nectar flowing perennially' that has given strength to the nation from time to time. The appearance of the Lord as Perserver of human race and human values in different Avataras in this land supports this view description of Nine Avataras is given in the following pages.

Avataras of Lord Vishnu-Incarnations of God

The purpose of God coming into different Avataras is to bring enlightenment and establish righteousness by eliminating the evil on earth. Vishnu is the Preserver of the World and therefore, to maintain its balance, he takes different forms to descend on the earth for the protection of Dharma or Truth.

"The 'devil' then, as now, is that adverse element in Nature which seeks to keep man's consciousness imprisoned in lower form of matter. That adverse element has existed from the very beginning of creation. It is nothing new, and it has its place because it gives us the opposition we need to bring out the latent strength within us. Without that strife we could never grow. Evil has its place, but it has to be overcome. And this is the battle which is not entered into once an finished with, it continues from plane to plane"[1]

The Ten Avatars of Vishnu are;

1. Matsya Avatara – Fish Incarnation
2. Kurna Avatara – Turtle Incarnation
3. Varaha Avatara - Boar incarnation
4. Narasimha Avatara – Man-Lion Incarnation
5. Vamana Avatara - Dwarf Incarnation
6. Parashurama
7. Rama
8. Krishna
9. Buddha
10. Kalki— yet to be born

It is to be noticed that upto the full-grown man stage, the Avataras have followed the Darwins law of evolution. The Lord first appears as Matsya-as fish a life on water. The life started by protoplasm on water as per latest scientific discoveries. Next in evolution is the water-earth creature i.e. turtle. Then comes the earth animal-boar. It is followed by half animal half man-Narasimha. After it comes a dwarf man, and then full–grown men Parshurama, Rama, Krishna and Buddha.

Matsya Avatara

Though some details have been given in Chapter-1 of this book, the same is briefly narrated as below in different context. Majority of people were practicing falsehood and indulging in evil ways at some period of time. None could correct their perversity. But there lived one kind soul Vaivasvata Manu, the Son of sun-God. He used to spend time in prayers and pious activities. Once Manu came to river to worship the Sun-God. As he put his hands in the water, he found there was a small fish in his half-closed hands. Before he could throw it out back in water, it said "Save me from the dangerous creatures of water". Manu put it in a pot but soon it became big (in different stages as described in chapter-1) and finally Manu shifted it to the ocean. The fish said " Manu I am the creator of this universe. I have taken this form to warn you that I will deluge the world soon. You build a big boat and put a pair of every kind of animal, other species, trees and plants and let your family enter it". As soon as Manu filled the ship with creatures as advised by the 'Fish', it started raining heavily till the whole land was covered with water and everything destroyed save this ship. Manu was also warned of tidal waves against which he was to tie the ship to the horn (of this fish) protruding out of water. When the destruction was complete, the rain ceased and the ship came near the ground to enable all creatures to come out of it and multiply their race on the earth. Manu conducted a Yagna in which a girl named Ida was born. She became the source of creation of the whole human race.

The deluge story does point out to the concept that human creation took place from one source. The modern day anthropologists believe that whole of human race is the creation of Black African Eve, who lived some 2 lakh years ago in Africa. The creation through a woman Ida, therefore, is not an unbelievable story.

The Kurma Avtara

In this Avtara the Lord takes the form of a turtle. In the ancient times there was a war between the *Devas* (Gods) and the *Daityas* (Demons). Seeing that they are losing the war, the gods prayed to Vishnu to save them from the demons as they are likely to die at their hands. Vishnu as their protector told them that they can overcome death through nectar of immortality, the nectar to be obtained by churning of milky ocean (*Khir Sagar)*.

Devas made the demons to agree for churning the ocean jointly, sharing its outcome whatever it be. The mountain Mandara was to be used as the churning rod, but it could not be lifted from its base. Snake Vashuki was asked to do this work. He placed it amidst ocean, part of it coming up above the water. The problem then came how the earth below shall bear the load and attrition of the mountain. Vishnu agreed to become its base as a tortoise, allowing the mountain to be placed on its back. The snake Vasuki was used as a rope with gods taking its tail and demons the head after reversing the decision of Devas to hold the head. As the churning started, the demons suffered due to occasional throwing of poisonous puffs by the snake as they were holding its head. Vasuki through fatigue omitted huge quantity of poison that started destroying the whole universe. All prayed to Shiva to save the worlds, as without his permission the total destruction can not take place. Shiva consumed the poison, due to which his throat became blue and that is why he is also called *Nilakantha*, blue at throat.

Out of the churned ocean the first thing to come out was the beautiful moon. Laxmi the goddess of wealth and beauty came out next which went to Lord Hari. Then came out Varuni the goddess of intoxicating drinks. It was claimed by Asuras. Next came the white horse Uchchaishrava taken by the Asura King. Then emerged a diamond Kausturba which went to Vishnu. The wish-fulfilling tree Parijata and the Cow Surabhi came afterwards. The God of health Dhanvantri came out with a big jar full of nectar *(Amrita)* moving towards gods. The gracious elephant Airavata with four white tusks came next which was taken by Indra. The demons snatched the Amrita from the hands of Dhanvantri and started fighting among themselves for its distribution. Vishnu who wanted only Devas to get immortality transformed himself into a beautiful woman Mohini.

Asuras with their Rajasic-Tamasic mind were easily charmed by her and they handed over the *Amrita* to her for distribution as she liked. She asked Devas and Asuras to sit in separate rows and started giving *Amrita* from Devas side. It was finished by the time Asuras row started. But Rahu, a Asura, disguised as Devas was able to get some Amrita before he was spotted by the Son-God and Moon-God and brought it to the natice of Vishnu. The Lord Vishnu cut the head of Rahu with his *Chakra*. But Rahu had got immortality by then and he still 'swallows' occasionally the sun and moon during eclipse for their complaint to Vishnu, which scene can not be looked at with necked eyes when it happens. Rahu's presence in astrology horoscope is considered troublesome and people go for stones etc. as protection measures.

But what is the meaning of this churning to a man? This seems to be valid even today in thought process, to get discoveries and other objects as outcome. Consider milky ocean as Nature, the Vauski as the subject matter, mountain Mandara as the intellect and tortoise as the Life Eternal. The Devas and Asuras are represented by the mind forces of purity and impurity. The churning starts by the mind, grappling with a subject matter fixed around the intellect which gets sustenance from the life principle, the element of Atman in a man. All things good or bad comes out of this churning. If the churning is for self discovery, i.e., *Atman-manthan*, the Amrita of immortality comes up as a reward. If the churning is for worldly objects, discoveries of Nature's laws secular knowledge and technological inventions appear as the outcome like Laxmi, Airavat and Uchchaishrava etc.

Varaha Avatara

Brahma, the creator of entire universe created man and a woman and told them to go out and multiply their race. But they pleaded before Brahma as to how they could do so when the Bhu, the Earth lies buried deep in the ocean. Please bring it up for the sake of future creation of beings. While Brahma was meditating on the possible solution, a Boar of the size of thumb came out of his right nostril. It started growing bigger and bigger till it acquired an huge form and roared loud to shake the denizens of heaven. The Boar dived deep into the ocean and smelt where the Bhu was. As he was lifting the earth on its two white tusks, it was attacked by the deity king Hiranyaksha. The Boar pierced his tusks and gored the demon to death. He then brought the earth above the surface of water and carefully placed it so that it does not sink again in the water. The Devas were full of praise for Narayana for this act of kindness towards the future generation of living beings to appear on the earth.

But who is this Hiranyaksha? There was a rishi called Kasyapa with his wife Diti the daughter of Daksha. Kasyapa was a very pious person passing his time in performing good deeds towards creatures. One day in the evening while he was sitting in meditation, Diti approached him to bless with children. Kasyapa said this is the time for meditating on God, so let me finish this act first. But with the evil forces hovering around, Diti was blessed with two sons, Kasyapa telling her that these sons will be very wicked who will trouble the human beings and other creatures in all possible ways, sparing not even the sages. They will be so powerful in their evil deeds that only Vishnu will be able to kill them. Another son was Hiranyakasipu as dare devil, as the brother of Hiranyaksha.

The two brothers were Jaya and Vijay in their former life as gate-keepers of Vishnu, who through a curse of sage were born the devils on earth.

The earth was said to be hidden in *Rasatala* which could not be discovered through the normal sense of eye, ear, touch and taste. It was traced through the sense of small which is highly developed in a Boar.

Narasimha Avatara

After the death of Hiranyaksha, his brother Hiranyakasipu vowed to avenge his death. For this he went to mount mandara and performed there a great tapas. His body became covered with ant-hills and wild grass. The force of tapas was so great that the whole world was shaken by it. Unable to bear heat any longer, Brahma went to this Asura's place and was wonder-struck at the severity of his tapas. He made Hiranyakasipu alive and asked for the boon. The demon said 'Lord grant me that I do not die at the hands of any being created by you, nor at the hands of any god, man, demon, or even inanimate thing. Let it not be by day or by night, outdoors or indoors, in the sky or the earth. Let is not be by any weapon whatsoever'. Brahma said 'So be it'.

On the strength of this boon Hiranyaksipu conquered all the world and heaven. He made people to worship him rather than the God. There was material prosperity but people were being terrorized. They prayed to Vishnu for early release from his terror.

Hiranyakasipu had four sons, youngest of whom was Prahlada. Even as a child he worshipped Lord Vishnu and chanted his glories. Teachers of daityas was a great Brahmin Sukracharya. It was his duty to teach Prahlada all daitya lesions. But his heart was not in it, and he will sing glories of Vishnu only. This greatly annoyed his father and he condemned Prahlad's teachers for it. Bu despite all this Prahlada continued to sing praise fo Lord Vishnu. Unable to control his anger,

Hiranyakasipu ordered to kill Prahlada by pointed and poisionus arrows. But this could not do any harm to the body of Prahlada. The demon ordered Prahlada to be trampled upon by mad elephant. The animal rushed forward but stopped before the boy and turned away. He then asked the boy to be dropped from the top of mountain, but this too could not harm Prahlada and he fell like a flower on the grass below. He was bitten by poisonous snakes, thrown into the sea and burnt alive. But he was always safe and sound through the grace of Lord Vishnu. The king was totally frustrated not finding ways to kill a little boy. He asked the boy how he is able to escape from death. The boy replied that all this is due to the protection of Lord Vishnu who is present everywhere in the universe. Hiranyakasipu thundered: "Is you Vishnu present in this pillar too". Prahalad said "Yes, he is in this pillar too".

"Well, then I am going to kick this pillar" said Hiranyaksipu. And as soon as he kicked pillar it broke into two with a sound that filled the whole world with fear. Out of the splilted pillar came a mighty being, half-man and half-lion. He was man-lion Avatara of Lord Vishnu. All Daityas fled after seeing his terrified form. Hirayaksipu lifted his mace to strike him. But Nara-simha picked him up with ease, placed him in his lap across high thighs. Then with a roar, he told the demon that he is neither man nor beast, neither he is in sky nor water or earth, neither in day nor night and tore his heart and threw away the carcass. Then he killed all the supporters of the dead king and seated himself on the throne. The flower and praise were showered by the gods and goddesses. But Nara-simha was still shaking with anger and no body dared to approach him. Brihma then sent Prahlada to him to prostrate in reverence. The great lord, lifted the boy with gentle touch and asked him to seek any boon. But the boy said

'My God, having seen you, I desire nothing else'. The Lord blessed him by saying that though he has asked no boon, yet His wish is that Prahlada should rule as a king of vast Kingdom. And as regards his father Hiranyakasipu, Nara-simha told that he was purified the moment he was touched by him, even though to kill him.

Vamana Avatara

Bali, the king of Asuras, was the grandson of Prahlada. In order to win over Indra- the Lord of heaven- he performed Viswajit yagna on the advice of his Guru Sukracharya. He obtained divine weapons from this sacrificial fire on the strength of which he attacked Indra and captured his capital.

For this success, Bali performed one hundred Aswamedha yagnas. Aditi, mother of Indra was sad to see her son defeated and told of it to her husband Kasyapa. Kasyapa told her to meditate on Vishnu. She performed intense tapas, pleased with which Vishnu appeared before her and promised to be born her son. In time lord was born her son, but a dwarf (Vamana) one. There was rejoicing all over.

Bali was performing Aswamedha yagna at this time, who had invited all Brahmins on this occasion. Vamana also went to see the great sacrifice alongwith other Brahmins. Bali washed his feet with water and prostrated before him. He asked the Brahmin (Vamana) anything, like gold, land, house, cows.... Pleased with this devotion Vaman said that he (Bali) is indeed the fit grandson of Prahlada, an embodiment of Dharma. He (Vaman) asked for three paces of ground to be measured by his own (dwarf) feet. Bali laughed in amusement seeing his dwarf feet, and asked him to seek greater boon. But vaman insisted on three paces only. Alright, measure your paces said Bali, taking water pot in his hand to materialize the boon.

At this moment Sukracharya realized that something unexpected is going to happen. He warned Bali that this dwarf is Lord Vishnu himself and with three paces he will cover everything, and therefore, he should get back on the boon which the Vedas allow in grave condition. To ensure that water does not come out of the holy vessel for the purpose of effecting the boon, Sukracharya blocked the mouth of water outlet. Vaman pierced a straw into this blockage, which damaged one eye of Sukracharya who was inside it. Ever since the Guru of demons is one-eyed.

But he washed feet of Vaman and asked him to obtain his boon. Vaman immediately increased his size, growing bigger and bigger. With his first step he covered the entire earth. With the second covered the whole universe. Bali was amazed to see the entire creation in Vishnu. Asuras were filled with anger at this apparent treachery of vaman and picked up terrible weapons of destruction. But they were put to flight by the attendants of Vishnu. Vaman asked Bali for the place of his third step. Bali bowed his head and asked vaman to place his foot on it so that by this touch he is released for ever.

Vaman placed his food on the head of Bali and said that he first takes away all from him whom he loves. Bali was blessed with God's love. While Indra got the creation, Bali got the creator as an eternal companion. Even for the temporal world, Bali was promised Indira's kingdom after some time.

Parashurama Avatara

This is the incarnation of Parashurama or Rama with the axe. In ancient time there was a king by name Gadhi. He was sitting on his throne when a Brahmin by name Richika visited him and told that he wants to marry king's daughter. Gadhi was surprised with this proposal and in order to make the marriage impossible, asked for a thousand white horses, all with one black ear. The Brahmin produced before the king all such horses. King was convinced about the powers of this Brahmin and therefore, married his daughter Satyavati to him. Considering that this Brahmin was an extra-ordinary person, Satyavati asked for a male child for himself and her mother who did not have the one. Richika gave two lumps of milk-rice mix, one infused with Brahmin spirit and the other with Kshatriya spirit, the former for Satyavati and the latter for her mother. The two got mixed up and reverse of above was eaten by the two ladies. Richika came to know of it and warned his wife that she is going to deliver a child too terrible nature. She was frightened to hear this and request for its amendment. Richika, said that her grandson shall be of this nature.

Eventually Satyavati gave birth to a sage-like child Jamadagani who when grew up was married to Renuka, the daughter of king Parsanjit. Four children were born to them, the youngest was Rama. One day a king called Kartavirya came to their hermitage with all his royal attendants. This Brahmin still entertained him as his guest because he had a cow which could produce anything for asking. The king was attracted towards this wonderful creature and asked Jamadagni to part with it, who refused to do so. Kartavirya took the cow by force and went away to his kingdom.

When Rama came home and found what has happened, he grew angry and rushed to the king's palace with battle-axe *(parsa)* in his hand. He cut off all the arms of the king and killed him. The cow was brought back to his father. But when he (father) came to know of the killings at the hands of his son, a Brahmin, he advised him to go on pilgrimages to expiate the sins. Rama did likewise and came back to the hermitage.

One day Renuka was sent to bring water for the sacrifice. She went to a lake and saw a *gandharva* playing in water. Being half human one helf-god, they are very attractive to look at. Renuka was charmed by the play of this strange being and stopped to see him. She became late in bringing the sacrificial water. Her husband Jamadagni came to know of the reason for delay through his mental powers. Renuka felt ashamed of her thoughts. Jamadagni asked his sons to kill her, but no one came forward. At last he asked Rama to kill his mother and disloyal brothers. Rama acted accordingly and killed his mother and brothers. Jamadagni was pleased and asked Rama for a boon. Rama said, let my mother and brothers become alive and they forget this incident. Jamadagni brought all his brothers and the mother back to life. It is said that due to murder of his mother the *parsa* remained stick to his-hand and could be detached only by a bath in river Brihmputra.

One day when Rama was away, the sons of king Kartavirya came to Jamadagni's Ashram and killed him alongwith others. The mother Renuka started crying for Rama, 'see how they have killed your father'. Rama came from forest afterwards and knowing what has happened, set out not only to destroy the royal line of Karatavirya but also all such evil-minded Kshatriyas, twenty one times.

After some time Parashurama met Shri Rama Chandra of Ayodhya at Janakpuri after the latter had broken the Shiva bow as a marriage condition with Sita. In the last stage of his, this Brahmin was made to realize that all Kshatriyas are not alike, some are as powerful if not more, as he, full of divine merits. Parashurama retired to mount Mahendra after this incident, for meditation.

Rama Avatara

Rama is the hero of the Epic Ramayana. He alongwith his three brothers, Bharata, Laxmana and Satrughna was born to the solar dynasty of king Dasaratha. There is such a mix of human values in this Avatara that despite lapse of thousands of years, story of Rama appears and appeals to be as fresh as it was in ancient times. The main reason is that it is based on certain eternal principles of human life which remain valid for all times. Obviously, these will not be the sectarian deeds meant to serve a particular group of humanity. Unless the spiritual knowledge be of universal nature, meant for the whole of humanity, time will not permit such teachings to remain in existence. Let us see what was the character and element of Rama from his deeds very briefly described as below:

All the four brothers were trained in the arts of archery, Vedas and other royal conducts. In the matter of shooting arrows Rama excelled all. By his compassionate conduct, he became darling of all, including the common people. In his young age suddenly he developed distaste for the world considering its ever-changing nature brining no permanent happiness to the people but assured death to all. Rama was instructed on the meaning of life for several days by the sage Vashista and Valmiki, till he realized his deeper self and the essence of what is called life.

Viswamitra was a grat personality of Kshatriya race. He visited Dasarth's palace and asked for Rama and Laxmana to be sent alongwith him to the forest to fight Rakshasas who devour the human beings and not allow to perform fire worship. Dasaratha hesitated for such dangerous adventure for Rama aged sixteen only. But reluctantly agreed to maintain the promise given to Vishwamitra. The great sage Vishwamitra imparted safety mantras and knowledge of divine weapons to Rama and Laxmana while nearing the forest.

As they crossed river Ganga they entered the forest infested with snakes, scorpions and wild animals, the abode of demoness Taaraka. She was cursed to be so in this forest surving on human flesh. As the three entered some distance in the forest, Taaraka charged Rama with a huge boulder in hand. But Rama was far swifter, and killed her with arrows. The forest was made habitable like other ones afterwards.

They proceeded then to Vishwamitra's Ashram 'Siddhashram'. While the sage were about to lit the sacrificial fire, the sky was covered with black demons led by Maareecha ready to throw flesh and blood in the fire. Rama scattered all of them by arrows, enabling the yagna to go peacefully.

Vishwamitara told the two brothers to proceed towards Mithila the capital of king Janka where *Swamvar* of his daughter Sita was to be held. While at the outskirts of Mithila, Viswamitra explained to Rama how Ahalya the wife of sage Gautama became a stone. Rama touched the stone with his feet and released Ahalya of the bondage. On reaching Mithila, they found a huge Shiva's bow carried on eight-wheeled chariot pulled by hundreds of men. Earlier all contending princes had tried to lift and put a string to it, but failed miserably. Rama, with the permission of Vishwamitra lifted this bow with the ease and grace, put the string and stretched to the ear, finally breaking it into two with a sound that shook the earth. Marriage ceremony of Rama was performed later after his father Dasartha had been invited from Ayodhya. Parashurama, hearing such a deed from a Kshatriya came to Mithila and challenged Rama to put string to his Vishnu-bow. Rama gracefully held it is his hands, put an arrow and asked Parashurama what to destroy, his good deeds or the power of mobility (he was known to move places swiftly). Parashurama felt humbled before him and blessing Rama went to mountain for tapas.

Back at Ayodhya Ram was darling of all through his conduct of justice, fair play and compassion. After some time the king decided to crown him being the eldest son. His step- mother Kaikeyi who otherwise intensely loved him, on the advice of her maid-servant Manthara, asked the promised two boons from the king to materialize. With first boon the queen asked for the crown to be given to her son Bharata and with second the banishment of Rama to 14 years exile to forest. Rama accepted both conditions with calmness and sincerity though his brothers resisted these. With least concern for the Kingdom and its comforts he left for forest with his wife Sita and brother Laxmana in bare cloths but with bow and arrows. Dasaratha died of shock after Rama left the palace. Bharata who had gone to his maternal relations, returned back and came to know everything. He had such an intense love for Rama that he nearly killed his mother and the poisonous Manthra for their misdeeds. He did not accept the crown and went to fetch Rama back to the kingdom. Rama was living a simple life in the forest after having met his friend Guha, a low caste man. When Bharata started with his people to get back Rama, Guha thought that Bharata is coming to attack Rama, he therefore gathered all his man to fight him to finish. Some elder however advised Guha to first check motives of Bharata. Knowing that Bharata is walking in simple cloths to request Rama to claim his kingdom, he became friendly to Bharata. The two marched towards Rama and seeing such a large crowed Laxmana also got suspicious of Bharata and prepared to fight. But Rama rebuked him for having such thoughts for noble Bharata. Bharata pleaded Rama to return back but Rama said that pledge given to his father shall be honoured under all circumstances. Finally, Bharata settled for his sandals to be placed on the throne till he returned from banishment, Bharata only managing the kingdom on his behalf.

The purpose here is not to repeat Ramayana which story is broadly known to almost all Indians, being repeated annually as *Ramalila* in all towns of India. Rama passed his 14 years like a *Tapasvi*, confronting the demons whenever required, making the country safe to live in. He had told Bharata not to blame Kaikeyi, as she was merely acting under the force of destiny. Rama had shown exemplary courage in fighting single handed the army of Khar and Dooshan who were instigated by their sister Soorpanaekha. After be-friending Sugriv and Hanumanana, he attacked Ravana of Lanka. Rama with arrows forced the ocean to give way or remain silent while he builds the great bridge connecting the island of Lanks with the sea-shore. Ravana was a great learned Brahmana, who had become exteremely powerful for any mortal. He took away Sita from forest by deceit. Rama killed him and his invincible son Meghnad (Inderjit) and mountain-like brother Khumbhakarna in the epic battle, placing Ravana's brother Vibhishan on this throne.

Krishna Avatara

In this Avatara, which is said to be full Avatara of God himself (all 16 *Kala* Avatara as against 12 of lord Rama), Krishna is revealed to be one of the greatest revolutionaries in spiritual, social, religious and political field. The spiritual Guru of Lord Shri Krishna was Ghora Angirasha as given in Chandogya Upanishad (III.17.6):

"Ghora Angirasa, after imparting this meditation that was such to Krishna, son of Devaki, Said,.....".

Now what are the thoughts of Ghora Angirasa in Mundaka Upanishad? Listen;

"Saunaka, well known as a great house holder having approached Angiras duly, asked, 'O adorable Sir, (Which is that thing) which having known, all this become known" (I.i.3)

Angirasa replied:

"Thre are two kinds of knowledge to be acquired the higher and the lower; this is what as tradition runs, the knowers of the import of the Vedas say" (1.i.4)

"Of these the lower comprises the Rg-Veda, Yajur-Veda, Sama-Veda, Atharv-Veda, the science of pronunciation etc., the code of rituals, grammar, etymology, meter, and astrology. Then there is the higher (Knowledge) by which is attained that imperishable". (1.i.5)

Such bold thoughts against Vedas could come only from the Guru of Krishna, who himself stopped the worship of Chief Vedic God Indra and demonstrated his might in childhood by holding Goverdhan mountain for 7 days on his little finger to protect the people from the fury of this rain God pouring destructive rains on them. By this act, of course, Krishna only subdued his superiority and did not mean any hostility towards him.

The whole life of Krishna is out brust of his infinite energy against darkness, social regidities, narrow thinking, arrogance of power, injustice in any form, attachment to worldly matters, individual weakness glorified as greatness through hypocrisy etc.

Krishna was born as eighth child to Devaki in the prison of Kansa at Mathura, where his father Vasudeva and mother Devaki were kept as prisoners. While Kansa was pulling the chariot in which his sister Devakhi (daughter of Ugrasena) and friend Vasudeva, newly wed were seated, a heavenly voice said "Fool ! know that eighth child born of this very girl will be the cause of your death". Kansa drew his sword to cut of her head, but she pleaded that she will hand over all his new-borns to him and so her life be spared. Kansa agreed to the term and accordingly killed all the earlier infants expect the seventh who was transferred to the womb of Rohini, another wife of Vasudeva at Gokula and became the mighty brother Balrama. When Krishna was born on eighth of *Bhadrapad* rainy month in the mid-night, he asked Vasudeva to take him to Gokul and exchange with the female child of Nanda. It was raining heavily when Vasudeva walked out of prison with Krishna on his head in a basket. All prison locks were opened and the guards felt asleep. After this exchange when the baby girl was brought back to prison, it started crying. News of eighth child went to Kansa. He caught hold of the child and was about to dash her on the ground when she slipped out of his hands and went into the air warning Kansa that his killer has been born already on the earth. Kansa was a great tyrant and his cruelties had crossed all limits.

Lord had to come down to earth himself to get rid of such demons. As soon as he heard this divine voice, he ordered all children of this age to be killed. Starting with Poothana, he sent a number of devils and evil spirits to kill baby Krishna, but they were all despathed by the Lord.

As a child at Gokul, Krishna showed many divine miracles and soon became the center of attraction to all in the village. After all, he was the centre of life itself. As he grew up he was sent out with cowherd boys to tend the cattle. But as a child he was all fun, frolic and full of darings. He will steel the butter from the 'Haves' and share it with the 'Have-nots'. The Gopa ladies used to complain about the mischievous activities of Krishna but always pleaded for no punishment to him. Once Krishna ate mud and was seen by his mother Yasoda in the act. She asked him to open the mouth so that mud could be taken out. But as soon as Krishna opened his mouth, she saw in it the entire universe. She was frightened but soon forgotten all, taking it as some sort of illusion. Such divine acts of Krishna's childhood are so numerous that it will fill the pages to record them all, it not being possible to describe such glorious deeds in few cold words without evaporating the charm in them. Records Swami Chinmayanandaji (Bombay); "Krishna is perhaps the only prophet (Avatara) that was never known to have wept, ever laughing, ever active, ever enthusiastic, thirsty to live, hungry to experience. He was in love with life be it on the Jamuna banks, in political discussions, in home scences, in the forest or on the war front. He was life itself the warm radiant life!!". After Kaliya Mardanam, that is, subduing the most powerful hundred-hooded snake by name kaliya, kansa was at his wits end and thought of killing this child without delay. He called Krishna to Mathura through Akrura a friend of Nanda, for taking part in a festival with many games and feats. As soon as Krishna and Balrama entered the arena, a mad elephant was let loose on them. They overcame it, but when entered the arena, they were challenged by four great wrestlers in a pre-planned scheme to kill the two. Krishna and Balrama, instead killed these wrestlers. The time for Kansa had also come. He ordered his attendants to kill Krishna, but he was too smart and powerful for them and therefore, Kansa himself was done to death, fulfilling one of the purposes of taking this Avtara.

The Kingdom was given back to Kansa's father Urgrsen. Althrough his life Krishna never claimed any kingdom won for himself. His father Vasudeva and mother Devaki were released from the prison. Krishna now entered the political field and never returned to Gokul or Vrindavan. He established his capital at the new place called Dwarka, inside Sea Island to provide security to its people from various evil-minded kings. Krishna cleared various kings like Jarasandha from this earth who were perpetrating cruelties on the people.

Having established his rule at Indraprastha (now Delhi) Yudhishira decided to perform grand Rajasuya Sacrifice where acquiescing kings would attend in token of acknowledgment of his supremacy. Pandawas accordingly invited all kings after slaying of the only stumbling block of Jarasandha. The custom was to render the first honour to the guest who was considered most worthy of taking precedence over all others. The Pandavas and the grand sire Bhisma were of the opinion that in the present times Krishna deserves this honour, and so he was worshiped for first honour. But Sisupala, the king of Chedi hated Krishna, as any wicked person always does to a good one. He laughed aloud in derision and hurled abuses after abuses on Krishna. The Lord kept quiet althrough which inflamed Sisupala even more. At the count of 99 abuses, Krishna warned Sisupala to hold, else face the consequences, as his promise to his mother to pardon one hundred acts each punishable with death, is coming to end. Susupala laughed even more contemptuously, challenging Krishna to do whatever he liked. Krishna materialized his *Chakra* on the finger and cut the head of Sisupala. All kings accepted (mentally) the prowess of Krishna, of calmness backed by infinity of strength, and were satisfied at the rightly deserved first honour to him.

Krishna later played prominent part in Mahabharata war. He saved the honour of Draupadi the wife of Pandavas, when she was being disrobed at the command of Duryodhana in the assembly hall. Krishna went to Hastinapur on a peace mission, asking Kaurvas to return half kingdom (or at least five villages) to Pandavas once they have completed the condition of 13 years living in forest. Duryodhana said that even the ground that can be covered by the tip of a needle will not be given. The war became inevitable. Krishna became charioteer of Arjuna and promised not to use any weapon in the war against Kaurvas. When Arjuna was hesitant to start the war against great personalities like Bhisma, Daronacharya etc. Krishna gave the teachings to Arjuna which are enshrined in Bhagwad Geeta. As a proof of his divinity as requested by Arjuna, Krishna showed on the battle field his Cosmic Form, covering the entire universe in it. Arjuna was frightened of this Cosmic Deity as one Great Being and prayed for normal vision. It is in Bhagwad Geeta that Krishna Said, "Arjuna whenever there is decline of righteousness and unrighteousness is in ascendant, then I body myself forth"

– Geeta IV :7

Budha Avatara

Lord Buddha has been mentioned as Ninth Avatara of Vishnu in Agani, Matsya, Bhagavata, Linga and Garuda Puranas. But presently, only the essence of his teachings have been absorved in Hinduism and the form is not its part.

"It was the great Buddha who never cared for the dualist Gods, and who has been called an atheist and materialist, who yet was ready to give up his body for a poor goat. That man set in motion the highest moral ideas any nation can have. Wherever there is a moral code, it is a ray of light form that man".

-Swami Vivekananda (Complete Works Vol.II P.143)

On attaining the enlightenment at Bodh Gaya, Buddha came to the Deer Park Sarnath, Benares and he gave the first sermon to his five disciples who had been his colleagues earlier. With this sermon he set in motion the Wheel of Law: *Dharma chakra pravartanah.* He initiated the *Middle path* as the right way of living by saying that Thathgatha does not seek salvation in austerities, though by that reason it should not be understood that he seeks worldly pleasures or abundance of material wealth. For a seeker of freedom to keep his body in good health is a duty, otherwise he shall not be able to burn the lamp of knowledge in it. But any amount of penances do not clean a person who is not free from anger, bigotry, deception, envy, self praise and evil intentions. He preached first the four fundamental truths, as below:

1. There is existence of sorrow in life.
2. There is a cause of sorrow.

3. There is a way out of sorrow.
4. There is cessation of sorrow or Nirvna possible for man.

For the fourth Noble Truth he preached that cessation of suffering can be attained by following the noble Eight-fold path. Removal of selfishness from one's inside was the basis of this Eight-fold path. The Eight-fold path is, 1. Right understanding, 2. Right Thought, 3. Right Speech, 4. Right action, 5. Right liveli-hood, 6. Right Efforts, 7. Right mind fullness, 8. Right concentration.

"To abstain from falsehood, to abstain from back-biting, to abstain from harsh language and to abstain from frivolous talks, is called right speech", Buddha said.

Practicing such strict moral laws was the Buddh's teaching for achieving Nirvana. There was no necessity of introducing personal god into it as practicing these laws alongwith meditation led to the state of cessation of sorrows, i.e., Nirvana. Buddha's teachings was, therefore, that of high order of asceticism. Buddhism expended in all directions initially so long the moral laws were followed by the Bhikshus and the populace. The Buddha has repeatedly said that metaphysical and intellectual knowledge is of little avail in the absence of moral knowledge and its practice, though allowing freedom to a rational intellect.

Some one has rightly said "The three cycles of Buddhism were five hundreds years of Law, five hundred years of Images, and five hundred years of Tantras". Buddhism remained active religion in India for about 1500 years, i.e., till 1000 AD, with its decline starting after the death of king Harshvardhan in 647 AD.

"The Buddha believed that fulfillment of worldly duties is not directly helpful for attainment of eternal salvation. He has said full of hindrances is the house hold life, a path defiled by passion; free as air is the life of him who has renounced all worldly things. How difficult is it for a man who dwells at home to live the higher life in all its fullness, in all its purity, in all its bright perfection. Let me then cut off my hair and beard. Let me clothe myself in the orange colored robes and let me go forth from the household life into the homeless state". [2]

With the God gone as mental prop and the householder not directly catered for Nirvana, the preservation and expansion of Buddhism depended on the Bhikhus following the moral law. The moment laxity came into it, in the later period, there remained nothing to prevent its popularity sliding down. Then the external factors of hostility of some Brahmin Hindus and invading Muslims (Bakhtiyar Khilji 1197 AD), in addition to Buddhism's own internal weaknesses developed, ensured that this great religion goes out of India into oblivion. But this is the religion which gave glorious spots in Indian history when the teaching of Lord Buddha were followed in true spirit. The two Chinese Visitors, Fa-Hien (405-411 AD) and Yuan-Chwang (629-645 AD) have recorded on the glory of this period apart from Ashoka's achievements visible everywhere even now.

The life of Buddha is an exemplary life of scarifices in the world history for the cause of suffering humanity. He was a born prince of the kingdom ruled by Sakya clan with capital at Kapliavastu (Presently on foot hills of Nepal) in solar dynasty. He was born on full moon day (Purnima) at Lumbini in 563 BC. His childhood name was Sidharta Gautam. The astrologer proclaimed that the child will become a grat émperor or a sanyasi. Sidharta showed all the greatness in his childhood as an archer or a compassionate prince. Once his cousin Devadatta hit a swan with arrow. Siddharta lifted if up and claimed after removing the arrow, saying that saver of a life has more right on it than the killer. His father provided every comfort to this child so that he remains entrapped in the comforts and luxuries and does not think of *Sanayas* life. But the destiny willed otherwise. He was married in early age to a girl Yasodhara and had son named Rahul. Some time later, the prince desired to see the world outside the palace. The king allowed the request but asked the attendants to ensure that nothing unpleasant crosses his path. But it was not to be so. The prince saw an old man in unspoken misery. Then he saw four persons carrying a dead body. He questioned the charioteer and came to know that all men have to similarly die. Then he saw a sannyasin of serene countenance beyond misery.

Sidharatha spent days thinking of the misery people are facing. The king learning of all this, was scared with apprehension that Siddhartha may take to ascetic life.

One night when all was quiet, the prince felt restless. He stood gazing at his wife and child. Finally decided to says 'Leave this world of misery and seek enlightenment'. He called Channa, the faithful charioteer to bring the horse. He mounted on it accompanied by Channa while the world was fast sleep. When the river came, he halted, cut off his hair and divested himself of robes and ornaments and gave all to Channa. He proceeded alone to the path of enlightenment, by sacrificing everything of worldly possessions. A rare act of selflessness in attaining the truth!

By begging alms, the prince came to Rajagriha the capital of Magadha. Its king persuaded Siddharta to hold reins of empire rather than the beggars bowl. But he was late for this. Siddharta moved to the forest near Bodh Gaya and came across five ascetics. For six years he continued his penances till his body was a mere skin and bones. Realization came to him that it is a mistake and he changed his way, so as to keep body in good condition. The five ascetics left him considering that he is not a fit sanyasin. One day Siddharta took some *Khir* from a low caste girl Sujata who had come to offer it to the Aswattha tree deity. He set in full determination, not to rise from meditation till he attained the light. And despite tempting forces of Mara the evil spirit, he obtained the enlightenment on this day-which was again Purnima. Siddharta thus became a Buddha. Then he proceeded to Sarnath to deliver his sermons of peace and happiness to the sorrowful world.

Buddha lived upto the age of about 80 years, giving his universal message to the humanity with emphasis on casteless society. The kings, Brahmins, merchants and masses had followed and absorved his message. He attained his Mahaparinirvana in 483 B.C. at Kushinara, again on Purnima, third time, the earlier two being his day of birth and achieving of enlightenment.

The Temple of Universal Religion

The teaching of this ancient religion are freely available now to all those who care to read and follow them. Rama Krishna Mission have published a series of books, with English translation of almost all ancient scriptures like Upanishads, Bhagwad Geeta etc. In fact, it has published books of other religions like Buddism, Christanity, Islam, Sikhism, as well, in 'Thus Spake' series and other forms. There is a fascinating story relating to the Kali Temple of Calcutta whose priest was Rama Krishna Pramahansa himself. This temple was built by a shudra woman Rani Rasmani. Mr. Christopher Insherwood in his book *'Rama Krishna and Disciples'* (Advaita Ashrama Calcutta) describes the events (abridged) as below:

There were many Bengalies of determined character who were not afraid to challenge the authority of foreigners and make themselves respected by them. Such a one was lady named Rani Rasmani. She was well known throughout the city and highly popular because of her generosity, courage and piety. By a paradox by no means unusual in India, this lady belonged to Shudras (fisher woman), the caste of the servants..The British had the good sense to recognize with humour one hope- that they had met their match. She got the tax abolished.... The Rani was an ardent devotee of goddess Kali, and in 1848 she decided to make a pilgrimage to Benaras, which is regarded as the holiest city in all India. But, on the night before her departure, she had a dream in which the goddess appeared to her and said "There is no need for you to go to Benaras. Build me a temple here in Calcutta on the Ganges bank and install my image in it. Arrange that I shall be worshiped there daily and offered food. I will manifest within that image and accept your worship". This temple was built in 1855 and became the famous Dakshineswar Temple of Kali. It's priest, who was named Gadadhar in young age, became the world famous Rama Krishna Pramahansa, the Guru of Swami Vivekananda. The Rani did not realize what she has created and who its priest would be. That she would get the best fruit of her efforts, she did not know. She was not aware that the disciple of this priest will be the one who will move the world towards universal Religion in harmony with the scientific developments and that the Guru Rama Krishna Pramahans, himself will be the one who can say that God can be reached through any religion. But all this was not without sever strain on her mind. On completion of the temple, no Brahamin priest was prepared to offer worship *(Puja)* in a temple constructed by a Shudra. With great difficulty one Brahmin named Khetranath came to officiate in another temple-Radha and Krishna temple as part of this very temple. For main Kali temple none was prepared to officiate. Ram Kumar, the elder brother of Gadadhar persuaded the latter but with no effect. Ultimately Gadadhar accepted priesthood of this temple after showing a little hesitation of an orthodox Brahamin and became its famous priest Rama Krishan Pramahansa, the exponent of enlightened Religion for all, irrespective of their caste and clan. Kali perhaps was taken by these great saints a form of cosmic energy as personal form of worship. Swami Vivekananda says about her;

"Kali worship is not a necessary step in any religion. The Upanishads teach us all there is of religion. Kali worship is my special fad, you never heard me preach it, or read of my preaching it in India. I preach only what is good for universal humanity".

Complete works Vol.-VIII P.522.

The Supreme Power

Lord Krishna shows his cosmic form to Arjuna on battlefield, as revealed in Chapter-XI of Bhagwad Geeta.

"Arjuna, then saw in the person of that supreme Deity, comprised in one limb, the whole universe with its manifold divisions". XI:13

Says Arjuna "You are the prime Deity, the most ancient person; you are the ultimate resort of the universe you are both the knower and the knowable and the highest abode. It is you who pervades the universe, assuming endless forms". XI:38

Says Krishna, "Neither by study of Vedas, nor by penance, nor by charity, nor by ritual can I be seen in this form as you have see me". XI:53

"Through single minded devotion, however I can be seen in this form (with four arms later revealed to Arjuna)". XI:54

Founder of modern science, Sir Isaac Newton believed that the solar system appeared too contrived to have arisen solely from the action of blind forces. Let us have glimpses of the extent of physical universe known to the scientist till date.

In this cosmos the scientist have discovered millions of galaxies (10 billions as per photograph capacity of Palomar telescope, California, USA), each galaxy being lakhs of light years in diameter. The distance of sun from our earth is about 8.3 minutes by the light speed. One can only imagine the distance which light can travel in one year (light-year) at its speed of about 3 lakh Kilometer per second. One amongst these billions of galaxies is our Milky Way Galaxy. It contains about 100 billions of stars, in a space which is about one lakh light years across. One amongst these billions of stars is our sun, situated at two third distances from the center of its spiral arm. The solar system have nine planets, one amongst which is our earth. Compared to the distance of our star-the sun, as 8.3 light minutes, the distance of our nearest star- Alfa Centoury is 4.4 light years. This is the extent of our known cosmos where even the sun hardly gets a place to be represented by a dot. Whole of the infinite cosmos is governed by certain laws, "Laws of physics discovered in the laboratory apply equally well to the atoms of a distant galaxy" says Paul Devies the great philosopher scientist. On the earth more than two-third area is under water. On the remaining land portion, we have about 200 countries. One amongst them is India. What an insignificant place we have in this great universe, but what an arrogance we display of our position obtained from man-made laws and for our worldly intellect not capable of looking towards the higher truth. The account of vastness of the universe given by our present day scientists attempts to see the body of the infinite, though still to a limited extent. Whole of this cosmos is governed by nature's laws which do not apply selectively to any part of it. Only the Supreme Intelligence of the infinity can control such unimaginable gigantic universe to keep the stars and planets in their places, moving with designed exact speed and orbit without collision, except colliding where there is purpose of further creation.

The Voice of God reflected in scriptures of various religions, always calls for well being of all people. But the teachings of Lord Krishna as given in Bhagwad Geeta are more direct in this regard. "Those, however, who controlling all their senses, and even-minded towards all, and devoted to doing good to all creatures constantly ador as their very self the Unthinkable, All-pervading, Imperishable, Ineffable, Eternal, Immobile, Un-manifest and Immutable Brahma, they too come to me"

BG XII:3,4

Two great personalities of the modern India who gave fresh impetus to the ancient religion of Hindus are Swami Dayananda Saraswati and Swami Vivekananda (in end of 19th century AD). Swami Dayananda gave a call 'go back to Vedas' and formed Arya Samaj to do away with various evils of Hindu society like casteism based on birth. He laid stress on Mantra portion of Vedas. Swami Vivekananda who created Rama Krishan Mission laid emphasis on the end portion of Vedas, i.e., the Upanishads or the Vedanta Philosophy. No modern saint of standing has given any push to the Brahmana portion (rituals and sacrifices) of Vedas, but it survives as a momentum of the past. The seed of Brahmanic caste system lies in this second Brahamana section of Vedas (first is Mantra, second Brahmana and the third Upanishads). Neither Swami Dayananda nor Swami Vivekananda took up the preaching and practicing of Brahmana portion of Vedas. Rather both ignored it. Several other saints like Anandmurti Guru Maan have also preached (still preaching) the knowledge portion of Hindu Philosophy in modern times, enlightening the gatherings. They equally appeal to awakened minds. Alongwith the medieval saints, we can revere the modern ones (including some foreigners) who have probed deeper into the mystery of universe. Like a swan we should be able to separate milk from water and discover the true saints, ancient, medieval or modern, who have uplifted the human race. Entry to the top of mountain may be from any side, but reaching at its peak, the differences should merge in higher vision.

Living a meaningful life for a human means the satisfying or developing all the four personalities of him viz.: the physical, the mental, the intellectual and spiritual. An animal may remain satisfied with its physical needs of food and shelter, but a man needs satisfaction of emotions and thoughts at mental level, curiosity for higher probes, discoveries and ideologies at intellectual level, and yearning for higher truths of God, Soul, Life, Super power or Moral law at spiritual level. The importance of man's true need is in ascending order starting from the physical. It is for this reason that the sages lived spiritual life of deeper contemplation by begging alms. Even Lord Buddha left the kingdom to become a *Sanyasi,* living on casual food and least physical needs, for the sake of attaining enlightenment. The wisdom which finally dawned on him taught that middle path is the best i.e. excessive materialism is as bad as torturing one self in the absence of minimum physical needs. Such balanced living remains ideal for human growth even today, the world over.

Unless the hunger of four different personalities in man is satisfied, he does not reach on top of human evolutionary ladder. Crucification of Jesus Christ imparts this lesson. While the first three are being addressed to in the present day democratic era, even if by promises, the fourth is to be taken care of by oneself looking inside. Fortunately, the time has removed fetters on the spiritual or higher knowledge which was hitherto an exclusive preserve of a few. It is for us to look towards enlightenment, which is open to all as a possibility, in this universe created by the Supreme Intelligence.

References

1. The Inner Reality (P.40) by Dr. Paul Brunton B.I Publications Pvt. Ltd.
2. Glimpses of World Religions P. 69-70, Jaico Books (2005 Impression).

13
Lawless State-A Dalit Girl Protects Her Honour by Losing One Arm

The Integrity in Public Service

For all government/public servants, particularly in officers class, there is system of writing confidential report (CR) annually. The CR invariably always contains a column 'Integrity', which is generally taken as relating to corruption. This is its limited meaning as the integrity of a person means much more. Even in the sense of corruption, the column is filled in by the Reporting Officer routinely, it being difficult to establish corruption charges against an individual. It is therefore, not surprising that even the official who purchased the posting 'through auction' finds this column filled in as 'Nothing adverse to notice'. But as said earlier, integrity means more, it is to render selfless service to the public. A person who does not indulge in corruption himself but allows others, above and below him, to play with public funds to keep himself away from the hazards, can not be said to be a man of integrity. Two cases are recent where an upright officer has paid with his life the price for maintaining the integrity. One is of Satyendra Dubey, a brilliant engineer from IIT Kanpur who was posted as Deputy General Manager in National Highway Authority of India (NHAI) project in Bihar. He was murdered on 27th Nov. 2003 in Gaya, Bihar in highly suspicious circumstances statedly by the hired killers. Dubey had exposed serious irregularities being committed by the Agencies and Officials of NHAI, in a confidential letter addressed to the Prime Minister's office in Nov 2002, requesting that his identity be not disclosed. But this letter was forwarded as it is to the Ministry of Road Transport and Highways, which in turn sent it to the NHAI against whose officers and contractors Dubey had complained. No doubt, Dubey paid with his life this bureaucratic indifference. Another case is of Manjunathan, an engineering graduate and MBA from IIM Lucknow, employed as Sales Officer in the Indian Oil Corporation. This 27 years young boy from Banglore had dreamt of serving his country with honesty and efficiency. He was aware that adulteration in petrol is going on mass scale in some petrol pumps. He performed his duty with the highest notion of integrity and booked the owner in Uttar Pradesh after detecting and establishing adulteration. But this mixing business fetched so much of money that it could influence high levels and engage criminals at any cost. This young lad was killed on 21 November 2005 at Gola (Lakhimpur Kheri) 150 km from Lucknow, leaving behind a hot depate in Media on adulteration of petrol.

We have seen the court judgment of 21 February 2006 on the murder of a girl Jessica Lal. On refusing drink to the son of an high profile politician, in company of similar elite boys at New Delhi, she was shot point blank in the presence of many people. The accused, son of a former Union Minister in the company of another son of a Rajya Sabha member, fled from the scene of crime but later caught by the Police. The case went on for 7 years but ultimately all the nine accused acquitted by the court as the prosecution dealt with the case in sloppy manner failing to recover even the murder weapon.

During such a prolonged period the key witnesses turned hostile. After the accused were granted bail, the family member of Jessica had stopped attending the hearing in the court. Delhi High Court has now taken suo moto cognizance of the lapses, due to public outrage. Not only this case, but several others like former Navy Chief's Grandson moving douse six pavenment dwellers with his vehicle in a drunken state speaks of the laws of land being applied differently for the powerful and the rich. Tardy investigations by the police gives enough scope to the influential criminals to go scot-free on the basis of benefit of doubt given by the courts. The third case of Priyadarshini Matto, who was a third year student of law. She was brutally raped and murdered in Delhi's Vasant Kunj Colony on 23 January, 1996. The alleged rapist and murder was son of an IPS Officer. Due to faulty investigation by the police, he was set free by the judge on the benefit of doubt.

Such cases of loose integrity are not in police alone, news papers are filled with the cases of public servants acting against public interest in various fields be it administrative, financial or technical. Mass scale unauthorized or illegal construction being done in the capital, has forced the court to pass order for their demolition. While lot of prestigious buildings on public land were demolished (others in progress) in February 2006, Delhi High court has ordered action against some 95 engineers.

Why is this failure of integrity so common amongst the public servants, the need quickly giving way to the greed? without going into the finer details, lack of integrity can be directly traced to the missing element of ethics in his/her character. Unless a majority of people in any country have some minimum consideration for the other's concern situation is bound to become like, that of a traffic chaos at the signal free crossing. Cases still occur where a person at the end of a long queue is not entertained at the window because the official time is up. The same person so meticulous of the timings spends much of it in gossiping on telephone or entertaining his friends or acquaintance out of turn. No doubt he himself receives this treatment at the hands of other working in different occupation. In 'We the People' (strand Book Stall) NA Palkhivala, a legal luminary, says;

> "To India Nature has given immense intelligence and skills but no sense of public duty, discipline or dedication.
>
> Our besetting sin is secular Fundamentalism. Fundamentalism is the triumph of the letter over the spirit. It spurns the lesson taught two thousand years ago that the letter killeth but the spirit giventh life. In our unwitting addiction to the fundamentalism we are fully supported by two defects in our national character-lack of sense of fairness and lack of sense of moderation".
>
> He further writes,

"The quality of our public life has reached the nadir. Politics has become tattered and tainted with crime. The moral standards of our politicians, policemen and criminals are indistinguishable from one another. India today is a living example of the fact that cynicism corrupts and absolute cynicism corrupts absolutely".

That this condition of lack of morality in dealing with public and its interest by the public servants emanates from his internal thinking based on materialism of selfishness, is clear from the following words of wisdom of James Allen in 'As A Man Thinkth' (The Peter Pauper Press) ;

"Thoughts and character are one and as character can only manifest and discover itself through environment and circumstances, the outer conditions of a person's life will always be found to be harmoniously related to his inner state".

And ;

"Every man is where he is by the law of his being ; the thoughts which he has built into his character have brought him there, and in the arrangement of his life there is no element of chance, but all is the result of a law which can not err".

So, therefore, to remedy the situation of selfishness prevailing alround, the thought process of people have to be channelised. They have to be taught in school the basic principles of character building, of tolerance towards other's views, openness of mind to absorb new thoughts alongwith creating analytical abilities, of universal brotherhood, of sacrifice towards the higher cause of public or the nation. Presently the humane qualities do not find any place, even a minimal of it, in the Confidential Report Performa of a public servant, all of it being devoted to the performance. Even this performance is a subjective grading, by and large.

Like the wild vegetation of all sorts growing on its own in a neglected field not cultivated, the thoughts in a person will grow of wild variety if the mind is not kept clean of selfish and cruel thoughts. He will not mind ditching his Department, society and even nation for the sake of his personal power and enjoyment. He can go to any extent of compromising his duties and honour.

Demoniacal Traits

What better description can be there of present situation than that given by Lord Krishna is Bhagwad Geeta :

- They say "The world is without any foundation and altogether false, godless and brought about by mutual union (of man and women); what else". - 8/XVI
- Embracing this view, these lost souls with little understanding, ill deposed and devoted to cruel actions are born for the destruction of the world. - 9/XVI
- Possessed of hypocracy, conceit and arrogance and given to insatiable passion, and adopting false doctrines due to delusion, they take to action with impure views. - 10/XVI
- ---- given to the enjoyment of sensuous pleasures they believe the highest limit of joy to consist only in this. - 11/XVI
- Held in bondage of a hundred ties of expectations given over to passion and anger, they strive to obtain by unlawful means hoards of money for enjoyment of sensuous pleasures. - 12/XVI
- This has been won by me today, that ambition I shall realize now ; this wealth is mine already; that will be mine again. - 13/XVI
- This enemy has been already disposed off by me, and I shall make short of other too. I am Lord, I am the enjoyer, I am perfect, powerful and happy. - 14/XVI
- I am wealthy and high born. Who else is like unto me? I shall perform sacrifices, give alms and rejoice. - 15, 16/XVI
- Self-important, unbending, filled with the intoxication of wealth and honour, performing nominal sacrifices for show and contrary to scriptural ordinance. - 17/XVI
- Given over to egoism, violence, insolence, passion and anger, these malicious persons hate Me that dwell in the bodies of others as well as their own. - 18/XVI

- Passion, anger and greed these constitute the triple gate to hell leading to the damnation of the soul. Therefore, one should shake off all these three. - 21/XVI
- A Man released from these three gates to hell, Arujna works his own salvation and thereby reaches the highest goal (i.e. myself) – 22/XVI

If Lord Krishna were to write the Annual Confidential Report of officials today and the Performa were to contain column on subjective personality, one, more or all of the above would have found place as entry in it for majority of us.

A Dalit Girl put up brave fight in a Corrupt System

Vigilance means watchfulness. Human weakness being what it is, it is not always possible for an official to apply self-corrections. He falls into temptations and after a time becomes so engrossed in it that he goes to accumulate money by crossing barriers after barriers of probity. Punitive action by any Government than becomes inevitable. Preventive vigilance of course is preferable to the punitive one, as it gives chance to an individual to come to right track. But as per Transparency International for the year 1999, India ranks 73 out of 99 countries, showing that India is recognized as one of the most corrupt countries in the world. Basic reason is again not need but greed. Mind boggling corruption details have been reported in the press of the officers who have been occupying top posts and thus far removed from the needs. Since such officers go to any extent to make compromise with their duties, public interest no longer remains safe in their hands. They not only threaten public exchequers but its security as well. Some time back Bihar was the worst example in this regard. The kidnappings, murders, gangs warfares, deep corruption, caste rivalries were order of the day. Bhagalpur blinding was only a symbolic expression of it, with little to distinguish between police, politician and the criminal. Political interference was norm rather than exception. But it will not be fair to single out Bihar, though it stood at higher pedestal. Other states like Uttar Pradesh are not far behind. There was a news item (The Pioneer dated February 14, 2006) with the heading 'Dalit girl fends off attackers, loses right arm', showing the girl's photo. " The 15 years old girl, Anju, put up a daring fight against the four men who tried to rape her in the fields near Achalda Village in Auraiya district 250 km from here" (Lucknow), says the newspaper report. The report further says "Frustrated at the daring resistance put up by Anju, the men chopped off her arm and abandoned her, leaving her bleeding profusely in an unconscious state. They allegedly carried away her arm, police said". The incident took place near the hometown (Etawaha) of the Chief Minister Mulayam Singh Yadav. When the girl approached police station to register her complaint, the cops refused to register the case. It was only after her father approached district superintendent of Police that a formal report was lodged. Anju has named Veeresh Yadav as the key accused alongwith three others who abducted her while she was on way to the local market. The cuprites are still at large. The father of this girl had told the police that earlier too Veeresh Yadav had threatened to sexually assault her, but the local police under influence of powerful Yadavs paid no heed to it. It is an irony that Dalit feel so threatened in the state ruled by higher OBCs. There was yet another operation 'Yamraj' on a TV Channel in this period where the Gaziabad (UP) policemen were shown accepting money for eliminating opponents of a fake complainant. Yet another TV Channels had shown the Jail conditions where the criminals enjoy all facilities including free use of mobile phones and free entry of their acquaintance. A Minister was shown talking of his VIP Car to transport drugs from eastern UP to Delhi at a price of 20 lakhs per trip.

Why are the government officials, the police and the administration allowing the criminals to run the state"? In one word, they lack in integrity. Majority are more than willing to carry out the illegal dictates of their political masters, to get their choice postings, timely promotions and other favours. No doubt, in the above instance of a Dalit girl, the superintendent of police has shown some integrity but the same was altogether missing in officials down below:

Where does one go to lodge complaint against the tyrannical system where the higher level in the hierarchy have formed a gang with the lower ones to jointly exploit the people. The Media of late, is doing wonderful job in this regard. It is exposing the scandalous episodes forcing the government to take action even if half-heartedly. The latest case in the state is of Meher Bhargava, a brilliant Parsi lawyer, married to Luv Bhargava, who was shot point blank in the heart of Capital (Luknow) for objecting to obscene remarks on her daughter in law. The culprit is still at large though one of them was caught after a month due to public outrage in the Media.

Though common people were not much concerned with the vigilance set up in the government hitherto-before, but now it has become necessary to know its basic details, as it only can keep the public officers on alert. Not that the officials are to be kept under constant threat and thereby making them shirk from taking decisions but to instill a legitimate fear into those who take public interest for a ride, is not wrong.

System of Vigilance in India

(a) Central Bureau of Investigation (CBI) :- [1] The CBI is constituted under the Government of India, Ministry of Home Affairs Resolution dated 1st April 1963. The investigation wing of CBI is Delhi Special Police Establishment (SPE). Delhi Special Police Establishment Act, 1946 was amended in 1952 to enlarge its scope to cover the employees of statutory corporations and other Govt. Bodies. The SPE enjoys with the respective State Police force concurrent powers of investigation and prosecution under Criminal Procedure Code. Cases which substantially and essentially concern Central Government employees or the affairs of central Government, even though involving certain state government employees, are to be investigated by SPE. The state police is, however, kept informed of such cases and will render necessary assistance to the SPE during investigation. The SPE, which now forms a Division of the CBI, functions under the administrative control of the Ministry of Personnel, Public Grievances and Pensions. The Director, CBI also functions as the Inspector General of Police in charge of SPE. The SPE has two Divisions ie (1) Anti-Corruption Division and (2) Special Crimes Division. The Anti-Corruption Division will investigate all cases registered under the Prevention of Corruption Act and cases registered under Sections 161 to 165-A and 168 of IPC. The Special Crimes Division will investigate all cases of Economic offences, which are at present being investigated by Economic Offences Wing, and all cases of conventional crimes such as offences relating to internal security, espionage, sabotage, narcotics, murders, decoities/robberies, cheating, criminal breach of trust, forgeries and other IPC Offences notified U/S 3 of DPSE Act, dowry deaths, suspicious deaths and offences under other laws notified under section 3 of

the DPSE Act. The SPE has its branches located in the different states, the jurisdiction of each branch extending over the state in which it is located. The central units under the Anti-Corruption Division and the Special Crimes Divisions located at Delhi have all India jurisdiction and generally take up only important cases against senior public servants or cases having inter-state or international ramification or offences of national importance.

(b) Central Vigilance Commission (CVC): The Central Vigilance Commission was set-up by the Government of India in February, 1964 on recommendation of the Committee on Prevention of corruption under the Ministry of Home Affairs Resolution dated 11 February 1964. In cases where it appears after a preliminary inquiry, that a public servant had acted or refrained from acting, for improper or corrupt purpose, the commission advises the appropriate disciplinary authority regarding suitable action to be taken against the public servant concerned. While the jurisdiction of CVC extends to all matters to which the executive power of the union extends and to all employees of Government and Central Public Undertakings for practical consideration, it has been decided that the commission will for the present advise on cases pertaining to Gazetted Offices of Central Government; the SHOs of Delhi Police; the Board level appointees in the public sector undertakings; the officers in scale III and above in public sector banks, officers of certain range in cooperative societies and other societies receiving grant from the central Government autonomous and other similar bodies. The commission exercise a general check and supervision over vigilance cases and anti-corruption work in all organizations within its jurisdiction, through periodical returns and

reports which are required to be submitted to the commission by the Chief Vigilance Officers. The functions of CVC are advisory but they are advisory in the same sense as those of Union Public Service Commission, with the same measure of independence and autonomy. The commission is required to submit an annual report to the Department of Personnel and Training about its activities drawing particular attention to any recommendation made by it which has not been accepted or acted upon the Government. A copy of annual report is required to be laid by that Department (Personnel and Training) before both Houses of Parliament together with a memorandum explaining the reasons for non-acceptance of the recommendations of the commission, if any.

Information about corruption and malpractices on the part of Public Servants may also be received from their subordinates or other Public Servants. While normally a Public Servant is required to address communications through proper official channel, there is no objection to entertaining direct complaints or Communications giving information about corruption and other kind of malpractice. While genuine complaints, should be afforded protection against harassment or victimization, serious notice should be taken if a complaint is, after verification, found to be false and malicious. There should be no hesitation in taking sever departmental action or launching of criminal proceedings against such complaints.

Complaints received in the CVC may be acted upon by it as below depending upon its nature:

1. It does not merit any action and may be filed, or
2 It should be sent for inquiry and disposal/report

to the administrative Ministry/Department concerned.
3. It should be sent to the CBI for investigation/ inquiry or,
4. The commission should undertake the inquiry itself.

The Government of India have reason to believe that a good many anonymous complaints are false and malicious and that such complaints are not a reliable source of information. Inquiries into such complaints have an adverse effect on the moral of the services. The Government of India have accordingly decided that no action should be taken on anonymous complaints against Government Servants. The Govt. have also decided that pseudonymous complaints against Govt. Servants should be treated similarly.

(c) Chief Vigilance Officers (CVOs):- While the primary responsibility for maintenance of purity, integrity and efficiency in his organization vests in the Secretary of the Ministry or the Head of the Department, the CVO acts as his special assistant in all matters pertaining to vigilance and provides a link between his Ministry/Department and the CVC. The CVOs in the Ministry/Department are appointed after prior consultation with the CVC. No person whose appointment is objected by the commission will be so appointed.

In big departments/organization, the CVO should be whole time, that is, the should not be burdened with other responsibilities. To be effective, he should normally be an outsider and should not have been an employee of the organization in the past. Officers of all Services and cadres should be considered and the field of selection should not be restricted to a particular service or state.

The CVC has also been given the power to assess

the work of CVO and the assessment is recorded in the character rolls of the officer. Similarly, the CVO of a Ministry/Department has been given the power to assess the work of Vigilance Officers working under him and to record his assessment in the character rolls of the officer(s).

*(d) The Central Vigilance Commission Act, 2003:-*The following Act of Parliament received the assent of the President on 11 September, 2003.

The Central Vigilance Commission Act, 2003.

The Commission shall consist of-

(a) a Central Vigilance Commissioner- Chairperson

(b) not more than two vigilance commissioner- Members.

The CVC and VCs shall be appointed from amongst persons:-

(a) Who have been or are in All India Service or in any Civil Service of the union or in a civil post under the Union having knowledge and experience in the matters relating to Vigilance policy making and administration including police administration; or

(b) Who have held office or are holding office in a corporation established by or under any central Act or a Government company owned or controlled by the Central Government and persons who have expertise and experience in finance including insurance and banking, law, vigilance and investigations.

The CVC and VCs shall be appointed by the

President, provided that every appointment shall be made after obtaining recommendation of a Committee consisting of:-

(a) The Prime Minister.
(b) The Minister of Home Affairs.
(c) The Leader of the Opposition in the House of the People.

The CVC and VCs shall hold office for a term of four years or till he attains the age of sixty five years, whichever is earlier.

Among other functions and power, the commission shall exercise superintendence over the functioning of the Delhi Special Police Establishment in so far as it relates to the investigation of offences alleged to have been committed under the prevention of corruption Act, 1988.

The Commission shall, while conducting any inquiry referred to in clauses (b) and (c) of sub-section (I) of Section 8 shall have all the powers of a civil court trying a suit under the code of civil procedure.

(e) Is the vigilance serving public interest?:- Due to some constraints on the functioning of CVC general impression amongst the public servants is that while the lower/middle levels are being caught the higher and bigger sharks are left untouched. In fact this is in-built into the very system of CVC Act. Para 6 A of this Act reads as below:-

6A(I) The Delhi special Police Establishment shall not conduct any inquiry or investigation into any offence alleged to have been committed under the prevention of corruption Act 1988 except with the previous approval of the Central Government where such allegation relates to:

(a) The employees of the Central Government of the level of Joint Secretary and above, and
(b) Such Officers as are appointed by the Central Government in corporations established by or under any Central Act, Government companies, Societies and local authorities owned or controlled by that Government.

Despite lot of noises against this provision, it remains intact. Higher Officers of the level of Joint Secretary and above remain in touch with their political masters in the Ministry and any exposure to such levels may touch the politicians also. It is therefore, no wonder that approval of the Govt. rarely comes forth in these cases, in fact it is rarely sought by the Vigilance itself. Take the case of Indian Railways, the biggest employer of public servants in the Govt. (near half of the entire strength of central Govt. employees). The accidents occur continuously, resulting into the loss of human lives every year. But what is the vigilance system there? The Advisor, Vigilance Railway Board, who is the nodal authority at the Headquarters of Railway Board, is the person from Railways only. Even a serious complaint is only forwarded to the concerned Zonal level, who investigate the cases and submit report to the Advisor where required. The Vigilance system at Zonal level functions under the General Manger (GM). There is Chief Vigilance Officer (CVO) in the Zone under whom are placed many Vigilance Officers (VOs) or Dy. CVOs each concerning its specific discipline. The Annual Confidential Report (ACR) of the CVO is written by the

GM and that of VOs by the CVO, received and accepted by the GM. Thus, the entire Vigilance set up functions under the GM. Now if the GM himself is involved in a case (and it happens), there will be no action against him unless he decideds to punish himself. At least the Zonal CVO should have been freed from the control of GM and placed directly under the Advisor, Railway Board for ACR and other purposes. Such a simple change has not happened in the last 56 years. The politician is happy, the entire staff is free (GM acts routinely) and of course the CVC is at peace. If people die due to negligence of staff, let it continue to be so, there will be some noise in the Parliament and Press and than subside.

The advice of the CVC is not for mandatory acceptance by the Ministry/ Department of the Central Govt. There are many cases where this is ignored or diluted to protect the high ups. Also, the jurisdiction of CVC and CBI does not extend to the State Governments. It is upto them to seek CBI investigation where they desire so, otherwise it is by the state's own vigilance system which is politicized almost everywhere. Of course there is some element of truth in the Central Govt.'s retaining final decision in its hand on the CVC advice. Para 2.1 of the Vigilance Manual Says "——. The prosecution of a Government servant for an offence challenging his honesty and integrity has also a bearing on the morale of the public service. The administrative authority alone is in a position to assess and weigh the accusation against the background of their own intimate knowledge of the work and conduct of the public servant and the overall administrative interest of the state". As per the para 2.2, the sanctioning authority has an absolute discretion to grant or to withhold sanction. But at least this discretion should be speaking one, giving details of disagreement.

How India has Survived ?

Despite the chaotic situation alround due to apathy of public servants and corruption at top level, this country is the only surviving democracy in the continent. In fact in the whole of world it is the largest democracy. Accept for a brief period of emergency during 1976, the change over to governments at center and state had been generally peaceful. The misdeeds of Governors of Goa, Jharkhand and Bihar is a recent phenomenon. And to add to the problem, there is so much of variety in the national composition in terms of caste, religion, language, region etc. that it is difficult to find the same elsewhere in other democratic countries. Still, the affairs of state are being run on secular basis, by and large. In fact the majority community, the back bone of secularism, has started complaining now that it is being ignored in various matters due to opportunistic policies of the political leaders. What is the secret of this success? While the Roman, Egyptian, Chinese and other ancient cultures of the world have been wiped out by the element of time, the Indian's still lives. The main factor is the teaching of universality in Upanishads, taking every human being as manifestation of one Divine soul. All different religious thoughts have been absorbed without conflict. So long this liberty of thinking prevails in India, its culture will not come to destruction.

While working in a senior position in Arunachal Pradesh, I was asked by All India Radio to give a talk on "National Integration with Social Justice" in 1986. This was given by me as below and the same was broad cast on 24 November, 1986.

National Integration with Social Justive

(Talk on All India Radio-broad cast on 24 Nov, 1986 at Tezu, Arunachal Pardesh)

What is national Integration? To me that means that we move as one body with no cleavage in it's constitution and no escape from its gravity. It is something like our Earth rotating on its axis and moving around without permitting even a single particle of its atmosphere to escape into space. Any particle has to overcome its given escape-velocity to be able to get out. This earth is not constituted of one single homogeneous mass. Exactly opposite of it. It has infinite variation in its constitution. You can find all basic elements of matter in it, in their varied form and shape. But here we are certain of one thing beyond doubt, and that is, it has one centre and one centre alone. There can't be two centres in a circle or sphere. The billions of stars and planets in this cosmos obey this law of one centre, to be able to retain their integrity under the great pulls of gravity. No exception is permissible.

Likewise, a Nation can exist as one heterogeneous mass only when there is on centre. That centre has to be necessarily equidistant from every point of it surface. Despite all the wonderful variety on its face, our Nation does have that centre. That is not merely a political, religious or social centre, but it is a cultural centre. On political or religious plane, we are near the one ideology and farther to another. But not so on cultural plane. The cultural Identity permeates every space of this land. It is one indivisible whole. It has been chiseled and hammered through the preachings of universal love, tolerance and brotherhood by galaxy of sages and saints through Centuries. Lord Budha, the Enlightened one, the Light of Asia; Adi Sankra-Charya, the exponent of Universal Philosophy of Vedanta, capable of grappling with the Infinite; Chaitanya Mahaprabhu, Ramanju, Sant Tuka Ram, Guru Nank, Kabir, Suffi Saints Ramakrishna Paramahans, Swami Vivekananda, Swami Dayananda,

Ramna Maharishi, Theosophical philosophers and host of other luminaries from Hindu, Muslim, Christian and Sikh religions have preached this message. Even Akbar the great on this land felt charmed to create a religion to express this universality, by its name, Dine-Ilahi. It is here that Lord Krishna declares in Geeta that He reinforces in a true devotee that faith by which the pure-minded one worships higher principles of Godhood. On this land is preached in the same Geeta the ideal of achieving liberation through work:

योग: कर्मसु कौशलम्।

Here itself is a Ashoka born to rule over the heart of all, irrespective of any faith. It is coming on this land from far off that the Chinese pilgrims Fa-hien and Huen-Tsang find their journey rewarded and life-time ambition fulfilled by seeing this spirit face to face. Lamented the pilgrims how they could not be born during the period of Budha's sojourn on this land. Here is a Tagore Singing भारत भाग्य विधाता... And Iqbal सारे जहाँ से अच्छा...

This Cultural Identity over which have rolled the centuries of political upheavals, stands undiminished, like a Beacon light, unaffected by storm. But it has a lesson to impart. Let everyone note carefully and makes no mistake about it; this spirit does not accept fanaticism and narrowness in religious and social thanking. We need not make further experiments to realize this fact. That is going to be unnecessarily costly.

We can see that political Integration in India has much to do with social renaissance. The glorious spots in Indian History are those where social divisions were not rigid in water-tight compartments and where there were hearty, healthy inter-action between them, though that did not mean leveling down of social identities but having a basis on the principle of intelligible differentia. In the epic period of Mahabharata, its author Ved Vyasa himself was born and brought up by a fisher-women in her cottage. And for this period Dr. Oak is putting his head to find out as to what sorts of nuclear fissions were used in the great war being televised live more than 100 miles away in king's palace. In Budha period, the Tathagatta's whole philosophy was based on social equality. In Maurya period, Chandra Gupta Maurya himself was born of a socially low woman. In subsequent Gupta Empire, known as Golden period of Indian History around 4th Century A.D, records the Budhist Fa-hien, that there were trade guilds for various professions with no social, religious conflict anywhere. Similarly recoards the pilgrim Huen-Tsang of Harsh Vardhan period around 7th Century A.D. about the healthy interaction amongst religious and social groups. During the period of 8th to 10th century A.D. Known to historians as dark period of Indian History, where no light is available, there stands the society completely dived in endless groups with cleavage developed in all faces. Muslim travelers like Ferishta, Alburani in 11 century A.D. following the attacks of Gaznavi, bring out this fact in their recordings. And since then we did not have stable Nationhood, though there are intermittent glorious lights of those unmatched mighty heros Prithvi Raj Chuhan, Rani Padmini, Maharana Pratap, Shivaji, Guru Govind Singh, Maharani Laxmi Bai, Tatya Tope and Maharaja Ranjeet Singh, all shining out. And when after a long spell, the dark clouds of slavery are on the move and light is visible again, while India is attaining Independence from foreign rule, what is the scenario opening up on Indian screen ? what do we see there ? There is that Mahatma Gandhi crusading against social tyranny and absurdities. The Socialism has entered into the soul of Father of Nation. That saint is seeing the core of National Freedom as social liberation of masses. He is refusing to live better than the ordinary Indian. The whole country is up. Look in the East, there is that rising sun awakening the land with its saffron light, Subhas Chandra Bose. It's light as coming from the Land of Rising Sun, Japan, are striking straight at Red Fort, Delhi. Saffron rays of this luminary Bose are emanating from the socialism of that fire, Swami Vivekananda. And see in the West, there is that dazzling spirit, soaked in socialism, hovering over the Empire, Saheed Bhagat Singh with other youngs and Azad. Also, round there is that Iron-man before whose movements unroll the divisive kingly states, Sardar Vallabh Bhai Patel. In the North, see that Friend, Philosopher and Guide, that Architect of Modern India, that image of secularism, unleasing dynamism into masses to get over orthodoxy and unscientific ways, Pandi Jawahar Lal Nehru. He is saying 1927, "Liberation of poor and oppressed from all exploitations is over and above the necessity of freedom from foreign rule". By his side is surging forward that pride of Prophet Mohemmed, fearless leader of Indian renaissance, that freed one, already named Azad, Abul Kalam. He is refusing to pay obeisance to bigotry. In the South, see coming those rulers of Indian homes, representing best in the Indian womanhood, Mrs. Annie Besant and Mrs. Sarojini Naidu. Who else could be better suited for launching Home Rule Movement against the Empire than those goddesses of learning and sacrifice. They are generating social waves reminiscent of ancient height in womanhood. South has gird up its loins to fight against social lunacy.

And at Centre, in that Maharastra including Nagpur, see that torch bearer of Liberty, held-high, asking for Swaraj, Bal Gangadhar Tilak. And right there is that modern Manu, giving constitution to this Swaraj, that heart of socialism, Messiah and voice of exploited millions, Dr. Bhim Rao Ambedkar.

So, this is the scene when light of freedom returns to this ancient land of Bharata. And it appears as if that spirit of liberty and Nationhood would not reveal itself until we clean ourselves of social impurities. That light does not percolate through this dark media of social obscurancy. Even on date we can see the most backward states (not merely economical) of the country as those which have such obscurancy in thicker shade. The words "National Integration with social changes", therefore, are self-speaking. I have tired to convey it's feeble voice upto you.

And Let us Prostrate unto this Mother of Nation, Because, when its spirit rises, the gods are ready to obey its command

Reference

1. From the Vigilance Manual Vol.I.

14
Basic Tenets of Hindu Philosophy

Reincarnation of Soul or Laws of Karma

All the India-originated religions like Hinduism Buddhism, Jainism and Sikhism including all the sects of Hinduism like Arya Samajist, Radha-Soami Satsang Beas etc. believe in the reincarnation of soul ie its rebirth in different bodies. This is a concept which is most misunderstood and sometimes dubbed as the fatalistic one for leaving the destiny of man in the hands of his fate. This is not so. It is the law of the nature of cause and effect or 'as you sow, so must you reap'. The law of cause and effect ie of action and its reaction is fully applicable in the physical world as discovered by the scientists. There is no reason that it should not be applicable to the mental world, which is only the finer state of material outside. All forms outside emerge out of the thoughts inside is the assertion of the great men like James Allen. In brief, the law of karma is that whatever you are doing presently is getting stored in the memory as a software to be projected in future on the screen of monitor (body). What is being projected right now is the past software ie the bundle of memories stored carefully in a very fine form, birth to birth. It does not get destroyed on the destruction of physical body. While exhausting the past karma presently we are creating the new one simultaneously which is getting stored up in the ultimate storage house of 'Sanchit Karma' to be expressed in future. The new karma can be created only in the present movement of NOW, therefore it is the opportunity also for happy future while reaping the fruits of past Karma, good or bad. The Karmic debt has to be paid, willingly or unwillingly. But by understanding it can be made more favorable. The right self efforts of man in the present moment can offset to some extent the bad part Karmas. If through good thoughts or meditation intermittently we allow the play of higher powers, the effect of past sins get reduced gradually. One has only to read "THE POWER OF NOW" by Eckhart Tolle of British Columbia, Canada, to realise the intense liberating powers of the present moment. The so-called bed circumstances are given to man to make him learn certain lesson from it. He has to suffer it either grudgingly or wisely. Under a tree if an apple falls on our head and injures it, we as a natural reaction shall curse the tree or our fate. But not Sir Isaac Newton. He shall discover the law of gravitation, apply it to suns and stars of the universe and lay the foundation of the modern science. The central message of Bagwad Geeta on action is to do it through detachment ie without caring for its fruits. In time this will reduce the binding Karmas, as the bindings come through attachment.

The Karmas are of three types as below:

1. *Sanchita Karmas*: These are the stored-up unexhausted Karmas colleted through countless past lives. Sanchita means accumulated ones.

2. *Prarabdha Karma*:- Karmas that have ripened at the time a soul takes birth, are called

prarabdha Karmas. The birth in different bodies depends upon the quality of this Karma and pleasures and sorrows in life are the outcome of expression of this Karma, also called as destiny. The body falls apart (dies) the moment Prarabdha Karmas are exhausted.

3. *Agami Karma*:- The actions being performed in the present moment with a sense of ego, creates the Karmas for future. These get merged into the Sanchit Karmas when the body is given up in the present incarnation.

On attaining the liberation or the enlightenment, all the seeds of Karmas are brunt up rendering them incapable of further fructifications. There remains, therefore, no need for taking another birth and the soul merges into the Infinite and Eternal Being.

Questions can be asked whether there is any proof of this theory of rebirth. First of all this will be replied in theory and then through practical examples.

Look around and you will find infinite variety of human beings. Some are in good health others are suffering from serious ailments like blindness, leprosy TB etc. Some are rich and others facing grinding poverty. Some are gently, loving and happy. Others are cruel, murderers, robbers, some are givers of happiness to all around others are distributors of miseries and agonies. Every man is a different variety having no similarity with the other in internal make up. Even the sons born to the some present in the similar circumstances, are widely different in their character. You can have a Ravana and a Vibhisan as brothers and as a late example Aurangzeb and Dara Sikho (having views of opposite directions) as sons of the same parents. Examples can be multiplied ad-inifinitum in all parts of the world. Now, if you do not hold the person concerned, responsible for his state, the other alternative remains to attribute this variety to the creator or God or the Nature. These impartial beings or non-beings then become the most whimsical, arbitrary and tyrant ones who give misery and happiness at random without any cause to different people. Nature being impartial can not do it. And if there is a god behind it, then he is the most irrational being. The theory of Karma answers this question satisfactorily and rationally. God plays no part in it except allowing the events or consequences to happen or fructify. He remains in impartial background, allowing the individuals to exercise his free choice in words, deeds and actions and get the exact fruit of the same.

How does one acquire the knowledge? Through experience. How is the experience made? Through memory. I can not have any knowledge of the things in the world unless the new sensation tallies with the past impression of it. Let it be explained further. Mind is like a lake and as a stone thrown in it creates waves which becomes smaller as it reaches out of the centre of disturbance (it never dies) so the impressions of the five senses like eyes, ear etc. create waves in the mind which are stored there permanently. When I see an object outside its identity becomes known to me only with reference to the similar impressions stored already, otherwise I remain ignorant. How is it that a duckling hatched recently by the duck starts swimming when it comes to the water. Because of past knowledge. The body and not the mind or the brain gets destroyed at the time of death. It is an immaterial consciousness that retains the past impressions of the jeeva in extremely finer form; it is like audio, video waves in a room emanating from a

TV station, which do not get destroyed by any amount of fire in the room. The jeeva with these peculiar impressions remains in search of right type of future body and gets birth the moment it finds one.

The argument against this theory is that we do not remember any of our past lives. But the existence does not depend upon one's memory. Even in this life we have hardly any memory of childhood, but we definitely existed as a child. And has not the Nature shown mercy on us to black out memory of past lives? We are troubled by the sad memory of even this life, what will be the condition if we were to know a large number of tragedies in previous lives. The enlightened masters say that a time will come when the soul will know all its incarnations when it gets freedom or *moksha*. It will then be too powerful to withstand any amount of shock.

But the cases of such past memory returning to some individuals keep on coming to the press from various parts of the country and outside. The latest case being reported by the Newspapers (November 2005) is the one of five years old Durgesh of Hathras district of Uttar Pradesh, which is being heard by the court involving un-heard-of legal precedence. But before this, let me give some details of two other earlier cases.

This relates to West Bangal, as reported in the Indian Express dated 10.7.1989. Being a small piece, I am reproducing it, as it is:

Wonder Girl
Calcutta, July 9: Photo produced

Having conquered Purulia, she has stormed Calcutta.

The city is agog with stories of the six year-old whiz kid, who talks of nuclear physics, knows about world affairs, solves tricky mathematical problems and quotes out of the hands from Indian constitution.

The todder, holding the hands of her parents, called on the state Minister for rehabilitation, Ms Chaya Bera, at the Writers' Building here two days ago. The Minister was zapped. Patitely ensconced in a chair opposite Momusami Chakraborty could red out the names of all the state Cabinet Ministers. And as Ms Bera listened wonder-struck, the tiny-tot informed she know about the UNO affais in Japan. She was grieved at the death of the former Soviet President, Andrej Gromyko, she let the Minister know. Pulling a typewriter, she gave an impromptu display of her flawless typing skill. Her little fingers danced over the key board and her speed was an astonishing 46 per minute.

The above presentation was before the Minister of a Marxist Government. Other cases were reported in quite detail in the Pioneer dated April 11, 2004. Only their substance is being produced here. One pertains to the village Sendra (near Belawar in Rajasthan). A boy Raghu Nath walking alongwith his father suddenly points out to two women coming their way as his wives. The father rebuked him but the boy supplied all the details to his satisfaction by going to their (woman's) house on his own and narrating various episodes known only to these women.

Another case, which made newspaper headlines about 75 years back, was got investigated by Mahatma Gandhi. It relates to nine-years old Shanti Devi of Delhi who started speaking about her husband at Mathura. She confounded everybody by recognizing all her relatives in addition to her previous life's home. She lived as a living testimony to the incidence of 'reincarnation' and died only a few years back.

The case of Mrs. Swaran Lata Tiwari is rather distinctive. At present teaching botany in a Bhopal College was approached to know about her past memories. She said I still tie 'rakhis' to the wrists of my brothers of the last birth. A 57 years-old (previous life) son of this 48 years old lady touched her feet in obeisance. Her narration of the correct details of the house and its neighborhood of 60-70 years ago impressed everyone.

A little boy Aishwarya of Chander Village born in 1999 taunted his parents as to why they don't give him money for the marriage of his (boy's) daughter. The boy replied he was Veerpal of Kamalpur village. His parents lived in Bulandshahr, while he was employed in a factory at Faridabad where he lived with his wife Rani, Sons Akash, Vikas and a daughter Sheetal. He had died in an electrical mishap. Learning of this, some people came to Chander who recognized them promptly. His Father took him to Kamalpur, where he recognized all his past life relations.

Now we come to the case of Durgesh mentioned earlier. It was reported in the Pioneer of November 27, 2005. Being lengthy in details its gist is given as below (Photo of mother and the child was produced).

This is the story of a five year old boy Durgesh who told a packed court in Hathras (UP) that he was reborn as Mahipal to avenge his own killing by friend Ved Prakash. The case is pending in the court for decision. The boy says that he was Mahipal in previous birth and that he had been reborn as Durgesh in Mahipal's origional family to avenge his own murder. He says my Friend Ved Prakash had killed him in an altercation over his wife who was being eyed by Ved and in ensuing scuffle Ved killed him (Mahipal). The judge took cognizance to find precedence if any existing.

The five years-old boy talks about his previous birth effortlessly. In this birth he claims to be born to the woman with whom he had affair sometime. Durgesh's mother tell that he smokes and has eating habits exactly like Mahipal. As for Durgesh, the mission is single-point, to get his murderer booked. His version is "I was the center of admiration and envy among villagers for having marred a good looking Bengali Girl. Ved Prakash and others used to ask me to get them married to Bengali girls like my wife".

Once, we had gone for a function to a nearby village when it was time to return Ved Parkash started insisting that he would escort my wife back home and that I should stay back to look for a similar Bengali girl for him to marry. It was then that I realized that he was eying my wife. So I refused. This led to an altercation and in the ensuing scuffle Ved Prakash and two my other friends throttled and murdered me".

No doubt it is a puzzle for the legal admissibility. The case dates back to the year 2000 when 21 year old Mahipal an Assistant District Government Counsel, was murdered and his body found in the fields on February 27, 2000. Not satisfied with strangling the victim, the killers had even mutilated his genitals. Mahipal's grand father Lalaram got an FIR lodged against his murderers. During preliminary investigations, the cops stumbled upon evidence suggesting that Ved Prakash was the real perpetrator of murder. Subsequently, he was arrested and charge-sheeted. Ved Prakash was released on bail and relocated at Aligarh. The case has come to stand still where it is not possible to predict the outcome.

These are some details of rebirth. The Law of Karma puts the responsibility on man for his state of being. It of course does not mean that we are not to struggle against the unjust circumstances imposed by the exploiters or the tyrants. Such a struggle itself is the Karmic debt to be paid and earn glory in the process. That is why we all honour the freedom fighters of our country's independence and those who struggled against social obscurantism.

Towards Evolution

From the state of an hot ball, our planet earth cooled down through millions of years at its surface, retaining to some extent still the hot material at its core. The life appeared on it billions of years later. Man as homo-sapiens was just one species out of endless others. In the initial period of life dinosaurs were the ruling class of the jungle. The lion became the ruler of jungle subsequently, at times the wild elephant performing this role. But there was something different in the homo-sapiens that made it to evolve fast and rule this earth as man today. Nay, he is aspiring to lay claim to other planets and stars in our galaxy, having already reached the moon. The lion or elephant remains even today where they were billions of years back, infact only to exist in his everyday shrinking territory. Its very existence is at the mercy of man. And in physical strength and faculties, man was nowhere near them. So, what has made this change, the descendants of homo-species ruling the universe and the offspring's of other species remaining almost as it is in the jungle with some variation in their physical characteristic. It is the difference of mind in the two, it evolving continuously in the man and remaining only instinctive in the animal. While the animal kingdom reacts through instinct, the man-world reacts through feelings and thoughts. All this evolution of man is the evolution of thought process in him. Says Swami Vivekananda;

"Like fire in a piece of flint, knowledge exists in the

mind; suggestion is the friction which brings it out" (CW: I:28)

"All knowledge, secular or spiritual is in the human mind. In many cases it is not discovered, but remains covered and when the covering is being slowly taken off we say ' We are learning', and the advance of knowledge is made by the advance of this process of uncovering. The man from whom this veil is being lifted is the more knowing man; the man upon whom it lies thick is ignorant, and the man from whom it has entirely gone is all-knowing, omniscient". (CW: I:28)

It is this evolution of mind that has produced the current civilization of the world, the agriculture, the transport, the flying machines, the weapons of defence far superior to those employed by the most ferocious species of the jungle, the industries,- capable of producing any material necessity and comfort and even recording millions of information on practically invisible silicon chips. A satellite has been launched (Feb 2006) by NASA for the planet Pluto located at the outer boundary of solar system, which is situated at such a distance that it will take 10 years for this mission to reach it, traveling at a speed of about 30,000 km per hour ! This is the wonder of physical body evolving into the mind and mind evolving into the intelligence. But there is something deeper than intelligence in a man. It is his existence itself as a conscious being, the Life Centre.

Material possession alone never satisfied any human being, either in the past or today. Lord Buddha, the Prince of a Kingdom, left all its comforts for the sake of acquiring higher knowledge of this Life Center surrounded by bliss. Once a person does not have this goal of searching higher in his self and still he goes for material accumulations then he remains dissatisfied by any amount of this possession. It is like pouring ghee in the fire, its addition only inflames the fire further. A Hitler does not stop merely at running the European countries under his feet he attached Russia. Ravana is not satisfied merely by possessing the mightiest generals of army and the golden city of Lanka with a space vehicle, he wants to exhibit his power of arrogance by forcefully taking away the wife of some other well known personality. For Stalin Joseph, it is not enough that he becomes the dictator of Russia after Lenin's death and brings about rapid industrialization and other forms of material intelligence, he must exterminate his opponents even in lakhs, to develop a personality cult. Alexander the great will not stop merely at conquering empires from Greece to Indus Vally, Egypt, he must come to India to capture it till his army rebels against this adventure after coming in contact with the bravery of Indians. Going further back, it is not enough for Duryodhan to capture the kingdom of Pandavas, he must publically insult their wife, send them to forest and even there harass these Pandavas in all possible ways what to say of returning back their kingdom after 12 years of exile. God is not against human prosperity, had it been so, a magnificent Indraprastha would not have been built by Pandavas with Krishna's advise. It is the lust of human mind riding rough-sod over the ethical values that has He put an end to. This world has seen all the mighty tyrannical empires crumbling into dust and we are still left to sing in praise of those who have brought about this change. So, beyond the intellect there is still a factor in human affairs, call it by the name of ethics or moral laws or God or spirituality or freedom. This is non-worldly. For its sake a Jesus Christ will sacrifice everything including his life. A Socrates will drink the cup of poison in the prison to uphold this state.

But do we have any scriptural basis for the above observations on human affairs ? It is exactly as above, given by no less than the Lord of Death itself in Katha-Upanished to Nachiketa. Dharmaraja ie Lord Death had tempted Nachiketa with every conceivable gift of worldly plane to ensure that he does not ask questions on spirituality. But Nachiketa persisted with his query and as a reward got the teachings of highest wisdom from the lips of Lord himself, the Deity presiding over the death of all living beings, without any exception. He also teaches what is beyond Death. Lord Death is therefore, not an ordinary Hindu deity. He knows the fate of every single creature of past, present and future. Death does not take place casually, at random, it has a precise timing and purpose for each being. Says the Lord Death;

"Beyond the senses are the sense-objects; beyond these objects is the mind; beyond the mind is the intellect and beyond the intellect is the Great Self." - III:10

'Beyond' here means the subtleness or pervasiveness, mind is more subtle or pervasive than the senses, intellect is more subtle than the mind. Self or the Life centre is of course said to be all pervasive. Sense objects are the impressions of sense-perceptions on the mind. Take for example a tree outside, which my eyes are seeing. The image of this tree fall on sense-instrument ie retina of eye in this case. The sense impression travels like waves through finer nerves to the brain centre. It is lodged there as an 'impression'. But there are so many other impressions simultaneously falling on the mind. Only that impression which gets registered and invokes thought as a reaction, is known, others go into waste basket as it were, get lost and remain meaningless. That is why when you are seeing the tree, so many other impressions like horn of passing vehicles, chirping of birds etc. go unnoticed. All such impressions are gathered by the mind and put up to intellect for decision. The intellect analyses, classifies it with reference to the similar previous impressions and conveys its decision to the mind for execution. The mind works like a receiving and dispatch clerk and the intellect like the executive Officer. But, all this formation of ideas and emotions is not possible unless there is conscious principles underlying below on which all this drama takes place. It is like a screen of cinema hall on which various pictures are being projected. This is the spirituo-physical constitution of man, a five-in-one personality, i.e., body, senses, mind, intellect and consciousness. Strangely, the subtler layer is more important than the grosser. It is due to this reason that for the sake of an ideology (intellect) the thoughts and feelings are sacrificed and all pains of body forgotten. You can see people braving heat and cold, standing for hours without food, protesting against assault on their ideology. The question here is not of ideology being right or wrong, but so long it is sustained by a particular group they virtually die for it forgetting physical and mental pains. Going beyond intellect a Bhagat Singh sacrifices his life itself to achieve highest goal of the soul-freedom. This freedom is not his personal freedom but that connected with his soul at its core, one aspect of spirituality devoid of religiosity. For the sake of the same freedom, Maharana Pratap fought the fierce battle with limited resources and remained in jungle for 10 years practically eating the grass and bearing all inconveniences to his family. I am not saying that Akbar was bad; he was great. But the question here is of one's conviction. Pratap was convinced that any compromise with Akbar would mean curtailment of his freedom, particularly when no attempt was made by Akbar to let him rest free due to constant prompting by Man Singh.

For a self-centred Hindu detached from the concerns of his soul, there is no bottom limit for his fall.

The evolution of a living being depends upon the state of his mental and intellectual faculties. A plant exhibits but rudimentary mind, it minds the neglect you show to it by no-watering or over-watering. The animal kingdom has better developed mind and intellect compared to the vegetation life, though they have no choice to exercise the intellect as they mostly act on instincts. It is in the man that mind and intellect have developed to a great extent. But where such development is not controlled by the concerns of his soul or deeper self or saner voice from inside, such development does not lead towards true goal. The goal is not to eat drink and make marry at others or public cost, to remain totally unconcerned with the sufferings of fellow human beings, to ditch the national interest for the sake of personal power. Here the example of freedom fighters and the kings or Princes supporting the British power is appropriate. We all know the glorious role played by the freedom fighters for the country's independence. They listened to the voice of their soul and were guided by it for the higher purpose. On the other hand we had the Indian princes or the Rajas, who, with some honorable exceptions, indulged in grossest form of pleasure, having least concern for its people. A Maharaja of Alwar will not mind picking any human child as bait for the tiger-shooting if animals like sheep and goats are not available immediately. He will burn his poney in a polo match failure in full public view by drenching the poor animal with kerosene oil and setting it on fire by his own hands. The deeds of Maharaja of Patiala and other such kings can not be described here. One has only to read the chapters 'Places and Tigers, Elephants, and Jewels' and 'A Day cursed by the stars' of the Freedom at Midnight by Larry Collins and Dominique Lapierre. These were the goals of these soulless people having reached the top of worldly possessions in terms of wealth, power and territory. On the other hand we see a foreigner Abraham Lincoln, who reached the top position in the United States of America, as it President twice, sacrificed his life for the sake of freeing Negroes from the slavery of Americans. Lincoln reached the highest position of America almost in the same period of our Rajas and Maharajas (1861-65), and laying the foundation of mightiest empire on the earth.

Continuing the teachings of Lord Death on vital matters concerning the human beings, it says;

> "This Atman (ie soul) can not be obtained by study of the Vedas, nor by intelligence, nor by much learning. He whom the Self chooses, by him the self can be gained. To him this Atman reveals its true nature". (II:23)

Here the choosing by self is not a random incidence. It is the result of a long period of self-cleansing by an individual.

Dharmaraja further says;

> "Know the Atman as the Lord of chariot, the body as the Chariot; know intellect as the charioteer and mind again as the reins" (III:3)

> "They say, the senses are the horses and their objects are the roads; the Atman, the senses and the mind united, the wise call the enjoyer" (III:4)

> "He who has no discrimination and whose mind is always uncontrolled, his senses (horses) are not controllable like vicious horses of a driver" (III:5)

> "But he who has understanding and whose mind is always controlled, his senses are under control like good horses of a driver" (III:6)

The Lord death says that whose horses are not under control moves from birth to birth and whose mind is under control reaches the destination where he is not born again.

The setting of Arjuna's chariot in Mahabharta war depicts the above philosophy. Arjuna's chariot is like his body, the horses like his senses, the reigns like his mind, Krishna the charioteer like his pure intellect. Keeping the mind fully under control is himself, a Arjuna- who was an egoistic weak master when he lost control on his senses and later the invincible hero who could face the entire might of Kaurvas after he gained control on his senses and mind through the teachings of Krishna in Bhagwad Geeta.

Here is something said by Swami Vivekananda on the Mind and its control:

> "Mind is like a lake, and every thought is like a wave upon that take. Just as in the lake waves rise, and than fall down and disappear, so these thought waves are continually rising in mind-stuff, and then disappearing, but hey do not disappear for ever. They become finer and finer, but are all there, ready to start up at another time, when called upon to do so. CW-II:268-69

> "Every vicious thought will rebound, every thought of hatred which you have thought, in a cave even is stored up and will one day come back to you with tremendous power in the form of some misery here. If you project hatred and jealousy, they will rebound on you with compound interest. No power can avert

them; when once you have put them in position, you will have to bear them. Remembering this will prevent you from doing wicked things CW- I:262

"My idea is to brig to the door of the meanest, the poorest, the noble ideas that the human race has developed both in and out of India, and let them think for themselves........ Liberty of thought and action is the only condition of life, of growth and well being. Where it does not exist, the man, the race, the nation must go down........... Caste or no caste, creed or no creed, any man, or class, or caste, or nation, or institution which bars the power of free thought and action of an individual – even so long as that power does not injure others- is devilish and must go down. (CW:V:28-29)

15
The Liberator of Indian Slavish Psyche -Swami Vivekananda

The lifting up

It has been said earlier that it is because of mind-intellect faculty in man that he has developed to this stage while animals remain where they were millions of years back. It was the depressed psyche of Indian masses that was slave to the Britishers. Physical reality is the automatic reflection outside, of this inner mind. Not only Swami Ji raised this mentality with reference to the British rulers but also he made a great dent on the attitudes of Hindus with reference to the socials evils like caste.

> "Do you think our religion is worth the name? Ours is only don't touchism..... A country, the leaders of which have for last two thousand years been only discussing whether to take food with right hand or left, whether to take water from right hand side or from the left, if such a country does not go to ruin what other will." C.W. Vol. IV P-253

Swami Vivekananda was the foremost disciple of Sh. Rama Krishna Pramahansa, who was the priest of Dakshineshwar temple built by a Shudra Lady Rani

Rasmani. When this temple was completed in 1855, no orthodox Brahmin was prepared to be its priest. Thus not only in worldly possessions but in matter of spirituality also the effort of a shudra was rewarded by the priesthood of Rama Krishna Pramahans. There is something beyond mind-intellect also. It is the Life Centre or God or Soul. The evolution of a man remains incomplete unless all faculties ie., physical, mental, intellectual and spiritual are developed. In fact, the final liberation comes only through the spiritual attainment. This is a matter connected with the soul. Now 'Soul' has become a vague term denoting no specific concept to us. Let it be explained by a sketch, as below:

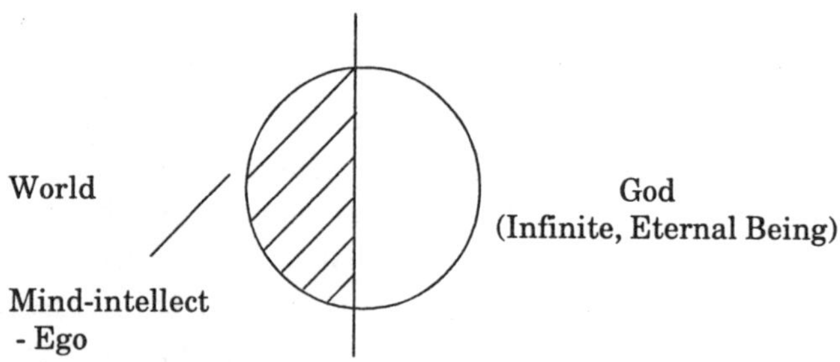

There is some place deeper in us which is in touch with the Infinite and Eternal Being and at the same time forming part of worldly mind-intellect-ego equipment. A normal human being identifies himself with the dark side, which is nothing but sort of chip having record of his infinite past impressions or Karmas, or desires. A particular body-mind-intellect equipment is manufactured by Nature according to this load of existing impressions. If the impressions are dark, very little light of the Higher Being percolates through it, and the man behaves in various cruel ways, going to any length to satiate his worldly desires. But through good actions and better understanding when the same become lighter, more light passes through it and the person expresses it in happy, harmonious, liberal but firm disposition and wise interaction with the world outside. Mundaka Upanishad says it as below:

> "On the same tree, the individual soul remains drowned (ie struck) as it were and so it moans, being worried by its impotence. When it sees thus the other, the adored Lord, and His glory, then it becomes liberated from sorrow." (III:2)

It is the glory of Swami Vivekananda that he taught man to develop all his personality layers. In America and other western countries, he was able to convey deeper spiritual teachings of Upanishads in the modern scientific language. It worked in two ways; one, by softening the racial pride of British masters and second, by lifting up the depressed psyche of Indian masses groaning in slavery. The life-sketch of Swamiji given below should be enlightening and encouraging to us.

Swami Vivekananda- His Life Sketch

It is said that seven stars in the sky represent seven sages in deep meditation. The great saint Rama Krishna Pramahans saw in a vision that as a small boy he went to one of the seven sages he knew, put his arms around him and brought back the sage to awareness from deep meditation. The boy implored the sage to come down to earth alongwith him, the sage agreed and was born as Swami Vivekananda.

In Calcutta, a lady Bhuvaneshwari used to worship Lord Shiva, for gifting her a son, as she had only daughters. A child was born to her on 12th January 1863, a Marker Sankranti day. She and her husband Vishwanth Datta thanked Shiva for this gift. Child was named Biley initially and Naren afterwards. From the beginning child was naughty but kind to the beggars and sages. He will give them any gift in his control. His mother once locked him in the room so that he does not give away house articles like this. A begger approached near the house, Biley opened the trunk in the room and threw a sari from the window towards the begger. He gave instances of strong will in the childhood. Biley used to play games like court and king, and always chose to be king to dispense justice. Even as a boy he will sit in meditation like Buddha. Once he was so sitting when a snake crawled near him. Other children ran out in fear, but Biley kept on sitting unware of the creature. It passed away without any harm to him. At the age of six he knew by heart the stories of Ramayana and Mahabharata. He remembered what he heard once. The child learnt various games of lathi-play alongwith other physical exercises. Children were always happy in his company. He was not scared of such things a ghosts. Biley now grown as Naren had a number of pet animals to play with- a monkey, a goat, a peacock, pigeon, a pony and family cow. In school, his memory was so sharp that he could repeat anything once heard. Once there was talk by Naren to his friends in class room hearing which the teacher asked him to explain the conduct. Upon this, Naren repeated word by word what the teacher had been teaching and was thus pardoned. His father wanted Naren to learn music, so Naren became a good singer with his sweet voice. Naren's father had many clients, of various castes including muslims who were friendly to him. Each was provided with his own hookah. What will happen if all smoked only from one. Boldly he went round the hookahs and took a whiff from each. When his father saw Naren doing this and questioned him Naren said "Oh, father ! I was trying to see what happens if I broke caste ! Nothing has happened to me when I smoked from all hookahs". Father laughed it away. Once Naren had gone to a fair with his friend. When they were returning home in the dusk, a carriage came dashing towards them. Naren to his horror discovered that life of his companion was in danger. Naren rushed to the lad's help unmindful of his own safety. He grabbed the child instantly from the approaching horses hoofs and saved him. Everybody who saw this was in praise of Naren and patted at his back His mother heard the storey and wept in happiness, blessing the boy to save human lives like this.

Due to some reasons Naren had to be out of Calcutta for two years alongwith is father. When Vishwanath returned back, there was problem to take Naren in the school. But the teachers loved him and his ability and so made exception for him. The boy mastered three years lession in one and passed Entrance examination in first division, being the only student to attain that position. Naren entered the first year Arts class of Presidency College in 1880 at the age of 17. He passed the B.A. in 1884.

Naren used to ask the saints and learned masters one question. Have you seen God ? But nobody answered it satisfactorily and Naren with rational intellect will not believe anybody blindly. He joined Brahmo-Samaj started by Rajarammohan Roy, where God was worshiped in formless form. Some one gave reference to Rama Krishna Pramahans, going into trance at times. Naren met Rama Krishna and asked the same question 'Have you see God, Sir'. Rama Krishna replied 'Yes, I see him just as I see you here, only in much intenser, sense'.

Naren returned to Dakshineswar which was Rama Krishna's temple after a passage to time. The master touched Naren with his foot where upon Naren saw the physical world slowly moving into nothingness. Naren was frightened and cried 'I have still my parents'. The sage laughed saying enough for the present.

After passing BA, Naren took admission in the three-years Law course of BL in Metropolitan Institution of Calcutta. But he had to abandon it due to death of his father in 1884. There was no one else in the family of seven persons now to took after it. There was no fixed income. Even his ancestral house had been grabbed by his relatives and the family forced to shift to a rented house and then to maternal grandmother's home. From comfort Naren was thrown into abject poverty, facing starvation at times. He was poorest of poor in the college and grown weak due to insufficient diet. His family was obviously passing bad time in appalling condition. Naren approached Rama Krishna to pray God to help him in this condition. Rama Krishna said that Naren should go to Mother Kali and request himself for the blessings. Naren went to Kali darshan three times, but always forgot to ask for any worldly gain, rather prayed for her mercy in keeping him engaged in selfless devotion. Rama Krishna was told everything by Naren, who consoled Naren by saying that henceforth his family will not suffer in food and clothing.

Ramakrishna did not attack social custom in the sense of a reformer, but performed such menial services which even the lowest of outcastes will hesitate doing it.

Once Naren came to Rama Krishna and said 'I wish to remain in Samadhi for days to experience the bliss of Godhood'. Rama Krishna was apparently annoyed and disapprovingly said 'Naren you have become so selfish to think of your salvation only what about the humanity at large?' In 1886, Rama Krishna fell ill and asked Naren to be by his side. He passed on some secrets of Brahm-Vidya to Naren and one day a great current of power emerged out of his body and entered Naren's as the spiritual power. Rama Krishna breathed this last on 16 August 1886. Naren established a Math at Barangore, keeping all the disciples of Rama Krishna there. Holy Mother Sarda Devi stood behind the boys. Naren now thought of visiting holy and other places in India to understand the country by direct experience. He first went to Varansi, Ayodha, Lucknow, Agra, Varandavan, Hathras, Haridwar, Rishikesh, but due to illness returned back to the Math. When he left the Math in 1990 he did not return to it till 1897, after the triumphant visit to America and other Western countries. As a wandering monk in 1888 he had a water pot, a copy of the Geeta and 'The Imitation of Chirst' in his bundle. He went to Deer Park in Sarnath (Varanasi) where Buddha gave his first Serman to the five disciples. Next he visited Ayodhya, then to Agra. From Agra, he went on to Vrindavan in early part of August 1888. Before reaching Varindavan, he saw a man smoking hookah by the wayside. Swamiji wanted to have a puff, but this person shrank in horror saying 'I am a low caste untouchable, you are a holy man, I can not pollute you'. But Swamiji said that this caste is man-made and particularly for a sannyashi it is meaningless. He smoked it, and passed ahead to Varindavan. Laer Swamiji told about this incident that it happened to convey the message that one should not despise others, thinking all as children of God.

From Varindavan Swamji wanted to go to Hardwar, then to Kedarnath and Badrinath in Himalyas. He reached Hathras where Sharat Chandra, the Assistant Station Master, became his disciple. Handing over the charge to his substitute, he accompanied Swamiji to Rishikesh. Now Sharat fell ill, so they returned back to Hathras and finally to the Math at Baranagore. Sharat gave up the job and became Sanyashi by the name Sadananda. After some time, they went to Tehri, Mussorie, Rajpur, Dehradun, Rishikesh, Hardwar, Saharanspur and Meerut.

From Meerat, Swamji went to Delhi. In February, Swamiji went to Alwar. Maharaja of Alwar, Mangal Singh had become too much anglicized in thoughts and speaking. He asked point blank to Swamiji that he has no faith in idol-worship. Upon this, Swamiji asked, looking at a Photo, as to whose picture is this ? Staff of the Maharaja answered that it is of the King himself. Swamiji asked the staff to bring it down and spit on it. Every body was horrified. But Swamiji said, it is only a piece of paper after all, why not do as I say. No one obeyed this command. Swamaiji said talking to Maharaja that your people do not consider the photo merely a piece of paper. They take it your reflection in it and hence have the same regard as for you physically. Thus devotees also who worship stone and metal images of god and goddesses do not consider them as mere stones or metal but as a reflection of their deity. Maharaja said with folded hands that he admits his mistake and seek for Swamiji's mercy (A National flag denotes the same sense). Swamiji thereafter, left for mount Abu and reached there on 30 April 1891. Here he met Raja of Khetri. The Raja asked him.

> "Swamiji what is life? "Swamiji replied", Life is the unfoldment and development of a being under circumstances tending to press it down".

The Raja Ajit Singh of Khetri invited Swamiji to his state. Both started together and reached Jaipur and then to Khetri. Once the Raja asked " Swamiji, what is truth". Swamiji replied "Truth your Highness, is one and Absolute. Man travels constantly towards it, from truth to truth, and not from error to truth". Raja also learnt basic principle of science in physics, chemistry and astronomy from Swamiji. Raja also sought for the blessings of Swamiji for a son as heir, which he did not have. Swamiji blessed him and in time a son was born for this kingdom The name Swami Vivekananda was given here by the Maharaja.

After Rajasthan, Swamiji proceeded towards Gujrart and Maharshtra. He visited Ahmedabad and then Wadhwan in Kathiawar. He went to Limbdi whose Raja Thakore Saheb Jaswant Singh for the first time suggested to Swamiji to go to America for religious discourses. He visited Junagarh. He moved to Veraval, Somnath, in Prabhas area. Thereafter, he want to Porbandar and Dwarka where he meditated on the future of India, and visited Bet Dwarka. Further went to Nadiad, Baroda, then to Mahableshwar to see Thakore Saheb in May 1892. The personal diary of Thakore Saheb, which was published in his life time contained the following:

> "............. 12th May: At the end of Yesterday's discussions it was proved that in ancient times the caste system was based only upon Guna and Karma......"

Swamiji then came to Poona, to Khandawa (MP) and to Indore. From Indrore, he proceeded to Bombay by train. At Bombay he met Lok Manya Bal Gangdhar Tilak. Through Kolhapur he went to Belgaum on 15 Oct., 1892. Swamiji went by train to Dharwar and Banglore, At Banglore, he was guest of Dr. P. Palpu, Municipal

Medical Officer, belonging to Ezhava Caste. He told Swamiji that due to his low caste he could not get any job in Kerala in Trawancoare state, also telling about the high handness of Brahmin caste. Swamiji told him "Why do you go after Brahmins ? Find out some good noble person from among your own people and follow him". Soon, Dr. Palpu found Sh. Naranya Guru to be followed. Swamaji then went to Trichur, Cochin Trivancoare, Nagarcoil and finally to Kanayakuamri at Southern-most tip of India. Kanyakumari is the vigin girl manifestation of Divine Mother. Reaching this shrine Swamji prostrated before the image in deep reverence. The rock is about ½ km away from the seashore. Swamiji wanted to go for meditation on this spot;. He had no money for boatmen. He jumped into the shark-infested water and swam across. Sitting here, he passed into deep meditation on past, present and future of India. The centuries of India's past rolled before him. He realized that religion was not the cause for India's downfall, but that true religion was nowhere followed. He saw how the poor have been oppressed. In a subsequent letter dated March 19, 1894 from Chicago, Swamiji wrote about the experience at this rock.

"In view of all this, specially of the poverty and ignorance, I got no sleep........".

Swamiji meditated on this rock for 3 days. From Kanya Kumari, Swamiji proceeded to Rameshwaram Via Madhuari. He met Raja of Ramnad, Bhaskar Setupati, at Madurai. This great enlightened ruler, became admirer and disciple of Swamiji. Swamiji went to Rameshwaram finally, worshiping Shiva Lignum which was established by Lord Ram before marching to Lanka to rescue Sita. Swami Vivekanand's India darshan ended at this sacred place, one of the four dhams (Sacred Place).

Swamiji was asked by someone as to why he came in contact with the Rajas of state. He replied that if he can mould the king and put him on right track then it will be easier to take care of the subject masses of the kingdom through him by establishing benevolent rule.

From Rameshwarm Swami returned to Madras in the beginning of 1893. Liberal and broad ideas of Swamiji were not acceptable to some section of Brahmins, who were engaged in violent discussions with him. Swamiji insisted that it was the duty of educated Indians to spread the ideal of social equality, and to root out the tyranny of priest craft and the evils of perverted caste system.

Money was collected through subscriptions, from Rajas and common people for sending Vivekananda to America for religious conference. Swamiji ordered this collection to be distributed amongst the poor. Swamiji went to Hyderabad at the invitation of people there. Railway station was full with the people and officials. Hindus and Muslims, of Hyderabad state. After giving them his message, Swamiji returned back to Madras. Money was then collected for his journey again and all concerned contributed toward the cause. But Swamiji was still in two minds, and wanted to proceed only when guided by his Master. He wanted clear directions. He got it when lay half-sleeping. He saw Shri Ramakrishna, walking from seashore into the waters of the ocean, and urging him to follow. The vision was a divine command to him.

Ensuring the well being of his mother, he was now ready to go to America. When arrangements of his sailing had been made, secretary of Maharaja of Khetri had come to take him to Khetri to attend celebration on the birth of a son, which had received blessing of Swamiji. Reluctantly, Swamiji agreed modifying the plan to board the ship from Bombay (Maharaja of Khetri also to pay expenses). Swamiji came to Khetri, there was a grand reception, stayed there for few days and finally left for Bombay. On May 31, 1893, he boarded the ship, sailing towards Japan. The ship landed on the western coast of America on July 25, 1893. Travling by train further, he reached Chicago on July 30, putting up in a Hotel. Next day he went to see world fair. He was struck with wonder to see the scientific developments in world, being exhibited there. But Swamiji got a shock to learn that (i) Parliament of Religions would not be opened till second week of September (ii) No one would be admitted delegate to it without proper references (iii) that in any case the time for being so admitted has gone by. This was enough to break his spirit. Even to attend the Parliament as a spectator, he had to wait for one month and his money was fast getting reduced. He came to know that Boston city was relatively cheaper. Traveling by train to Bostan, he met 54 years old Miss Katherine Sanborn. She entered into conversation with him and felt so impressed that she invited Swamiji to her house in Massachusetts near Boston. Through this lady who was a lecturer, Swamiji met Dr. John Henry Wright, a professor in Harvard University, among others. Dr. Wright invited Swamiji to spend few days in end August with him. They discussed various subjects at length. Wright asked Swamiji to speak at the Parliament, but Swamiji said that he has no credentials. Wright replied "To ask, you, Swami, for credentials is like asking sun to state its right to shine". He assured Swamiji that he would get him into the Parliament. He wrote to the Chairman of the Committee for the Selection of Delegates "Here is a man who is more learned than all our learned professors put together". Knowing that

Swamji had had little money, he presented him with the fare to Chicago and gave him letters of introduction of committee in charge of accommodating and providing for oriental delegates. Swamiji took it as the mercy of God on him.

Back at Chicago station, he discovered that he had lost the address of the Chairman. Passerby could not guide him and night was approaching. He passed the night in an empty box in the railway yard. The person who was to shake America after two days, was sleeping without food in such a helpless condition. In the morning he came to the most fashionable area of the city. He was very hungry and therefore, started begging and asking for the address of the Committee. He was treated rudely because of his strange cloths. In disgust, he set on a spot on street side to go further by the will of God. The door of a house opposite him opened and a lady came to him asking whether he is a delegate to the Parliament of Religions. Swamiji told about the loss of address. She invited him into her house attended him properly, promising that after the breakfast, she herself would take him to the office of the Committee. She was Mrs. George W. Hale. Giving his credentials (by Mr. Wright) he was gladly accepted as delegate.

Parliament of Religion which was being held to mark the Colombian expedition over discovery of America, was the World's greatest event at that time. It opened on September 11,1893. Delegates of all religions came from all part of the world, becoming the assembly of world's humanity. On the dias set the leading delegates of various religions, on the centre being the highest priest of Roman Catholic Church. On the left and right were oriental delegates. In numerical order Vivekanand's position was 31. The hall below and gallery above was packed with six to seven thousand men and woman representing the best of their nation and religion. The delegates were introduced one by one, they stepped up and spoke briefly. Says Swamiji, "I was so nervous that I could not venture to speak in the morning. Other Indian (Hindu) delegates had come prepared with ready-made speeches". To speak extempo in front of such huge gathering of intellectuals required extra-ordinary confidence and skill. In the afternoon the Chairman insisted and Vivekananda arose. His face emitted radiance, the audience grew intent in silence, fall of a pin on the floor could be heard. Then Swamiji, bowing mentally to goddesses Sarswati, addressed the audience as, "Sisters and Brothers of America". Before he could utter further words, the whole Parliament was caught up in a frenzy. They stood up on their feet, and such a thunderous was the applause for more than two minutes continuously that it appeared as if the Parliament had gone mad with enthusiasm. With great difficulty, the order was restored, to allow Swamiji to speak further. He spoke on the Universal Religion, essence of Hinduism being the Mother of Religions, which has taught the world tolerance and acceptance. The short speech delivered is reproduced at the end of this chapter. The whole Assembly was captivated by the Universality of appeal in the name of ' most ancient order of monks in the world'. A lady as an eye witness recalled "......... I saw scores of women walking over the benches to get near him, and I said to myself, well, my lad, if you can resist that onslaught you are indeed a God"! The morning newspapers were full of praise for him, some going to the extent of calling him Messiah of the New World or the 'Prophet of New Dispensation'. His life-size pictures were placed on the streets of Chicago. New York Herald one of the most popular and widely read paper editorially remarked "He is undoubtedly the greatest figure in the Parliament or Religions. After hearing him we feel how foolish it is to send missionaries to this learned nation". And it were the Christians all the way to be so broad-mended to say all this (though some jealous ones of them tried to bring him down, every religion having such fanatics to express hatred). He read his detailed paper on Hinduism later, when the hall was overflowing its capacity. He spoke many times in the Scientific Section of the conference and its President Mr. M.M. Snel became great friend of him. As soon as he used to walk towards the platform for speaking, there used to be enthusiastic applause for him. In fact to ensure the crowds sitting till end, his talks were kept at the end of the programme. After the Parliament was over a Lecture Bureau was organized for him for various cities of America. At one place, a hall was booked for second floor, but other floor below including the ground was overflowing in the hope that if he can not be seen speaking, atleast his voice can be heard. Many Americans became his disciples and some came to India as well. After about two years of lecturing in America, he came to Paris and London. There also he received warm welcome and made some as his disciples.

After leaving England and travling through Europe, Vivekananda landed in Cylon on January 15, 1897. From there his journey to Caluctta was wading through the sea of humanity. Raja of Ramnad pulled his carriage through street by himself, disengaging the horses. At one Railway Station, the train was not to halt but people lay themselves on the tracks, forcing the train to stop and Swamiji to come out to give his darshan. On his first landing on Indian soil at Rameswaram, where the king himself had pulled his carriage without horses, Swamji said;

> "........ to worship shiva not in images alone, but in the poor in the weak, and in the deceased....... The

Raja of Ramanad was besides himself with the spirit of the occasion, and the very next day fed and clothed thousands of poor people...."

When the top intellectuals of the world had heard and accepted his message in the west, his words had impact on what he said in India. The words were not merely coming from the lips or pen but form the heart soaked in spirituality. Writing to a lady in his letter dated 3rd January 1899, Swamiji said;

"........ To advance oneself towards freedom-physical, mental, and spiritual- and help others to do so, is the supreme prize of man. Those social rules which stand in the way of the unfoldment of this freedom are injurious and steps should be taken to destroy them speedily. Those institutions should be encouraged by which man advance in the path of freedom. Complete Works Vol-V P.147

Swami Vivekanada had shaken the mental slavery and social rigidities of Indians, and racial pride of the white people, without malice in his spiritual heart.

Swami reached Calcutta amidst great welcome and established Rama Krishna Mission with universal aim of serving humanity. He took active part to serve the people in the time of plague, prepared even to sell the newly acquired land for Belur Math. Even the English government appreciated the efforts. He visited places in Rajasthan again, went to Almora, Kashmir, Lahore, Darjeeling, Amarnath and Bodh-Gaya. He established Advaita Ashram at Mayavati (Almora-Nainital belt) with the help of English couple. Last Visited Kamakhya, Shillong and Dacca. Finally, he came to Belur Math, Calcutta and entered into deep meditation on 4 July 1902, never returning back into physical body.

Swami Vivekananda's Address

At the world's parliament of religions, Chicago, 1893

Response to Welcome

At the inaugural session, 11 September 1893

Sisters and Brothers of America,

It fills my heart with joy unspeakable to rise in response to the warm and cordial welcome which you have given us. I thank you in the name of the most ancient order of monks in the world; I thank you in the name of the mother of religions; and I thank you in the name of the millions and millions of Hindu People of all classes and sects.

My thanks, also, to some of the speakers on this platform who, referring to the delegates from the Orient, have told you that these men from far-off nations may well claim the honour of bearing to different lands the idea of toleration. I am proud to belong to a religion which has taught the world both tolerance and universal acceptance. We believe not only in universal toleration, but we accept all religions as true. I am proud to belong to a nation which has sheltered the persecuted and the refugees of all religions and all nations of the earth. I am proud to tell you that we have gathered in our bosom the purest remnant of the Israelites, who came to southern India and took refuge with us in the very year in which their holy temple was shattered to pieces by Roman tyranny. I am proud to belong to the religion which has sheltered and is still fostering the remnant of the grand Zoroastrian nation. I will quote to you, brethren, a few lines from a hymn which I remember to have repeated from my earliest boyhood, which is every day repeated by millions of human beings; 'As the different streams having their sources in different places all mingle their water in the sea, so, O Lord, the different paths which men take though different tendencies, various though they appear, crooked or straight, all lead to thee'.

The present convention, which is one of the most august assemblies ever held, is in itself a vindication, a declaration to the world, of the wonderful doctrine preached in the Gita: 'Whosoever comes to Me, through whatsoever form, I reach him; all men are struggling through paths which in the end lead to Me'. Sectarianism, bigotry, and its horrible descendant, fanaticism, have long possessed this beautiful earth. They have filled the earth with violence, drenched it often and often with human blood, destroyed civilization, and sent whole nations to despair. Had it not been for these horrible demons, human society would be far more advanced than it is now. But their time is come; and I fervently hope that the bell that tolled this morning in honour of this convention may be the death-knell of all fanaticism, of all persecutions with the sword or with the pen, and of all uncharitable feelings between persons wending their way to the same goal.

Appendix-1

Caste of Guna and Karma in Bhagwad Geeta

"The four-fold caste* has been created by Me according to the differentiation of *Guna* and *Karma;* though I am the author thereof know me as non-doer and immutable. " Geeta IV:13

*Chaturvarna means four-fold caste, that is, four varnas.

Varna is shade or color. A man is what his basic temperament is. The temperament is what basic texture of thought is. The finest form of food or matter is the thought. As a man thinks, so he becomes, is a deep psychological fact, asserted so forcefully by James Allen in his masterpiece 'As a man thinketh'. Now, in Indian 'Yoga Sutra', the different type of thoughts have different shade or color. The thoughts fall basically in three types, Sattva, Rajas and Tamas. These are three Gunas of thoughts. Sattva is white, Rajas is red and Tamas is black. The varna of an individual is the varna or color of these basic thoughts of him.

Gunas: In Indian philosophical thought (particularly Sankhya philosophy given by Kapila) the basic constituents of Prakriti or nature or matter are these three Gunas, i.e., Sattva, Rajas and Tamas. The Prakriti includes not only the visible external matter, but also ego, mind, intelligence (Geeta Chapter VII:4, 5). So comprehensive is the operation of these Gunas that entire universe in all its expressions can be said to be the outcome of Gunas. "The whole of this creation is deluded by objects evolved from the three modes of Nature-Sattva, Rajas and Tamas hence it does not know Me, who am above these and imperishable "(Geeta VII:13). We can divide the physical world into these Gunas like this: all matter (dull and inert) is Tamasic, all energy (active state) as Rajasic and all knowledge/ consciousness as Sattvic. Almost the whole aspects of human expressions/behavior/thoughts have been defined in terms of these Gunas in Bhagwad Geeta, in the following slokas:

Chapter XVII	*Expression of Gunas*
Sloka 3, Faith	Whatever the nature of faith, that verily he is
Sloka 4, Worship	**Sattvic**, worship gods **Rajasic**, worship Yaksas **Tamsic**, worship Spirits and ghosts.
Sloka 8,9,10, Food	**Sattvic**, take nourishing and agreeable food. **Rajasic**, take bitter, acid, salted, hot and burning food. **Tamasic**, take stale, polluted and impure food.
Sloka 11,12,13, Sacrifice	**Sattivic**, offer it as a duty without desire for fruit.

	Rajasic, offer to get fruit
	Tamasic, offer without faith, only as formality.
Sloka 17,18,19, Penance	**Sattvic**, perform with supreme faith without desire for fruit.
	Rajasic, perform for winning respect, honour and worship
	Tamasic, perform to torture one's mind and body or with the object of causing injury to others.
Sloka 20,21,22 Gift	**Sattvic**, give with the idea that it is one's duty and with due regard to time place and recipient.
	Rajasic, give with the object of getting one's name or some service in return or grudgingly.
	Tamasic, give at improper place and time in disrespectful manner to undeserving person.

Chapter XVIII

Sloka 20, 21, 22, Knowledge	**Sattivic**, obtains the knowledge of the one imperishable—being appearing as divided among beings. **Rajasic**, obtains the knowledge that all being are separate. **Tamasic**, obtains the knowledge that an individual is whole, there is no rationale and truth in anything
Sloka 23, 24, 25, Action	**Sattvic**, does it without passion and prejudice. **Rajasic**, does it for his ego and to seek enjoyment. **Tamasic**, does it without understanding, causing loss to oneself and injury to others.
Sloka 26, 27, 28, Ego	**Sattvic**, is un attached, firm and unconcernedabout success and failure **Rajasic**, is passion ate, greedy, given to violence and impure conduct. **Tamasic**, is arrogant

	lacking in self-control and piety and generally vulgar.
Sloka 30, 31, 32, Reason	**Sattvic**, knows what is wrong, what is right, what should be done and what not, what is bondage and what is liberation. **Rajasic**, does not know what is right what is wrong and what should be done and what should not be done. **Tamasic**, is envelop-ed in ignorance, thinks the wrong to be right.
Sloka 33, 34, 35, Firmness	**Sattvic**, firmly controls the mind and senses. **Rajasic**, firmly holds on to prosperity, pleasure and Dharma. **Tamasic**, firmly does not abandon sleep, fear, despon-dency and arrogance.
Sloka 36, 37, 38, 39, Joy	**Sattvic**, find joy in meditation and worship and in those practices which appear like poison in the beginning but nectar in the end.

Rajasic, find joy in attachment to senses. **Tamasic**, find joy in that which deadens soul and in that which is derived from sleep, indolence and carelessness.

Appendix-2

Important Dates of Indian History

3000 – 800 BC	Vedas
1000 BC or back	Mahabharta, Ramayana is earlier to it.
599 – 527 BC	Vardhman Mahavira
563 – 483 BC	Gautam Buddha
327 – 325 BC	Invasion by Alexander
306 BC	Selaucos, the general of Alexander defeated by Chandragupta Maurya.
322 – 298 BC	Rule of Chandragupta Maurya.
298 – 273 BC	Rule of Bindusara
273 – 232 BC	Rule of Ashoka
191 – 185 BC	Rule of Brahadratha
185 BC	Pusyamitra Sunga – a Brahmin general, kills Brahdratha on prade ground.
185 – 148 BC	Rule of Pusyamitra Sunga
165 – 33 BC	Bactarian Greeks
58 BC	Vikramaditya of Ujjain

4 BC – 30 AD	Jesus Christ
130 – 150 AD	Sakas
120 – 160 AD	Kushans, Kanishka
106 – 130 AD	Andhras 100 AD
	Chola Kings
320 – 335 AD	Chandragupta-I
335 – 375 AD	Samudragupta
380 – 413 AD	Chandragupta-II
405 – 411 AD	Visit of Chinese Traveler Fa-Hien
414 – 455 AD	Kumar Gupta
475 – 495 AD	Buddha Gupta
495 – 510 AD	Bhanu Gupta
476 AD	Arya Bhatta Born
485 – 580 AD	Huna's invasion
580 – 647 AD	Harsh Vardhan of Kannouj rule
629 – 645 AD	Hiuen-Tsang(Yuan-Chwang) Chinese traveller visited India.
647 – 1192 AD	Rajputs rulers - Chauhans, Chandels, Rathoors, Parmars, Gurjar Pratiharas and Cholas (in South).
570 – 632 AD	Prophet Mohammed
712 AD	Mohammed Bin Quasim conquered Sindh.
1000 – 1026 AD	Mahmud of Ghazni invaded India 17 times (destroyed Somnath in 1025 AD)
1191 AD	Prithvi Raj Chauhan defeated Mohammed Ghori at Trai.

1192 AD	Mohammed Ghori defeated Prithivi Raj Chauhan of Delhi and established Muslim rule.
1221 AD	Chengiz Khan invaded India
1290 – 1320 AD	Khilji Dynasty
1320 – 1412 AD	Tughlaq Dynasty
1398 AD	Timur Lung's attack at Delhi
1411 – 1527 AD	Sant Ravidas
1451 – 1526 AD	Lodhi Dynasty
1469 – 1538 AD	Guru Nanak and Bhakti movement around 1500 AD
1497 – 1623 AD	Tulsidas
1526 – 1857 AD	Mughal Dynasty
1526 AD	First battle of Panipat- Babar defeated Ibrahim Lodhi
1527 AD	Battle of Khanwa – Babar defeated Rajput King Rana Sanga
1556 D	Second battle of Panipat-Akbar defeated Hemu.
1576 AD	Battle of Haldighati-Maha Rana Pratap against Akbar
1627 – 1680 AD	Chatterpati Shivaji, 1674 AD coronation of Shivaji
1659 – 1707 AD	Reign of Aurangzeb

1699 AD	Creation of Khalsa by Guru Govind Singh
1739 AD	Invasion of Nadir Shah
1761 AD	Third battle of Panipat- Marathas defeated by Abdali
1801 AD	Maharaja Ranjeet Singh coronated at Lahore
1857 AD	First Indian war of Independence against Britishers, won by latter.
1824 – 1883 AD	Swami Dayananda
1863 – 1902	Swami Vivekananda
1914 – 1918	First World War
1939 –1945	Second World War
1947	India achieved Independence
1950	Constitution of Indian came in force and India became a Republic
1952	First General Election held
1962	China invaded India in Ladakh and North East
1965	India Pakistan conflict on Kashmir
1971	India Pakistan war, Pakistan was defeated and Bangla Desh created.

Appendix-3

Rendering The Public Service

In India getting a government job is not only an employment to support oneself and family but also an opportunity to acquire status, connections with powers that be, either to render selfless service to the people for inner satisfaction or to use official powers to make money, get promotions and enjoy privileges, legitimiate and illegitimate. Immediately after the Independence, Government job was considered as a power seat to exercise authority over the people, on the lines of Britishers. People who gave Constitution unto themselves in 1949 and therefore, the ultimate master of the Governance, found themselves to be the dust (particularly the lower strata) to be kicked around by any person of authority in whatsoever field (with honorable exceptions of course in every such field). Some people also no doubt had their own fault of preferring to remain unenlightened, without higher cause guiding their spirit, as they voted (and still vote) even the hardened criminal to power. What will such a politician perpetuate except corruption, partialities, injustices, social and political discriminations and disturbances. A conscientious bureaucracy could balance to some extent such political offshoots, but if they themselves be more than willing to carry out their dictates for their own weaknesses, comforts and selfishness, who will save and serve the people?

Leaving aside some exemplary sacrifices by few public servants to contain their erratic masters for wider public cause, even normal will (with human errors) to serve people is not seen in the day to day administration. Mostly the establishments remain exploitive in nature and will continue to remain so unless higher sense of fair play dawns on the functionaries. Once one gives up his all to acquire higher powers, he is unlikely to get back those lost virtues on attaining the desired goal (seat of authority). Higher sense of public service need not always be expressed in the form of martyrdom, but even reasonable amount of conscience can keep the state machinery greased and running without friction. Problem comes when there is downright failure to protect the right and deserving and on the contrary all efforts made to cover up the wrong done against the employee, the public and even the nation. Whenever a cohesive group is formed in the organization from top to bottom, either it renders an excellent service as a **team** to the people or it works like a **gang** of criminals to aggrandize, loot and plunder, in which there is no chance of appeal against the excesses of any employee to his superior. It all depends on the top man of this group and his evolutionary stage. Formation of such criminal groups to share money amongst themselves and protect each other with the powers vested in different authorities, is the common feature of today's corruption in various sensitive Departments/Government Bodies. The employee does not remain a member of organization his is to be serve but converts to that of a gang through which he exploits the public, rendering service being a secondary ritual. Dimension of corruption shall remain controllable and punishable in organizations where such gangs are not formed.

Public service (Private sector not being discussed) is being rendered by the sincere and dedicated at one end of the scale and by the grossly corrupt and utterly selfish at its other extreme. Majority in between, have different degrees of the dedication depending upon their social or personal traits. Those falling in the range of enlightened self-interest are asset to the Government or organization, as they do not prop up their self advancement at the cost of public interest but rather alongwith it. Those falling outside this range, harm the organization in one way or the other, the final outcome of which is the tortuous delays, injustice or victimization, financial strains, insecurities, sufferings and dissatisfactions. The aim to take oneself in the lightened arena, however, is not easy to achieve as one has to come to it by crossing a river which is at times infested with dangerous crocodiles of self interest, sharks of inflated ego, and whirlpools of deep prejudices ever ready to swallow others, with state power vested in them. Since the Prakriti or nature generally protects the well-meaning individual, this belief can give support to the struggling one against the odds. Of course, this is valid only when he uses his own sources of intelligence, tact and riskiness.

In very brief, I am giving below the gist of true events (not in specific details) which were encountered by me, ultimately with success and peace of mind. These do not contain the ones of personal nature like increments not being released for first five years with absolutely no reasons for withholding the same for which appeal to higher authorities like CAG made no difference. Since I carry no negative impression of the happenings and the purpose here is not to expose individuals or buttress any view point but only to express the principles involved or the nature of problem existing in the system, the names and places have become irrelevant and therefore not mentioned. The aim is to give a cross section of rugged surface of public administration faced for a period of about 35 years to show its nature and functioning. Though limited to a particular field, some tendencies are the common phenomenon of work culture elsewhere too.

While serving as a junior Engineer in Government service to start with, I applied for leave to prepare and appear for engineering degree level examination of the country's premier Institute (not a regular college course but in which one could appear in different papers by studying at home and pass in any number of attempts). Not a single day's leave for preparation was sanctioned to me; it was only for exact exam. days. Despite this, I was able to clear all the nine papers of this second and final part in the first attempt without any coaching etc. This was a rare event considering that I was in hectic field assignment. My immediate boss greatly surprised informed his superior about this achievement, whose only reaction was 'What about the pending work'. My boss informed him in my presence, 'Nil Sir'. Later, I was selected in class A Engineering service of the Govt. of India as a direct recruit through the All India Examination Conducted by UPSC.

While in the office posting, I happened to be a witness for my colleague who was assaulted verbally by his junior official in the hall. My act was not taken kindly by my boss and his next. Till date I do not know what sort of conscience the above two superiors possessed, as the assaulting junior was a known bad element. Despite my performance being the best and visible one (having personally dealt an emergency project with zero delay), I could not get my next promotion even though it was a non-selection post, the Departmental rules for it requiring only satisfactory confidential report (CR). My representation led not to my promotion but to change of criteria of CRs for the post as 'Good' for future.

On the regular promotion after delay of one year, I was given the charge of an heavy field unit, newly created, without staff. Despite this tremendous handicap, the unit developed heavy workload. By next year some staff joined and my unit was the one amongst the heaviest loaded in the Department. The appreciations from the client Deptts. flowed freely on their own. But this was not possible without initiating some deterrent action against those who were stumbling blocks either as staff or powerful contractors of influence. They practically launched a plethora of complaints on daily basis on any flimsy ground. Apart from delivering the public goods, I was also engaged in replying to queries from nearly all quarters of Vigilance and Administration, none to support but only find fault. As the projects were delivered in time and with quality, even the toughest scrutiny by Vigilance could not discover any irregularities. I remained on this posting for 5 years, frustrating the design of the complainants for premature transfer. The top bosses of the organization found no cause to act unjustifiably.

My next posting was on deputation to a reputed Development Authority. Seeing my previous performance, I was given a sought-for posting, which I politely refused in writing. Afterwards, I was on an emergency project involving day and night working without any holidays including Sundays. It was an atmosphere of terror, partly justified and partly created to pressurize the officers to commit irregularities. The project requiring to be completed for a national cause, the staff was scared that any misreporting against them could lead to their removal from service without appeal.

Holding on to the solid base of devotion to duty, I in individual capacity objected in writing to that part of the project functioning which was outside the requirement of timely delivery of it and created only for self-interest. It had on effect, the relief was provided to all in the form of intermittent holidays once a fortnight (thereby increasing their efficiency) and more transparent working. The Chief appreciated my 'courage' publically for having suggested positive remedial measures. It was later inferred at the time of my next promotion, that he had given high grading of CR to me. The project was completed in time, all including me got apprecation certificate.

Following the above posting in the same grade, I was placed in the quality cell of this Authority which was created after a lot of buildings had collapsed due to poor quality and the public pressure was mounting to wind up the organization. My performance of duty in this cell without any care of pressures influences and threats (of course always keeping practical side of field in mind) brought together those who were indulging freely in baffling corruption and irregularities of high orde, having no concern for the public interest. A Physical mafia attack was launched on me while I was returning from my duty on a two-wheeler scooter. At just the start of attack by iron rods on me, with helmet on my head, providential help came instantly in the form of my colleague in a jeep appearing on the spot. This was not his route and he was there by sheer chance. He took me to hospital where after some treatment I was discharged. But the organization was charged and most of the top men visited my house in the night. It was a prominent item news on all the nation dailies with several Parliament Questions asked (without my knowledge). The quality was definitely improved for years to come without any collapse taking place thereafter.

I was back to my parent Department and was serving under an officer who was extremely negative and who will not leave even a tiny error unexploited for the purpose of condemnation. But this was nothing compared to deep prejudice of the Head of organization who will deny me the next promotion on any available pretext, despite my excellent records. Earlier, he attempted to exclude my name on the plea that I am outside the Deptt.. (such exclusion was entirely against the rules) but the panel had to be cancelled on my representation that there are others in the panel who are on deputation. Again he prepared ad-hoc panel excluding my name, against which I represented that now I am back in the Deptt. and not even on deputation. The immediate boss, however, was not happy to forward my above simple representation and for this I had to request the Deptt. to shift me to a relatively insignificant post in the office, though it was not accepted. This panel too was cancelled and orders came from the Ministry to prepare regular panel, where my name found place in it, there being no ground for exclusion. But this Head will simply not issue my promotion order, even using arguments that he is waiting for deputationist to return back, the deputationist who were not in the panel but those who were to return in future for whom a huge lot of additional posts were available as a result of cadre review, waiting for formal orders. This Head went for long leave and the one who took over charge from him issued my promotion orders on his own, as by now everyone was aware of this case of gross injustice. On return from the leave, the earlier Head was so infuriated that he issued my transfer order to hard and remote area of India, where no one had acted on his earlier transfer orders. Being mid-session, I represented to the Govt. bringing out all above facts of prejudices (I had never worked under this Head at any level, his prejudice was not personal) which were considered and I was retained till the end of current session, after which I joined this hard area posting. But my basic theme of representation against the grossest form of provable misconduct by a Head remained unaddressed and this person (Head) was given plum U.N. assignment after the retirement, even by a so called secular central Government of that time.

I had pleasant experience in working in this tribal area 20 years back because of peace and purity of environment, though reaching some of its places was a tough job. I had the healthy team spirit with my seniors in early stage, till they were replaced by others. I had the satisfaction of focusing my attention on completion of long pending bridges over rivers in different terrain of deep gorges and fast currents. This was to provide instant relief to the people by shortening their hill journey on foot. The reasons for pendency was that the officials were not interested to take risks and responsibilities while easy works were available to use their discretions in spending funds. My immediate juniors and the senior were non-tribals. In the last stage of tenure, some of the direct juniors were seen to be having no regards whatsoever for any norms, financial and administrative after having enticed the local political leadership through mis-information about working conditions. The requirement of flexible condition in difficult areas was confused with loose working in all areas. It was very easy to draw line between the two if one was interested in doing so. Such juniors were literally working under the law of Jungle, being master of their will throwing all norms to winds, even the written directions of higher authorities. Themselves extending leave and even absconding, they will terminate the service of non-tribal labourers in employment for 5 years for proceeding on leave with prior intimation. They will not take back them despite written directions of competent higher authority, because they had kept some one in their place. The papers for urgent project works will not be forwarded for several months but still manage to get blind structure passed for delay against all from the senior. This my immediate senior was a personification of sadism and negativism fused together, generally believing in double standards. Though having one of the most prestigious field postings of the Deptt. in the state., I wrote to him, with copy to the highest in the state administration, to recommend my transfer to any place in the state, as this loose working can not deliver any public goods. There was no action or response from the senior, as he was quite satisfied by my embarrassment caused due to his direct support to this junior. He will order me to furnish by a fixed date huge records (specified by him) on grave irregularities, but quickly abandon the pursuit after having received such records and discovering the involvement of above juniors with no role of mine in the same. There were missing links in his conscience which could not be bridged over only by his professional intelligence, which he no doubt possessed. The state finally acted by ensuring graceless exit of this lot after I had left the place to be back in my parent Department.

Coming back from this tenure, I was posted on a prestigious big project. This was competed in time, within the cost and with required quality. The client was so satisfied that I and some others were given the appreciation letter by the Head of the organization, stating "........ I am happy that you have .... earned laurels for the Department. I take this opportunity to congratulate on your achievements". But such achievements were not possible without properly dealing with some officers totally devoid of duty-consciousness. Since they were having links with higher levels, there was no possibility of shifting them elsewhere. I gradually reduced their quantum of charge to the barest minimum, thus limiting the damage to small area. The project was completed to the satisfaction by the dedicated team once the non-performing elements were shown their worth and not allowed to affect the morale of dedicated officials.

Rather than exercising self-control, the manipulating aspect was seen to be the operating system wherever failures were noticed. Putting up some cross-section of the public service, I am left with no desire to repeat such experiences which definitely occurred later in my career, some of different variety. Suffice it to say that finally I reached the high level of my Department, heading one of its most prestigious Zone. There too, I faced some juniors who (backed by higher levels of the Department) utilized their inefficient and irresponsible working to lower down the image of this Zone. But again, as I was able to form a team of dedicated officers, the good and visible performance alround (action taken wherever it was not so) saw me retired with complete satisfaction and grace. Perhaps, my rural background in a 'low caste' (Western U.P) where working in the field even as a child, was the only way to manage existence, provided training ground to face vicissitudes of life standing up and looking ahead.

• Babu Jagjivan Ram, 120
Delhi Special Police Establishment, 257
Deputy Magistrate, 179
Dharma Shastra, 14, 44, 99
Dharam Sutra, 99
Dhritrastra, 78, 97-98
Divine Abode, 73
Divine Life Society, 172
DPSE Act, 252-53
Drafting Committee, 177
Duryodhana, 98, 277

E

Earth, 14
East India Company, 152, 154
Economic Offences Wing, 252
Ego, 14
Eknath, 76
English Culture, 18
Eternal Cycle, 30
Eternal Light, 72
External World, 159

F

Fa-Hien, 104, 142-43, 263
• Chinese Traveller, 104
Famines, 154-55
Fire, 14
Famous Chinese Travellers, 142-43
• Yuan-Chwang, 142-43

G

Gandhiji, 181
General Dyer, 178
• Jallianwala Bagh, 178
George W. Bush, 94
• President of America, 18
George Washington, 18
Germany, 182
German Philosopher, 34, 46
• Prof. F. Max Meuellor, 34, 46
Ghazni, 110
Gitanjatli, 178
Galaxy of Sages and Saints, 261
• Adi Sankara Charya, 261
• Chaitanya Mahaprabhu, 261
• Guru Nanak, 261
• Kabir, 261
• Lord Buddha, 261
• Ramanuja, 261
• Swami Dayananda, 261
• Rama Krishna Paramhansa, 261
• Ramna Maharishi, 261
• Sant Tuka Ram, 261
• Swami Vivekananda, 261
God of Justice, 97
Good Nature, 76
Gopal Krishna Gokhle, 182
Greek Ambassador, 102
• Meghasthenes, 102
Guna, 303
Gunas, 14
Gupta Empire, 263
Gupta Period, 142
Gupta Rulers, 104
Guru Gobind Singh, 116, 147, 263
Guru Nank, 76, 148
Guru Ravidas, 114
• A Chamar Sant, 114
Gayatri Mantra, 167

H

Hanged, 181
- Ashfaqullah Khan, 181
- Rajinder Lahiri, 181
- Ram Prasad Bismil, 181
- Roshan Singh, 181

Harish Chandra, 75
Harsh Vardhan, 263
Harshwardhan's Death, 106
Harshvardhan Rule, 106
Harvard University, 296
Hastinapur, 62
Hierarchy, 141
Hinduism, 77
Hindu-Muslim Unity, 183
Hindu Philosophy, 21, 240
Hindu Religion, 13, 21, 61, 170
Hindu Scriptures, 41
Hindu Society, 13, 240
Homo Erectus, 25
Homo Sapiens, 25, 31
Home Rule, 178
Home Rule Movement, 264
Himalayan Blunder, 95
Huen-Tsang, 263

I

IIM Lucknow, 244
IIT Kanpur, 243
Iltutmish, 110
- Ruler of Gwalior, 110

Indian National Congress, 178
Indian Oil Corporation, 244
Indian Philosophy, 40
Internal Universe, 162
Ishwar Chandra Vidya Sagar, 179
Dr. Ishwari Prasad, 115

J

Jai Chand, 110
- king of Kannauj, 110

Jai Prakash Narayan, 182
- Freedom Fighter of 1942, 182

Jalaluddin Khilji, 110-11
James Allen, 164, 204, 267
Japan, 182
Jatindra Nath Das, 181
- Fasted unto Death, 181

Jawahar Lal Nehru, 183
- First Prime Minister of India, 183

J.C. Bose, 160
Jessica Lal Murder, 244
Jesus Christ, 159, 240, 277
Jhali Rani, 146
- Mother-in-law of Mira, 146
- Wife of Rana Sanga, 146

Joyatiba Phule, 174
Justice M.G. Ranade, 147

K

Kabir, 76
Kali Temple of Calcutta, 236
Kanishka, 104
Kannyakumari, 294
Karl Marx, 17
Karma, 14, 268
- Agami Karma, 269
- Prarabdha Karma, 268
- Sanchita Karma, 268

Kaurvas, 78, 145
Kaushik Brahmin, 80

Kautilya, 63
Kavasa Ailush, 21
- A Composer in Rig Veda, 21

Khudi Ram Bose, 181
- Threw Bomb, 181
- Muzaffarpur Judge, 181

King Parvataka, 101
King Ugrasena, 61
Krishna, 64-66, 77, 140, 238
Kshatriya, 13, 75
Kurukshetra Battle Field, 61
Kushinara, 235

L

Lal Bahadur Shastri, 183
- Prime Minister of India, 1965, 183

Lala Lajpat Rai, 180
- Lion of Punjab, 180

Laws of Manu, 44
Laws of Mother Nature, 13
Law of Karma, 274
Laxman, 75
Lokmanya Bal Gangadhar Tilak, 180
- Mandalay Jail, 180

Lord Buddha, 76, 83, 131, 276
Lord Death, 190, 278, 281
- Dharmaraj, 278

Lord Krishna, 22, 43, 53, 56, 60, 91, 195, 239, 247
Lord Rama, 68-70, 73, 187, 294
Lord Shiva, 75
Lord Shiva's Curse, 52
Lord Vishnu, 75, 148
Louis Pasteur, 26
- French Scientist, 26

Low Castes, 72
Lumbini, 233

M

Madras High Court, 64
Magesthenes, 63
- Famous Greek, 63
- Ambassador to Chandragupta Maurya's Court, 63

Mahabharata, 14, 75, 77, 98, 288
Mahapadmananda, 100
Maharaja of Alwar, 280
Maharaja of Baroda, 176
Maharaja of Patiala, 280
Maharaja Ranjit Singh, 263
Maharana Pratap, 113, 263, 279
Maharani Laxmi Bai, 263
Mahatma Gandhi, 16, 177-78, 183
- Nathu Ram Godse, 183

Mahmud of Ghazni, 62, 93, 105, 108-09, 143
Mandal Commission, 62
Marriage, 141
Maurya Empire, 101-02, 134
Maratha Empire, 175
Maurya Period, 21, 104, 263
Mulayam Singh Yadav, 250
- Chief Minister, 250
- Uttar Pradesh, 250

Messiah of the New World, 60, 298
Mira Bai, 146, 149
- Devotee of Krishna, 146
- Disciple of Ravi Das, 146

Modern Period, 22
Mohammad Ghori, 106, 109-10

Moro Pant Pingle, 118
Mrs. George W. Hale, 297
Mughal Empire, 113, 116, 149, 151
- Aurangzeb, 149

Mundaka Upanishad, 87
Munshi Ram, 176
Muslim Travellers, 263
- Al-Beruni, 263
- Ferishta, 263

N

Nagarcoil, 294
Namdev, 76, 148
Nanda, 101
Narayan Guru, 76, 170
NASA, 43, 161, 276
National Highway Authority of India, 243
Newton, 164
NHAI, 243-44
Nishad Raj, 71
Nishad Raj Guha, 72

O

OBC, 62-63, 250
Occupation, 141
Olympics, 161
Other Backward Castes, 62

P

Pakistan, 183
Palomer Telescope, 238
- California, 238

Pandavas, 22, 98, 145
- Arjuna, 98
- Bhima, 98
- Nakul, 98
- Yudhistir, 98

Parshurama, 100
Patanjali, 198
Patliputra, 101
Dr. Paul Brunton, 123, 159, 202-03
Pondicherry, 177
Position of Vedas, 52
Presidency College, 179
- Calcutta, 179

Prevention of Corruptiuon Act, 252
Prime Minister, 120
- Smt. Indira Gandhi, 120

Prithvi Raj Chauhan, 110, 263
Priyadarshini Moatto, 245
Prophet Mohammad, 264
Prophet of New Dispensation, 298
Pt. Jawahar Lal Nehru, 15
Pt. Motilal Nehru, 182
Puranas, 14
Pushyamitra Sunga, 104
- Brahmin Commander-in-Chief, 104
- Killed Brihdratha, 104
- Grandson of Asoka, 104
- On the Parade Ground, 104

Q

Quest of the Overself, 171
Quit India Movement, 173, 183
Qutub Minar, 159
Qutub-ud-din-Aibak, 110

R

Rabindra Nath Tagore, 16, 26, 177-78

- National Anthem of India, 177
- Our Universe, 65

Raikva, 21
Raja Ajit Singh, 292
- Khetri, 292

Raja of Ettaypuram, 180
Raja of Ramnad, 299
Rajagriha, 235
- Capital of Magadh, 235

Raja Ram Mohan Roy, 168
- Born in a Brahmin Family, 168
- Established Brahmo Samaj, 168
- Learned Man of
- English, French, Greek, Persian, Sanskrit, 168

Dr. Rajendra Prasad, 174, 182
Rama, 71-72
Rama Krishna Mission, 15, 169, 235, 240, 300
Rama Krishna Paramhansa, 22, 140, 236-37, 240, 286, 289
Rama and Sita, 145
Ramana Maharishi, 171
Ramanand, 140
Ramanuj, 76
Ramayana, 21, 71,148, 288
Rameshwaram, 295
Ranade, 175
Rani Padmini, 263
Rani Rasmani, 21
- Builder of Dakshineshwar Kali Temple, 21
- Calcutta, 21

Ravana, 71-72, 277
Ravi Das, 146
Right of Knowledge, 51
Rig Veda, 55, 96
Rishi Gautam, 193
Rishi Kavash Ailush, 34
Rishi Nahusa, 79
Rishi Valmiki, 79
- Author of Ramayana, 97

Rishi Vashistha, 187
- Court of Dashratha, 187

Robert Clive, 124
- Clerk in East India Company, 124
- Governor General of Bengal, 124

Rock Edict, 102
Round Table Conference, 177-78
Russia, 77-78

S

Sage Kapila, 13
Saibaba of Shirdi, 76, 170-71
Sambuka, 74
- a Shudra, 74

Sami Ramananda, 76
Samratha Ram Das, 149
Sanatan Dharma, 77
Sankhya Philosophy, 200
Sanskrit Language, 179
Sant Kabir, 148, 171
Sant Ravi Das, 21, 76, 144, 146-47
Sant Tuka Ram, 149
Sardar Vallabhbhai Patel, 183
- First Home Minister of India, 183
- Iron Man, 183

Sarnath, 159
Sarojini Naidu, 182, 264
Satyagraha, 183
Satyakama Jabala, 21, 193

Scheduled Castes, 64
Scientific Dicoveries, 28
Selucus, 100
- Alexander General, 100

Shaheed Bhagat Singh, 181, 264
- Rajguru, 181
- Sukhdev, 178

Shanti Niketan, 178
Shanti Parv, 81
Shivaji, 118, 149, 263
Shudras, 13, 75, 79, 139-40, 143
Shudra Lady, 236, 285
- Rani Rasmani, 236, 286

Siddhartha, 235
Sidhartha Gautam, 233-34
Simon Commission, 180
Sir Isac Newton, 238
Sisters and Brothers of America, 60
Socrates, 277
Somnath Temple, 93
Space, 14
SPE, 252
Special Crime Division, 252
St. Paul School, 177
- London, 177

Subhash Chandra Bose, 15, 125, 181, 264
- Resigned ICS in 1920, 181
- President of Congress, 1939, 181

Subramaniam C. Bharti, 180
Sujata, 235
Supreme Power, 237
Surendra Nath Banerjee, 182
Survival of the Fittest, 26
Svetaketu, 193-94
Swadeshi, 183
Swami Chinmayanada, 55
Swami Dayananda, 76, 176
Swami Dayananda Saraswati, 96, 169, 239-40
- Founder of Arya Samaj, 96

Swami Ramananda, 148
Swami Sradhananda Saraswati, 175
Swami Shivananda, 76, 171, 173
- of Rishikesh, 173

Swami Tapovan, 174
Swami Vivekananada, 14-16, 24, 29, 59-60, 75-77, 156, 169-70, 199, 239-40, 264. 275, 285, 287
- Parliament of Religion, 15
- Disciple of Shri Rama Krishna Paramhansa, 169
- of Dakshineswar, Calcutta, 169

Swami Vivekananda's Lecture, 26
- New York, 26

System of Vigilance, 252

T

Tamil Nadu, 171
Tarikhul Hind, 62
Tatya Tope, 263
Ten Avtara of Vishnu, 211
Taxila, 100
- Sind Region, 100

Theosophical Society, 178
Trai, 110
Trichur, 294
Tukaram, 76
Tulsidas, 71

U

Udai Singh, 114
Uddalaka, 193-94
Union Public Service Commission, 254
United States of America, 281
Universal Equality, 61
Universal Religion, 235, 298
Universal Science of Life, 16
UNO, 272
Untouchability, 150, 154
Untouchable, 53
Upanishads, 52, 55-57, 189-92, 194, 235, 240
USA, 60, 174, 176
Uttar Pradesh, 62, 244

V

Valmiki Ramayana, 75
Varanasi, 71, 159
Vasant Kunj Colony, 245
Vaushya, 13, 75
Vallabh Bhai Patel, 264
Vedanta, 189
Vedanta Philosophy, 174, 240
Vedic God, 61
Ved Vyasa, 14, 78, 97-98, 144, 263
- Mahabharata, 263

Vidur, 62, 78
Vir Sawarkar, 181
- Andaman Nicobar Jail, 181

Visaka Dutta, 101
Vishnu Bharti, 178
Vishwamitra, 75

W

Waren Hastings, 195
- First British Viceroy of India, 195

Water, 14
Western Philosophy, 201
- Mystry of Life, 201

Wonder Girl, 271
World Parliament of Religion, 60, 169
- in Chicago, 169

World War-II, 126

Y

Yadavas, 62
Yajnavalakya Smriti, 63
Yudhistir, 79-80
Yuan- Chwang, 104

Z

Zonal CVO, 259